Hierarchical Linear Models

Introduction to the Series:
Advanced Quantitative Techniques in the Social Sciences

The volumes in the new AQTSS series consider quantitative techniques that have proven to be, or that promise to be, particularly useful for application in the social sciences. In many cases these techniques will be advanced, not necessarily because they require complicated mathematics, but because they build on more elementary techniques such as regression or descriptive statistics. As a consequence, we expect our readers to have a more thorough knowledge of modern statistics than is required for the volumes in the QASS series. The AQTSS series is aimed at graduate students in quantitative methods specializations, at statisticians with social science interests, and at quantitative social scientists who want to be informed about modern developments in data analysis.

The AQTSS series aims to be interdisciplinary. We prefer to publish volumes about techniques that can be used, and have been used, in different social disciplines and, in some cases, in the behavioral, medical, or physical sciences. This also is reflected in the composition of our editorial board. The board consists of scientists from many different disciplines, all of whom are involved in creating the Interdisciplinary Program in Social Statistics at UCLA.

The series also seeks to be practical. Although a good mathematical background may be essential to understand some aspects of the techniques, we insist on an emphasis on real data, real social science problems, and real analyses. This means that both data structures and computer packages get a great deal of emphasis in the volumes of this series.

Statistics present us with a series of techniques that transform raw data into a form that is easier to understand and to communicate or, to put it differently, that make it easy for the data to tell their story. In order to use the results of a statistical analysis in a responsible way, it is necessary to understand the implementations and the sensitivities of the transformations that are applied. We hope that the volumes in this new series contribute to quantitative social science applications that are both persuasive and precise.

Jan de Leeuw
Richard Berk

List of Advisory Board Members

Hierarchical Linear Models:

APPLICATIONS AND DATA ANALYSIS METHODS

❖

Anthony S. Bryk, University of Chicago
Stephen W. Raudenbush, Michigan State University

Advanced Quantitative Techniques in the Social Sciences **1**

SAGE PUBLICATIONS
International Educational and Professional Publisher
Newbury Park London New Delhi

For information address:

SAGE Publications, Inc.
2455 Teller Road
Newbury Park, California 91320

SAGE Publications Ltd.
6 Bonhill Street
London EC2A 4PU
United Kingdom

SAGE Publications India Pvt. Ltd.
M-32 Market
Greater Kailash I
New Delhi 110 048 India

Printed in the United States of America

Library of Congress Cataloging-in-Publication Data

Main entry under title:

Hierarchical linear models: applications and data analysis methods/
Anthony S. Bryk, Stephen W. Raudenbush.
p. cm.—(Advanced quantitative techniques in the social sciences; 1)
ISBN 0-8039-4627-9 (cloth)
1. Social sciences—Statistical methods. 2. Linear models (Statistics) I. Bryk, Anthony S. II. Raudenbush, Stephen W. III. Series.
HA29.H64 1992 91-45334
300′.72—dc20 CIP

92 93 94 95 10 9 8 7 6 5 4 3 2

Sage Production Editor: Diane S. Foster

Contents

Acknowledgments

This book represents the culmination of 10 years of collaboration between its two authors. These interactions have been rich and numerous, so much so that it is now impossible to define where one's ideas end and the other's begin. The ordering of the authors is strictly alphabetical. This book is a joint endeavor to which we have contributed equally.

Many others also have contributed in various ways—colleagues have offered invaluable criticism of an earlier draft of the book, co-workers have typed, proofread, and retyped sections of the manuscript, and other colleagues have patiently collaborated with one or both of us in conducting research used as examples throughout the book. Each of these contributors deserves our thanks, though we alone are responsible for the content of the book.

Grants from the Spencer Foundation, the National Science Foundation, and the Benton Center for Curriculum and Instruction at the University of Chicago provided generous support for this work. Without this support, neither our research nor this volume would have been possible.

Darrell Bock, Adam Gamoran, Lindsay Paterson, Erin Phelps, Bob Prosser, Herb Weisberg, and Doug Willms read an earlier draft and provided many insightful comments. John Willett deserves special thanks for offering literally hundreds of suggestions for improvement with a special emphasis on making the book accessible to the broadest possible audience. Wing-Shing

Chan, Barry Sloane, and Ken Frank each spent many hours checking the accuracy of the statistical arguments and empirical results. Special thanks are due to Richard Congdon who played a major role in developing the statistical programs for analyzing hierarchical data. His "handiwork" runs throughout this volume. We also thank Michael Seltzer for his contributions in this regard.

Anonymous reviewers offered many useful criticisms of the earlier draft. We thank Sage Publications and, especially, Jan de Leeuw, the Editor of this series, for gathering these reviews and offering his own advice.

We express special gratitude to Carmen Valverde and Marjorie Hoffman who have worked tirelessly typing text, formatting equations, tables, and figures, proofreading, editing, and revising. Their efforts, skill, and patience have been exceptional.

We have drawn on the research of many others, cited in the text but too numerous to mention here, to illustrate arguments. We owe special thanks to colleagues who have collaborated with us in substantive research using hierarchical linear models. These include Yuk Fai Cheong, Mary Driscoll, Ken Frank, Jane Ellen Huttenlocher, Sang Jin Kang, Somsri Kidchanapanish, Valerie Lee, Brian Rowan, Michael Seltzer, Yeow Meng Thum, and Doug Willms.

Series Editor's Introduction to Hierarchical Linear Models

In the social sciences, data structures are often hierarchical in the following sense: We have variables describing individuals, but the individuals also are grouped into larger units, each unit consisting of a number of individuals. We also have variables describing these higher order units.

The leading example is, perhaps, in education. Students are grouped in classes. We have variables describing students and variables describing classes. It is possible that the variables describing classes are aggregated student variables, such as number of students or average socioeconomic status. But the class variables could also describe the teacher (if the class has only one teacher) or the classroom (if the class always meets in the same room). Moreover, in this particular example, further hierarchical structure often occurs quite naturally. Classes are grouped in schools, schools in school districts, and so on. We may have variables describing school districts and variables describing schools (teaching style, school building, neighborhood, and so on).

Once we have discovered this one example of a hierarchical data structure, we see many of them. They occur naturally in geography and (regional) economics. In a sense, one of the basic problems of sociology is to relate properties of individuals and properties of groups and structures in which the individuals function. In the same way, in economics there is the problem of relating the micro and the macro levels. Moreover, many repeated measurements are hierarchical. If we follow individuals over time, then the measurements for any particular individual are a group, in the same way as the school class is a group. If each interviewer interviews a group of interviewees, then the interviewers are the higher level. Thinking about these hierarchical structures a bit longer inevitably leads to the conclusion that many, if not most, social science data have this nested or hierarchical structure.

The next step, after realizing how important hierarchical data are, is to think of ways in which statistical techniques should take this hierarchical structure into account. There are two obvious procedures that have been somewhat discredited. The first is to disaggregate all higher order variables to the individual level. Teacher, class, and school characteristics are all assigned to the individual, and the analysis is done on the individual level. The problem with this approach is that if we know that students are in the same class, then we also know that they have the same value on each of the class variables. Thus we cannot use the assumption of independence of observations that is basic for the classical statistical techniques. The other alternative is to aggregate the individual-level variables to the higher level and do the analysis on the higher level. Thus we aggregate student characteristics over classes and do a class analysis, perhaps weighted with class size. The main problem here is that we throw away all the within-group information, which may be as much as 80% or 90% of the total variation before we start the analysis. As a consequence, relations between aggregated variables are often much stronger, and they can be very different from the relation between the nonaggregate variables. Thus we waste information, and we distort interpretation if we try to interpret the aggregate analysis on the individual level. Thus aggregating and disaggregating are both unsatisfactory.

If we limit ourselves to traditional linear model analysis, we know that the basic assumptions are linearity, normality, homoscedasticity, and independence. We would like to maintain the first two, but the last two (especially the independence assumption) should be adapted. The general idea behind such adaptations is that individuals in the same group are closer or more similiar than individuals in different groups. Thus students in different classes can be independent, but students in the same class share values on many more variables. Some of these variables will not be observed, which means that they vanish into the error term of the linear model, causing correlation between disturbances. This idea can be formalized by using variance component models. The disturbances have a group and an individual component. Individual components are all independent; group components are independent between groups but perfectly correlated within groups.

Some groups might be more homogeneous than other groups, which means that the variance of the group components can differ.

There is a slightly different way to formalize this idea. We can suppose that each of the groups has a different regression model, in the simple regression case with its own intercept and its own slope. Because groups are also sampled, we then can make the assumption that the intercepts and slopes are a random sample from a population of group intercepts and slopes. This defines random-coefficient regression models. If we assume this for the intercepts only, and we let all slopes be the same, we are in the variance-component situation discussed in the previous paragraph. If the slopes vary randomly as well, we have a more complicated class of models in which the covariances of the disturbances depend on the values of the individual-level predictors.

In random-coefficient regression models, there is still no possibility to incorporate higher level variables, describing classes or schools. For this we need multilevel models, in which the group-level model is again a linear model. Thus we assume that the slope of the student variable SAT depends linearly on the class variables of class size or teacher philosophy. There are linear models on both levels, and if there are more levels, there are more nested linear models. Thus we arrive at a class of models that takes hierarchical structure into account and that makes it possible to incorporate variables from all levels.

Until about 10 years ago, fitting such models was technically not possible. Then, roughly at the same time, techniques and computer programs were published by Aitkin and Longford, Goldstein and co-workers, and Raudenbush and Bryk. The program HLM, by Bryk and Raudenbush, was the friendliest and most polished of these products, and in rapid succession a number of convincing and interesting examples were published. In this book, Bryk and Raudenbush describe the model, the algorithm, the program, and the examples in great detail. I think such a complete treatment of this class of techniques is both important and timely. Hierarchical linear models, or multilevel models, are certainly not a solution to all the data analysis problems of the social sciences. For this they are far too limited, because they are still based on the assumptions of linearity and normality, and because they still study the relatively simple regression structure in which a single variable depends on a number of others. Nevertheless, technically they are a big step ahead of the aggregation and disaggregation methods, mainly because they are statistically correct and do not waste information.

I think the main gain, illustrated nicely in this book by the extensive analysis of the examples, is conceptual. The models for the various levels are nicely separated, without being completely disjointed. One can think about the possible mechanisms on each of the levels separately and then join the separate models in a joint analysis. In educational research, as well as in geography, sociology, and economics, these techniques will gain in importance in the next few years, until they also run into their natural limitations. To avoid these limitations, they will be extended (and have been extended) to more levels, multivariate data, path-analysis models, latent variables, nominal-dependent variables, generalized linear models, and so on. Social statisticians will be able to do more extensive modeling, and they will be able to choose from a much larger class of models. If they are able to build up the necessary prior information to make a rational choice from the model class, then they can expect more power and precision. It is a good idea to keep this in the back of your mind as you use this book to explore this new exciting class of techniques.

JAN DE LEEUW
SERIES EDITOR

1 Introduction

- Hierarchical Data Structure: A Common Phenomenon
- Persistent Dilemmas in the Analysis of Hierarchical Data
- A Brief History of the Development of Statistical Theory for Hierarchical Models
- Applications of Hierarchical Linear Models
- Organization of the Book

Hierarchical Data Structure: A Common Phenomenon

Much social research involves hierarchical data structures. In organizational studies, for example, researchers might investigate how workplace characteristics, such as centralization of decision making, influence worker productivity within these contexts. Both workers and firms are units in the analysis; variables are measured at both levels. Such data have a hierarchical structure with individual workers nested within firms.

In cross-national studies, demographers might examine how differences in national economic development interact with adult educational attainment to influence fertility rates (see, e.g., Mason, Wong, & Entwistle, 1983). Such research combines economic indicators collected at the national level with household information on education and fertility. Both households and countries are units in the research with households nested within countries, and the basic data structure is again hierarchical.

Similar kinds of data occur in developmental research where multiple observations are gathered over time on a set of persons. The repeated measures contain information about each individual's growth trajectory. The psychologist is typically interested in how characteristics of the person, including variations in environmental exposure, influence the shape of these growth trajectories. For example, Huttenlocher, Haight, Bryk, and Seltzer (1991) investigated how differences among children in exposure to language in the home influenced the development of each child's vocabulary over time. When every person is observed at the same fixed number of time points, it is conventional to view the design as occasions crossed by persons. But when the number and spacing of time points vary from person to person, we may view occasions as nested within persons.

The quantitative synthesis of findings from many studies presents another hierarchical data problem. An investigator may wish to discover how differences in treatment implementations, research methods, subject characteristics, and contexts relate to treatment effect estimates within studies. In this case, subjects are nested within studies. Although the development of methodological techniques for meta-analysis has proceeded independently of work on hierarchical linear models, such models in fact provide a very general statistical framework for these research activities (Raudenbush, 1984a; Raudenbush & Bryk, 1985).

Educational research is often especially challenging because studies of student growth often involve a doubly nested structure of repeated observations within individuals, who are in turn nested within organizational settings. Research on instruction, for example, focuses on the interactions between students and a teacher around specific curricular materials. These interactions usually occur within a classroom setting and are bounded within a single academic year. The research problem has three foci: the individual growth of students over the course of the academic year (or segment of a year), the effects of personal characteristics and individual educational experiences on student learning, and how these relations are in turn influenced by classroom organization and the specific behavior and characteristics of the teacher. Correspondingly, the data have a three-level hierarchical structure. The Level-1 units are the repeated observations over time, which are nested within the Level-2 units of persons, who in turn are nested within the Level-3 units of classrooms or schools.

Persistent Dilemmas in the Analysis of Hierarchical Data

Despite the prevalence of hierarchical structures in behavioral and social research, past studies have often failed to address them adequately in the data analysis. In large part, this neglect has reflected limitations in conventional statistical techniques for the estimation of linear models with nested structures. In social research, these limitations have generated concerns about aggregation bias, misestimated precision, and the "unit of analysis" problem (see Chapter 5). They have also fostered an impoverished conceptualization, discouraging the formulation of explicit multilevel models with hypotheses about effects occurring at each level and across levels. Similarly, studies of human development have been plagued by "measurement of change" problems (see Chapter 6), which at times have seemed intractable, and have even led some analysts to advise against attempts to directly model growth.

Although these problems of unit of analysis and measuring change have distinct, long-standing, and virtually nonoverlapping literatures, they share a common cause: the inadequacy of traditional statistical techniques for modeling hierarchy. In the past, sophisticated analysts have often been able to find ways to cope at least partially in specific instances. With recent developments in the statistical theory for estimating hierarchical linear models, however, an integrated set of methods now exists that permits efficient estimation for a much wider range of applications.

Even more important from our perspective is that the barriers to use of an explicit hierarchical modeling framework have now been removed. We can now readily pose hypotheses about relations occurring at each level and across levels and also assess the amount of variation at each level. From a substantive perspective, the hierarchical linear model is more homologous with the basic phenomena under study in much behavioral and social research. The applications to date have been encouraging in that they have both afforded an exploration of new questions and provided some empirical results that might otherwise have gone undetected.

A Brief History of the Development of Statistical Theory for Hierarchical Models

The models discussed in this book appear in diverse literatures under a variety of titles. In sociological research, they are often referred to as *multilevel linear models* (cf. Goldstein, 1987; Mason et al., 1983). In biometric applications, the terms *mixed-effects models* and *random-effects models* are common (cf. Elston & Grizzle, 1962; Laird & Ware, 1982). They are also called *random-coefficient regression models* in the econometrics literature (cf. Rosenberg, 1973) and in the statistical literature are often referred to as *covariance components models* (cf. Dempster, Rubin, & Tsutakawa, 1981; Longford, 1987).

We have adopted the term *hierarchical linear models* because it conveys an important structural feature of data that is common in a wide variety of applications, including studies of growth, organizational effects, and research synthesis. This term was introduced by Lindley and Smith (1972) and Smith (1973) as part of their seminal contribution on Bayesian estimation of linear models. Within this context, Lindley and Smith elaborated a general framework for nested data with complex error structures.

Unfortunately, the Lindley and Smith (1972) contribution languished for a period of time because use of the models required estimation of covariance components in the presence of unbalanced data. With the exception of some very simple problems, no general estimation approach was feasible in the early 1970s. Dempster, Laird, and Rubin's (1977) development of the EM algorithm provided the needed breakthrough: a conceptually feasible and broadly applicable approach to covariance component estimation. Dempster et al. (1981) demonstrated applicability of this approach to hierarchical data structures. Laird and Ware (1982) and Strenio, Weisberg, and Bryk (1983) applied this approach to the study of growth, and Mason et al. (1983) applied it to cross-sectional data with a multilevel structure.

Subsequently, other numerical approaches to covariance component estimation were also offered through use of iteratively reweighted generalized least squares (Goldstein, 1986) and a Fisher scoring algorithm (Longford, 1987). Finally, a number of reasonably sophisticated statistical computing programs have become available for fitting these models including GENMOD (Mason, Anderson, & Hayat, 1988), HLM (Bryk, Raudenbush, Seltzer, & Congdon, 1988), ML2 (Rabash, Prosser, & Goldstein, 1989), and VARCL (Longford, 1988). For a technical review of these computers programs see Kreft, de Leeuw, and Kim (1990).

Applications of Hierarchical Linear Models

As noted above, behavioral and social data commonly have a nested structure, including, for example, repeated observations nested within persons. These persons also may be nested within organizational units such as schools. Further, the organizational units themselves may be nested within communities, within states, and even within countries. With hierarchical linear models, each of the levels in this structure is formally represented by its own submodel. These submodels express relationships among variables within a given level, and specify how variables at one level influence relations occurring at another. Although any number of levels can be represented, the essential statistical features are found in the basic two-level models that are the principal focus of this book.

The applications discussed here address three general research purposes: improved estimation of effects within individual units (e.g., developing an improved estimate of a regression model for an individual school by borrowing strength from the fact that similar estimates exist for other schools), the formulation and testing of hypotheses about cross-level effects (e.g., how varying school size might affect the relationship between social class and academic achievement within schools), and the partitioning of variance and covariance components among levels (e.g., decomposing the correlation among set of student-level variables into within- and between-school components). Published examples of each type are summarized briefly below.

Improved Estimation of Individual Effects

Braun, Jones, Rubin, and Thayer (1983) were concerned about the use of standardized test scores for selecting minority applicants to graduate business schools. Many schools base admissions decisions, in part, on equations that use test scores to predict later academic success. However, because most applicants to most business schools are white, their data dominate the estimated prediction equations. As a result, these equations may not produce an adequate ordering for purposes of selecting minority students.

In principle, a separate equation for minority applicants in each school might be fairer, but difficulties often arise in estimating such equations, because most schools have only a few minority students and thus little data on which to develop reliable predictions. In Braun et al.'s (1983) data on 59 graduate business schools, 14 schools had no minorities, and 20 schools had only one to three minority students. Developing prediction equations for minorities in these schools would have been impossible using standard regression methods. Further, even in the 25 schools with sufficient data to sustain a separate estimation, the minority samples were still small, and as a result, the minority coefficients would have been poorly estimated.

Alternatively, the data could be pooled across all schools, ignoring the nesting of students within schools, but this also poses difficulties. Specifically, because minorities are much more likely to be present in some schools than others, a failure to represent these selection artifacts could bias the estimated prediction coefficients.

Braun et al. (1983) used a hierarchical linear model to resolve this dilemma. By borrowing strength from the entire ensemble of data, they were able to efficiently utilize all of the available information to provide each school with separate prediction equations for whites and minorities. The estimator for each school was actually a weighted composite of the information from that school and the relations that exist in the overall sample.

As one might intuitively expect, the relative weights given each component depend on its precision. The estimation procedure is described in Chapter 3 and illustrated in Chapter 4. For a related application see Rubin (1980), and for a statistical review of these developments see Morris (1983).

Modeling Cross-Level Effects

The second general use of a hierarchical model is to formulate and test hypotheses about how variables measured at one level affect relations occurring at another. Because such cross-level effects are common in behavioral and social research, the modeling framework provides a significant advance over traditional methods.

An Example from Social Research. Mason et al. (1983) examined the effects of maternal education and urban versus rural residence on fertility in 15 countries. It has been well known that in many countries high levels of education and urban residence predict low fertility. However, the investigators reasoned that such effects might depend on characteristics of the countries, including level of national economic development, as indicated by gross national product (GNP), and the intensity of family planning efforts.

Mason et al. (1983) found that higher levels of maternal education were indeed associated with lower fertility rates in all countries. Differences in urban versus rural fertility rates, however, varied across countries with the largest gaps occurring in nations with a high GNP and few organized family planning efforts. The identification of *differentiating effects,* such as this rural-urban gap, and the prediction of their variability is taken up in Chapter 5.

An Example from Developmental Research. Investigators of language development hypothesized that word acquisition depends upon two sources: exposure to appropriate speech and innate differences in ability to learn from such exposure. It is widely assumed that innate differences in ability are largely responsible for observed differences in children's vocabulary development. However, the empirical support for this assumption is weak. Heritability studies have found that parent scores on standardized vocabulary tests account for 10% to 20% of the variance in children's scores on the same tests. Exposure studies have not fared much better. Most of the individual variation in vocabulary acquisition has remained unexplained.

In the past, researchers have relied primarily on two-time point designs to study exposure effects. Children's vocabulary might first be assessed at, say, 14 months of age, and information on maternal verbal ability or language use also might be collected at that time. Children's vocabulary size then would be reassessed at some subsequent time point, say 26 months. The data would be analyzed with a conventional linear model with the focus on estimating the maternal speech effect on 26-month vocabulary size after controlling for children's "initial ability" (i.e., the 14-month vocabulary size).

Huttenlocher et al. (1991) collected longitudinal data with some children observed on as many as seven occasions between 14 and 26 months. This permitted formulation of an individual vocabulary growth trajectory based on the repeated observations for each child. Each child's growth was characterized by a set of parameters. A second model used information about the children, including the child's sex and amount of maternal speech in the home environment, to predict these growth parameters. The actual formulation and estimation of this model are detailed in Chapter 6.

The analysis, based on a hierarchical linear model, found that exposure to language during infancy played a much larger role in vocabulary development than had been reported in previous studies. (In fact, the effects were substantially larger than would have been found had a conventional analysis been performed using just the first and last time points.) This application demonstrates the difficulty associated with drawing valid inferences about correlates of growth from conventional approaches.

Partitioning Variance-Covariance Components

A third use of hierarchical linear models draws on the estimation of variance and covariance components with unbalanced, nested data. For example, educational researchers often wish to study the growth of the individual student learner within the organizational context of classrooms and schools. Formal modeling of such phenomena require use of a three-level model.

Bryk and Raudenbush (1988) illustrated this approach with a small subsample of longitudinal data from the Sustaining Effects Study (Carter, 1984). They used mathematics achievement data from 618 students in 86 schools measured on five occasions between Grade 1 and Grade 3. They began with an individual growth (or repeated measures) model of the academic achievement for each child within each school. The three-level approach enabled a decomposition of the variation in these individual growth trajectories into within- and between-school components. The details of this application are discussed in Chapter 8.

The results were startling—83% of the variance in growth rates was between schools. In contrast, only about 14% of the variance in initial status was between schools, which is consistent with results typically encountered in cross-sectional studies of school effects. This analysis identified substantial differences among schools that conventional models would not have detected, because such analyses do not allow the partitioning of learning-rate variance into within- and between-school components.

Organization of the Book

The book is organized into nine additional chapters. We have attempted to keep the presentation as nontechnical as possible, relying primarily on simple examples to explicate the basic features of the models. Although the book is primarily intended for behavioral and social scientists interested in using these methods in their research, we have also attempted to provide sufficient detail for the more methodologically oriented reader.

Chapter 2 introduces the logic of hierarchical linear models by building on simpler concepts from regression analysis and random-effects analysis of variance. In Chapter 3, we summarize the basic procedures for estimation and inference used with these models. The emphasis is on an intuitive introduction with a minimal level of mathematical sophistication. These procedures are then illustrated in Chapter 4 as we work through the estimation of an increasingly complex set of models with a common data set.

Applications of hierarchical linear models follow in the next four chapters. Chapters 5 and 6 consider the use of two-level models in the study of organizational effects and individual growth, respectively. Chapter 7 discusses use in the context of research synthesis or meta-analysis applications. This actually represents a special class of applications where the Level-1 variances are known. Chapter 8 introduces the three-level model and describes a range of applications including a key educational research problem—how school organization influences student learning over time.

The last two chapters further discuss the logic of statistical inference in hierarchical linear models. Chapter 9 reviews the basic model assumptions, describes procedures for examining the validity of these assumptions, and discusses what is known about sensitivity of inferences to violation of these various assumptions. Chapter 10 is intended for a more methodological audience desiring a formal derivation of the statistical methods used in this book.

2 The Logic of Hierarchical Linear Models

- Preliminaries
- A General Model and Simpler Submodels
- Further Generalizations
- Choosing the Location of *X* and *W* (*Centering*)
- Summary of Terms and Notation Introduced in this Chapter

This chapter introduces the logic of hierarchical linear models. We begin with a simple example that builds upon the reader's understanding of familiar ideas from regression and analysis of variance (ANOVA). We show how these common statistical models can be viewed as special cases of the hierarchical linear model. The chapter concludes with a summary of some definitions and notation that are used throughout the book.

Preliminaries

A Study of the SES-Achievement Relationship in One School

We begin by considering the relationship between a single student-level predictor variable (say, socioeconomic status [SES]) and one student-level outcome variable (mathematics achievement) within a single, hypothetical school. Figure 2.1 provides a scatterplot of this relationship. The scatter of points is well represented by a straight line with intercept β_0 and slope β_1. Thus, the regression equation for the data is

$$Y_i = \beta_0 + \beta_1 X_i + r_i . \qquad [2.1]$$

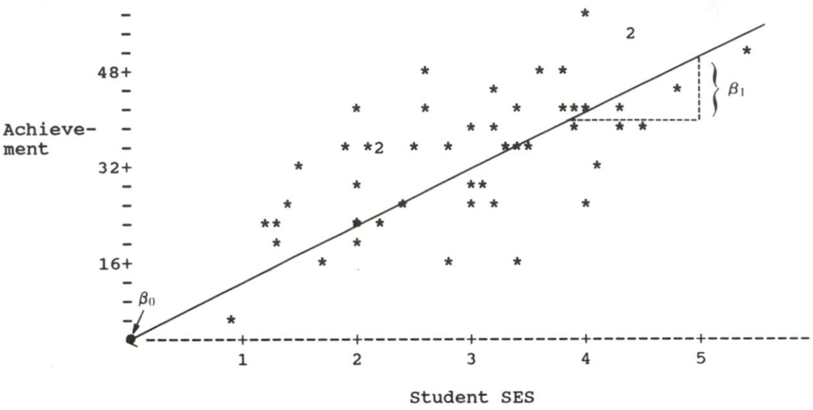

Figure 2.1. Scatterplot Showing the Relationship Between Achievement and SES in One Hypothetical School

The intercept, β_0, is defined as the expected math achievement of a student whose SES is zero. The slope, β_1, is the expected change in math achievement associated with a unit increase in SES. The error term, r_i, represents a unique effect associated with person *i*. Typically, we assume that r_i is normally distributed with a mean of zero and variance σ^2, that is, $r_i \sim N(0, \sigma^2)$.

It is often helpful to scale the independent variable, *X*, so that the intercept will be meaningful. For example, suppose we "center" SES by subtracting the mean SES from each score: $X_i - \underline{X}.$ where $\underline{X}.$ is the mean SES in the school. If we now plot Y_i as a function of $X_i - \underline{X}.$ (see Figure 2.2) with the regression line superimposed, we see that the intercept, β_0, is indeed the mean math achievement while the slope remains unchanged.

A Study of the SES-Achievement Relationship in Two Schools

Let us now consider separate regressions for two hypothetical schools. These are displayed in Figure 2.3. The two lines indicate that School 1 and School 2 differ in two ways. First, School 1 has a higher mean than does School 2. This difference is reflected in the two intercepts, that is, $\beta_{01} > \beta_{02}$. Second, SES is less predictive of math achievement in School 1 than in School 2, as indicated by comparing the two slopes, that is, $\beta_{11} < \beta_{12}$.

If students had been randomly assigned to the two schools, we could say that School 1 is both more "effective" and more "equitable" than School 2.

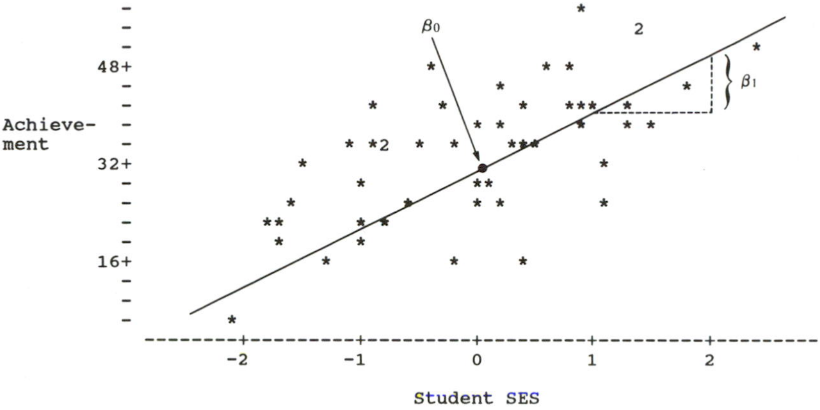

Figure 2.2. Scatterplot Showing the Relationship Between Achievement and SES (Centered) in One Hypothetical School

The greater effectiveness is indicated by the higher mean level of achievement in School 1 (i.e., $\beta_{01} > \beta_{02}$). The greater equity is indicated by the weaker slope (i.e. $\beta_{11} < \beta_{12}$). Of course, students are not assigned at random to schools, so such interpretations of school effects are unwarranted without taking into account differences in student composition. Nevertheless, the

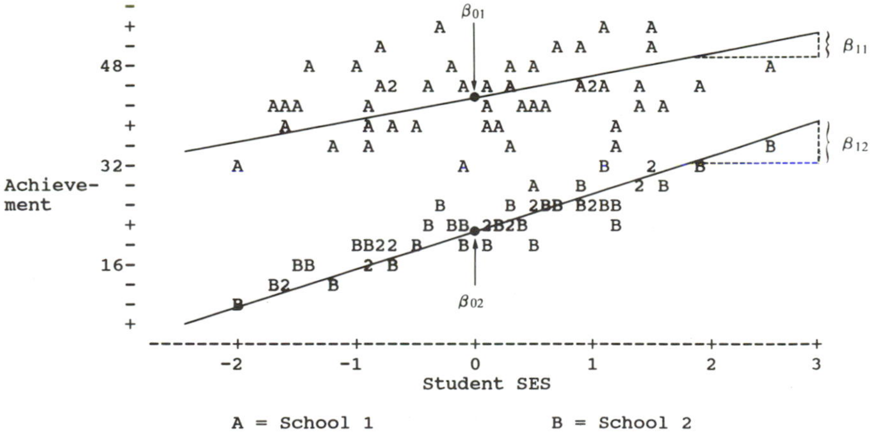

Figure 2.3. Scatterplot Showing the Relationship Between Achievement and SES Within Two Hypothetical Schools

fiction of random assignment clarifies the goals of the analysis and simplifies our presentation.

A Study of the SES-Achievement Relationship in *J* Schools

We now consider the study of the SES-math achievement relationship within an entire *population* of schools. Suppose that we now have a random sample of J schools from a population, where J is a large number. It is no longer practical to summarize the data with a scatterplot for each school. Nevertheless, we can describe this relationship within any school j by the equation

$$Y_{ij} = \beta_{0j} + \beta_{1j}(X_{ij} - \overline{X}_{\cdot j}) + r_{ij}, \qquad [2.2]$$

where for simplicity we assume that r_{ij} is normally distributed with homogeneous variance across schools, that is, $r_{ij} \sim N(0, \sigma^2)$. Notice that the intercept and slope are now subscripted by j, which allows each school to have a unique intercept and slope. For each school, effectiveness and equity are described by the pair of values (β_{0j}, β_{1j}). It is often sensible and convenient to assume that the intercept and slope have a bivariate normal distribution across the population of schools. Let

$$E(\beta_{0j}) = \gamma_0, \quad Var(\beta_{0j}) = \tau_{00}$$

$$E(\beta_{1j}) = \gamma_1, \quad Var(\beta_{1j}) = \tau_{11}$$

$$Cov(\beta_{0j}, \beta_{1j}) = \tau_{01}$$

where

γ_0 is the average school mean for the population of schools;
τ_{00} is the population variance among the school means;
γ_1 is the average SES-achievement slope for the population;
τ_{11} is the population variance among the slopes; and
τ_{01} is the population covariance between slopes and intercepts.

A positive value of τ_{01} implies that schools with high means tend also to have positive slopes. Knowledge of these variances and of the covariance leads directly to a formula for calculating the population correlation between the means and slopes:

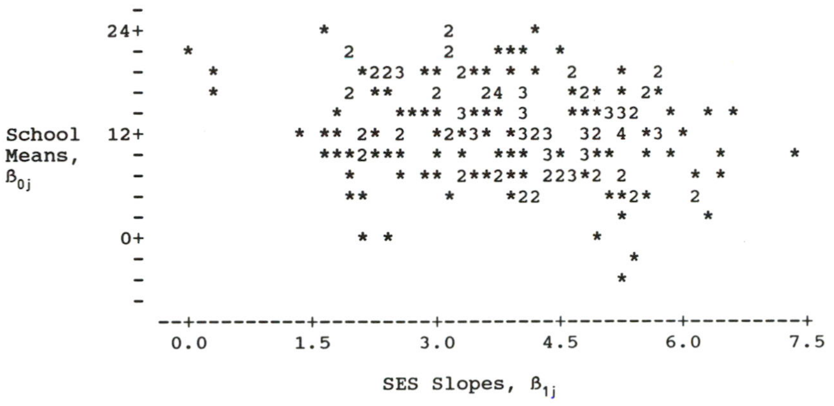

Figure 2.4. Plot of Mean (vertical axis) and SES Slopes (horizontal axis) for 200 Hypothetical Schools

$$\rho(\beta_{0j}, \beta_{1j}) = \tau_{01}/(\tau_{00}\tau_{11})^{1/2} \qquad [2.3]$$

In reality, we rarely know the true values of the population parameters we have introduced (γ_0, γ_1, τ_{11}, τ_{00}, τ_{01}) nor of the true individual school means and slopes (β_{0j} and β_{1j}). Rather, all of these must be estimated from the data. Our focus in this chapter is simply to clarify the meaning of the parameters. The actual procedures used to estimate them are introduced in Chapter 3 and are discussed more extensively in Chapter 10.

Suppose we did know the true values of the means and slopes for each school. Figure 2.4 provides a scatterplot of the relationship between β_{0j} and β_{1j} for a hypothetical sample of schools. This plot tells us about how schools vary in terms of their means and slopes. Notice, for example, that there is more dispersion among the means (vertical axis) than the slopes (horizontal axis). Symbolically, this implies that $\tau_{00} > \tau_{11}$. Notice also that the two effects tend to be negatively correlated: Schools with high average achievement, β_{0j}, tend to have weak SES-achievement relationships, β_{1j}. Symbolically, $\tau_{01} < 0$. Schools that are effective and egalitarian—that is, with high average achievement (large values of β_{0j}) and weak SES effects (small values of β_{1j})—are found in the upper left quadrant of the scatterplot.

Having examined graphically how schools vary in terms of their intercepts and slopes, we may wish to develop a model to predict β_{0j} and β_{1j}. Specifically, we could use school characteristics (e.g., levels of funding, organizational features, policies) to predict effectiveness and equity. For instance, consider a simple indicator variable, W_j, which takes on a value of one for Catholic schools and a value of zero for public. Coleman, Hoffer, and Kilgore (1982) argued that W_j is positively related to effectiveness (Catholic schools have higher average achievement than do public schools) and negatively related to the slope (SES effects on math achievement are smaller in Catholic than in public schools). We represent these two hypotheses via two regression equations:

$$\beta_{0j} = \gamma_{00} + \gamma_{01} W_j + u_{0j}, \qquad [2.4a]$$

and

$$\beta_{1j} = \gamma_{10} + \gamma_{11} W_j + u_{1j}, \qquad [2.4b]$$

where

γ_{00} is the mean achievement for public schools;

γ_{01} is the mean achievement difference between Catholic and public schools (i.e., the Catholic school "effectiveness" advantage);

γ_{10} is the average SES-achievement slope in public schools;

γ_{11} is the mean difference in SES-achievement slopes between Catholic and public schools (i.e., the Catholic school "equity" advantage);

u_{0j} is the unique effect of school j on mean achievement holding W_j constant (or conditioning on W_j); and

u_{1j} is the unique effect of school j in the SES-achievement slope holding W_j constant (or conditioning on W_j).

We assume u_{0j} and u_{1j} are random variables with zero means, variances τ_{00} and τ_{11} respectively, and covariance τ_{01}. Note these variance-covariance components are now *conditional* or *residual* variance-covariance components. That is, they represent the variability in β_{0j} and β_{1j} remaining after controlling for W_j.

It is not possible to estimate the parameters of these regression equations directly, because the outcomes (β_{0j}, β_{1j}) are not observed. However, the data contain information needed for this estimation. This becomes clear if we substitute Equations 2.4a and 2.4b into Equation 2.2, yielding the single prediction equation for the outcome

$$Y_{ij} = \gamma_{00} + \gamma_{01} W_j + \gamma_{10}(X_{ij} - \bar{X}_{.j}) + \gamma_{11} W_j (X_{ij} - \bar{X}_{.j}) \qquad [2.5]$$

$$+ u_{0j} + u_{1j}(X_{ij} - \bar{X}_{.j}) + r_{ij}.$$

Notice that Equation 2.5 is not the typical linear model assumed in standard ordinary least squares (OLS). Efficient estimation and accurate hypothesis testing based on OLS require that the random errors are independent, normally distributed, and have constant variance. In contrast, the random error in Equation 2.5 is of a more complex form, $u_{0j} + u_{1j}(X_{ij} - \bar{X}_{.j}) + r_{ij}$. Such errors are dependent within each school because the components u_{0j} and u_{1j} are common to every student within school j. The errors also have unequal variances, because $u_{0j} + u_{1j}(X_{ij} - \bar{X}_{.j})$ depend upon u_{0j} and u_{1j}, which vary across schools, and upon the value of $(X_{ij} - \bar{X}_{.j})$, which varies across students. Though standard regression analysis is inappropriate, such models can be estimated by iterative maximum likelihood procedures described in the next chapter. We note that if u_{0j} and u_{1j} were null for every j, Equation 2.5 would be equivalent to an OLS regression model.

Figure 2.5 provides a graphical representation of the model specified in Equation 2.4. Here we see two hypothetical plots of the association between β_{0j} and β_{1j}, one for public and a second for Catholic schools. The plots were constructed to reflect Coleman et al.'s (1982) contention that Catholic schools have both higher mean achievement and weaker SES effects than do the public schools.

A General Model and Simpler Submodels

We now generalize our terminology a bit so that it applies to any two-level hierarchical data structure. Equation 2.2 may be labeled the Level-1 model; Equation 2.4 is the Level-2 model, and Equation 2.5 is the *combined* model. In the school-effects application the Level-1 units are students and the Level-2 units are schools. The errors r_{ij} are the Level-1 random effects and the errors u_{0j} and u_{1j} are Level-2 random effects. Moreover, $\text{Var}(r_{ij})$ is the Level-1 variance, and $\text{Var}(u_{0j})$, $\text{Var}(u_{1j})$, and $\text{Cov}(u_{0j}, u_{1j})$ are the Level-2 variance-covariance components. The β parameters in the Level-1 model are Level-1 coefficients and the γs are the Level-2 coefficients.

Given a single Level-1 predictor, X_{ij}, and a single Level-2 predictor, W_j, the model given by Equations 2.2, 2.4, and 2.5 is the simplest example of a full hierarchical linear model. Mason et al. (1983) showed that when certain sets of terms in this model are set equal to zero, we are left with a set of simpler models, some of which are quite familiar. It is instructive to examine these, both to demonstrate the range of applications of hierarchical linear models and to draw out the connections to more common

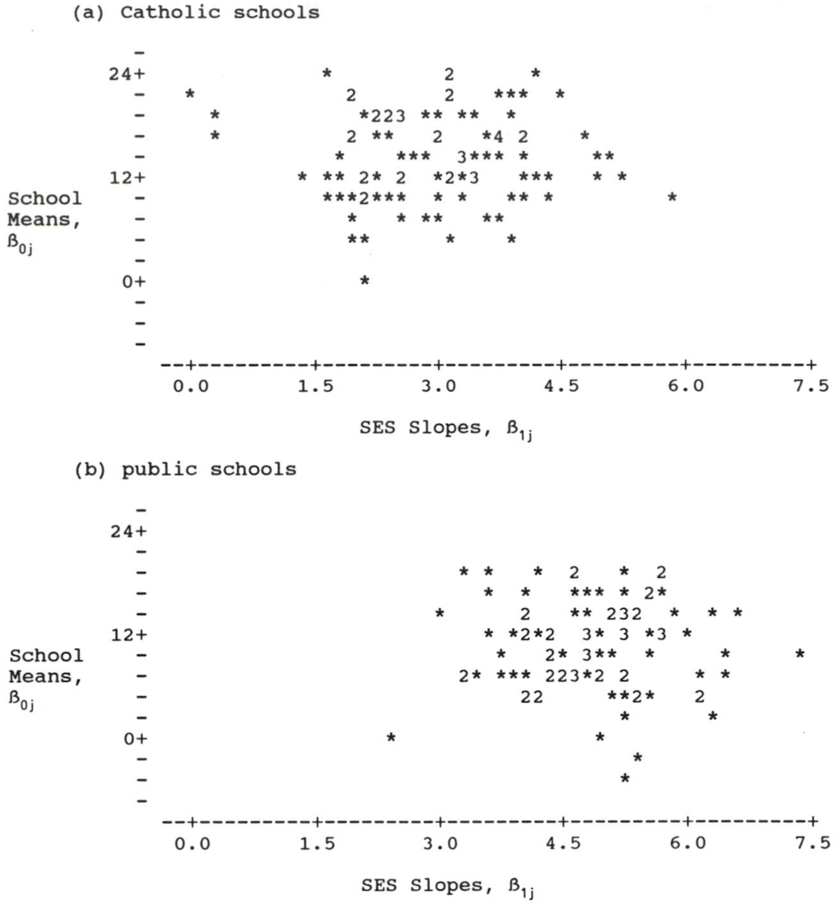

Figure 2.5. Plot of Means (vertical axis) and SES Slopes (horizontal axis) for 100 Hypothetical Catholic Schools and 100 Hypothetical Public Schools

data analysis methods. The submodels, running from the simpler to the more complex, include the one-way ANOVA model with random effects; a regression model with means-as-outcomes; a one-way analysis of covariance (ANCOVA) model with random effects; a random-coefficients regression model; a model with intercepts- and slopes-as-outcomes; and a model with nonrandomly varying slopes.

One-Way ANOVA with Random Effects

The simplest possible hierarchical linear model is equivalent to a one-way ANOVA with random effects. In this case, β_{1j} in the Level-1 model is set to zero for all j, yielding

$$Y_{ij} = \beta_{0j} + r_{ij}. \qquad [2.6]$$

We assume that each Level-1 error, r_{ij}, is normally distributed with a mean of zero and a constant Level-1 variance, σ^2. Notice that this model predicts the outcome within each Level-1 unit with just one Level-2 parameter, the intercept, β_{0j}. In this case, β_{0j} is just the mean outcome for the jth unit. That is, $\beta_{0j} = \mu_{Y_j}$.

The Level-2 model for the one-way ANOVA with random effects is Equation 2.4a with γ_{01} set to zero:

$$\beta_{0j} = \gamma_{00} + u_{0j}, \qquad [2.7]$$

where γ_{00} represents the grand mean outcome in the population, and u_{0j} is the random effect associated with unit j and is assumed to have a mean of zero and variance τ_{00}.

Substituting Equation 2.7 into Equation 2.6 yields the combined model

$$Y_{ij} = \gamma_{00} + u_{0j} + r_{ij}, \qquad [2.8]$$

which is, indeed, the one-way ANOVA model with grand mean γ_{00}; with a group (Level-2) effect, u_{0j}; and with a person (Level-1) effect, r_{ij}. It is a random-effects model because the group effects are construed as random. Notice that the variance of the outcome is

$$\text{Var}(Y_{ij}) = \text{Var}(u_{0j} + r_{ij}) = \tau_{00} + \sigma^2. \qquad [2.9]$$

Estimating the one-way ANOVA model is often useful as a preliminary step in a hierarchical data analysis. It produces a point estimate and confidence interval for the grand mean, γ_{00}. More important, it provides information about the outcome variability at each of the two levels. The σ^2 parameter represents the within-group variability, and τ_{00} captures the between-group variability. We refer to the hierarchical model of Equations 2.6 and 2.7 as *fully unconditional* in that no predictors are specified at either Level 1 or 2.

Intraclass Correlation Coefficient. A useful parameter associated with the one-way random-effects ANOVA is the intraclass correlation coefficient. This coefficient is given by the formula

$$\rho = \tau_{00}/(\tau_{00} + \sigma^2) \quad [2.10]$$

and measures the proportion of the variance in the outcome that is between the Level-2 units. See Chapter 4 for an application of the one-way random-effects submodel.

Means-as-Outcomes Regression

Another common statistical problem involves the means from each of many groups as an outcome to be predicted by group characteristics. This submodel consists of Equation 2.6 as the Level-1 model and, for the Level-2 model,

$$\beta_{0j} = \gamma_{00} + \gamma_{01} W_j + u_{0j}, \quad [2.11]$$

where in this simple case we have one Level-2 predictor W_j . Substituting Equation 2.11 into Equation 2.6 yields the combined model:

$$Y_{ij} = \gamma_{00} + \gamma_{01} W_j + u_{0j} + r_{ij}. \quad [2.12]$$

We note that u_{0j} now has a different meaning as contrasted with that in Equation 2.7. Whereas the random variable u_{0j} had been the deviation of unit j's mean from the grand mean, it now represents the residual

$$u_{0j} = \beta_{0j} - \gamma_{00} - \gamma_{01} W_j.$$

Similarly, the variance in u_{0j}, τ_{00}, is now the residual or conditional variance in β_{0j} after controlling for W_j . The advantages of estimating Equation 2.12 rather than performing a standard regression using sample means-as-outcomes are discussed in Chapter 5.

One-Way ANCOVA with Random Effects

Referring again to the full model (Equations 2.2 and 2.4), let us constrain the Level-2 coefficients γ_{01} and γ_{11} and the random effects u_{1j} (for all j) equal to 0. The resulting model would be a one-factor ANCOVA with random effects and a single Level-1 predictor as a covariate. The

Level-1 model is Equation 2.2, but now the predictor X_{ij} is centered around the grand mean. That is,

$$Y_{ij} = \beta_{0j} + \beta_{1j}(X_{ij} - \bar{X}_{..}) + r_{ij}. \quad [2.13]$$

The Level-2 model becomes

$$\beta_{0j} = \gamma_{00} + u_{0j} \quad [2.14a]$$

$$\beta_{1j} = \gamma_{10}. \quad [2.14b]$$

Notice that the effect of X_{ij} is constrained to be the same fixed value for each Level-2 unit as is indicated by Equation 2.14b.

The combined model becomes

$$Y_{ij} = \gamma_{00} + \gamma_{10}(X_{ij} - \bar{X}_{..}) + u_{0j} + r_{ij}. \quad [2.15]$$

The only difference between Equation 2.15 and the standard ANCOVA model (cf. Kirk, 1982, chap. 14) is that the group effect here, u_{0j}, is conceived as random rather than fixed. As in ANCOVA, γ_{10} is the pooled within-group regression coefficient of Y_{ij} on X_{ij}. Each β_{0j} is now the mean outcome for each Level-2 unit adjusted for differences among these units in X_{ij}. Specifically, $\beta_{0j} = \mu_{Y_j} - \gamma_{10}(\bar{X}_{.j} - \bar{X}_{..})$. We also note that the $\text{Var}(r_{ij}) = \sigma^2$ is now a residual variance after adjusting for the Level-1 covariate, X_{ij}. Aitkin and Longford (1986) provide a detailed discussion of the applications of this model in estimating the effects of individual schools.

An extension of the random-effects ANCOVA allows for the introduction of Level-2 covariates. For example, if the coefficient γ_{01} is nonnull, the combined model becomes

$$Y_{ij} = \gamma_{00} + \gamma_{01}W_j + \gamma_{10}(X_{ij} - \bar{X}_{..}) + u_{0j} + r_{ij}. \quad [2.16]$$

This model provides for a Level-2 covariate, W_j, while also controlling for the effect of a Level-1 covariate, X_{ij}, and the random effects of the Level-2 units, u_{0j}. Interestingly, all of the parameters of Equation 2.16 can be estimated using the methods introduced in the next chapter. This is not the case, however, for a classical fixed-effects ANCOVA. Also, the classical ANCOVA model assumes that the covariate effect, γ_{10}, is identical for every group. This homogeneity of regression assumption is easily relaxed using the models described in the next three sections (for randomly varying and nonrandomly varying slopes). We illustrate use of the random-effects

ANCOVA model in Chapter 5 in analyzing data on the effectiveness of an instructional innovation on students' writing.

Random-Coefficients Regression Model

All of the submodels discussed above are examples of *random-intercept models*. Only the Level-1 intercept coefficient, β_{0j}, was viewed as random. The Level-1 slope did not exist in the one-way ANOVA or the means-as-outcomes cases. In the random-effects ANCOVA model, β_{1j} was included but constrained to have a common effect for all groups.

A major class of applications of hierarchical linear models involves studies in which Level-1 slopes are conceived as varying randomly over the population of Level-2 units. The simplest case of this type is the random-coefficients regression model. Models of this type are illustrated by Dempster et al. (1981) and have been common in econometric research for some time (cf. Swamy, 1973). In these models, both the Level-1 intercept and one or more Level-1 slopes vary randomly, but no attempt is made to predict this variation.

Specifically, the Level-1 model is identical to Equation 2.2. The Level-2 model is still a simplification of Equation 2.4 in that both γ_{01} and γ_{11} are constrained to be null. Hence, the Level-2 model becomes

$$\beta_{0j} = \gamma_{00} + u_{0j} \qquad [2.17a]$$

$$\beta_{1j} = \gamma_{10} + u_{1j} \qquad [2.17b]$$

where

γ_{00} is the average intercept across the Level-2 units;
γ_{10} is the average regression slope across the Level-2 units;
u_{0j} is the unique increment to the intercept associated with Level-2 unit j; and
u_{1j} is the unique increment to the slope associated with Level-2 unit j.

We formally represent the dispersion of the Level-2 random effects as a variance-covariance matrix:

$$\text{Var}\begin{bmatrix} u_{0j} \\ u_{1j} \end{bmatrix} = \begin{bmatrix} \tau_{00} & \tau_{01} \\ \tau_{10} & \tau_{11} \end{bmatrix} = \mathbf{T} \qquad [2.18]$$

where

$\text{Var}(u_{0j}) = \tau_{00}$ = unconditional variance in the Level-1 intercepts;
$\text{Var}(u_{1j}) = \tau_{11}$ = unconditional variance in the Level-1 slopes; and
$\text{Cov}(u_{0j}, u_{1j}) = \tau_{01}$ = unconditional covariance between the Level-1 intercepts and slopes.

Note that we refer to these as unconditional variance-covariance components because no Level-2 predictors are included in either Equation 2.17a or 2.17b. Similarly, we refer to Equations 2.17a and 2.17b as an *unconditional* Level-2 model.

Substitution of the expressions for β_{0j} and β_{1j} in Equations 2.17a and 2.17b into Equation 2.2 yields a combined model:

$$Y_{ij} = \gamma_{00} + \gamma_{10}(X_{ij} - \overline{X}_{.j}) + u_{0j} + u_{1j}(X_{ij} - \overline{X}_{.j}) + r_{ij}. \qquad [2.19]$$

This model implies that the outcome Y_{ij} is a function of the average regression equation, $\gamma_{00} + \gamma_{10}(X_{ij} - \overline{X}_{.j})$ plus a random error having three components: u_{0j}, the random effect of unit j on the mean; $u_{1j}(X_{ij} - \overline{X}_{.j})$, where u_{1j} is the random effect of unit j on the slope β_{1j}, and the Level-1 error, r_{ij}.

Intercepts- and Slopes-as-Outcomes

The random-coefficients regression model allows us to estimate the variability in the regression coefficients (both intercepts and slopes) across the Level-2 units. The next logical step is to model this variability. For example, in Chapter 4, we ask "What characteristics of schools (the Level-2 units) help predict why some schools have higher means than others and why some schools have greater SES effects than others?"

Given one Level-1 predictor, X_{ij}, and one Level-2 predictor, W_j, these questions may be addressed by employing the "full model" of Equations 2.2 and 2.4. Of course, this model may be readily expanded to incorporate the effects of multiple Xs and of multiple Ws (see the section on "Further Generalizations"). Applications are illustrated in Chapter 5 in the context of organizational effects and in Chapter 6 in the context of studying growth curves.

A Model with Nonrandomly Varying Slopes

In some cases, the analyst will prove quite successful in predicting the variability in the regression slopes, β_{1j}. For example, it might be found that the Level-2 predictor W_j in Equation 2.4b does indeed predict the Level-1 slope β_{1j}. In fact, the analyst might find that after controlling for W_j the residual variance of β_{1j} (i.e., the variance of the residuals, u_{1j} in Equation 2.4b) is very close to zero. The implication would be that once W_j is controlled, little or no variance in the slopes remains to be explained. For reasons of both statistical efficiency and computational stability (as discussed in Chapter 9), it would be sensible, then, to constrain the values of u_{1j} to be zero. This eliminates τ_{11}, the residual variance of the slope, and τ_{01}, the residual covariance between the slope and the intercept, as parameters to be estimated.

If the residuals u_{1j} in Equation 2.4b are indeed set to zero, the Level-2 model for the slopes becomes

$$\beta_{1j} = \gamma_{10} + \gamma_{11} W_j , \qquad [2.20]$$

and this model, when combined with Equations 2.2 and 2.4a, yields the combined model

$$Y_{ij} = \gamma_{00} + \gamma_{01} W_j + \gamma_{10}(X_{ij} - \overline{X}_{.j}) + \gamma_{11} W_j (X_{ij} - \overline{X}_{.j}) + u_{0j} + r_{ij} . \qquad [2.21]$$

In this model, the slopes do vary from group to group, but their variation is nonrandom. Specifically, as Equation 2.20 shows, the slopes β_{1j} vary strictly as a function of W_j.

We note that Equation 2.21 can be viewed as another example of what we have called a random-intercept model, because β_{0j} is the only component that varies randomly across Level-2 units. In general, hierarchical linear models may involve multiple Level-1 predictors where any combination of random, nonrandomly varying, and fixed slopes can be specified. An application of this sort is illustrated in Chapter 8.

Section Recap

We have been considering a simple hierarchical linear model with a single Level-1 predictor, X_{ij}, and a single Level-2 predictor, W_j. In this scenario, the Level-1 model (Equation 2.2) defines two parameters, the intercept and the slope. At Level 2, each of these may be predicted by W_j and each may have a random component of variation, as in Equations 2.4a and 2.4b. The resulting full model, summarized by Equation 2.5, is the most general model we have considered so far. If certain elements of the full model are constrained to be null, we are left with a submodel that may be useful either as preliminary to a full hierarchical analysis or as a more parsimonious summary than the full model.

The six submodels we have considered may be classified in several different ways. We have distinguished between random-intercept models and randomly varying slope models. The one-way random-effects ANOVA model, the means-as-outcomes model, the one-way ANCOVA model, and the model with nonrandomly varying slopes are all random-intercept models. In such models, the variance components are just the Level-1 variance, σ^2, and the Level-2 variance, τ_{00}. We noted that in the ANOVA and means-as-outcomes models, no Level-1 slope exists. In the ANCOVA model, the Level-1 slope exists but is constrained or *fixed* to be invariant across Level-2 units. In the nonrandomly varying slope model, slopes were allowed to vary strictly as a function of a known W_j with no additional random component. In contrast, the random-coefficients model and the slopes- and intercepts-as-outcomes models allowed random variation for both the intercepts and slopes.

Another distinction is whether models include *cross-level interaction terms* such as $\gamma_{11} W_j(X_{ij} - \overline{X}_{.j})$. In general, the combined model will include such cross-level interaction terms whenever we seek to predict variation in a slope. Such terms appear in two of our submodels: the intercepts- and slopes-as-outcomes model and the nonrandomly varying slope model.

One of the purposes of this book is to help the reader to make sensible choices among the various possible models in the context of specific types of applications. Chapters 5 through 8 draw upon our experiences in using these models in the areas of organizational effects, growth, research synthesis, and certain three-level applications. In these chapters we clarify the logic that underlies model specification and model choice.

Further Generalizations

Multiple *X*s and Multiple *W*s

Suppose now that the analyst wishes to use information about a second Level-1 predictor. Let X_{1ij} denote the original X discussed above and let X_{2ij} denote the second Level-1 predictor. For now, assume that there is still just a single Level-2 predictor, W_j. The Level-1 model, assuming group-mean centering for both X_{1ij} and X_{2ij}, becomes

$$Y_{ij} = \beta_{0j} + \beta_{1j}(X_{1ij} - \overline{X}_{1.j}) + \beta_{2j}(X_{2ij} - \overline{X}_{2.j}) + r_{ij}. \qquad [2.22]$$

The modeling options for β_{0j} and β_{1j} at Level-2 are as discussed above. As for β_{2j}, one option is that the effect of X_{2ij} is constrained to be invariant across Level-2 units, implying

$$\beta_{2j} = \gamma_{20},$$

where γ_{20} is the common effect of X_{2ij} in every Level-2 unit. We say that the effect of β_{2j} is *fixed* across Level-2 units.

A second option would be to model the slope β_{2j} as a function of an average value, γ_{20}, plus a random effect associated with each Level-2 unit:

$$\beta_{2j} = \gamma_{20} + u_{2j}. \qquad [2.23]$$

Here, β_{2j} is *random*. Notice that Equation 2.23 specificies no predictors for β_{2j}. Suppose, however, that this slope depends upon W_j. One might then formulate the slopes-as-outcomes model:

$$\beta_{2j} = \gamma_{20} + \gamma_{21} W_j + u_{2j}. \qquad [2.24]$$

According to this model, part of the variation of the slope β_{2j} can be predicted by W_j, but a random component, u_{2j}, remains unexplained. On the other hand, it may be that once the effect of W_j is taken into account, the residual variation in β_{2j}—that is, $\text{Var}(u_{2j}) = \tau_{22}$—is negligible. Then a model constraining that residual variation to be null would be sensible:

$$\beta_{2j} = \gamma_{20} + \gamma_{21} W_j. \qquad [2.25]$$

In this case β_{2j} is a *nonrandomly varying* slope because it varies strictly as a function of the predictor W_j.

So far we have been interested in just a single Level-2 predictor, W_j. The introduction of multiple W_js is straightforward. Further, the Level-2 model does not need to be identical for each equation. One set of W_js may apply for the intercept, a different set be used for β_{1j}, another set for β_{2j}, and so on. When nonparallel specification is employed, however, extra care must be exercised in the interpretation of the results (see Chapter 9).

Generalization of the Error Structures at Level 1 and Level 2

The model specified in Equations 2.2 and 2.4 assumes homogeneous errors at both Level 1 and Level 2. This assumption is quite acceptable for a broad class of multilevel problems. Most of the published applications to date have been based on this assumption, as are all of the examples discussed in Chapters 5 through 8.

The model can easily be extended, however, to more complex error structures at both levels. The Level-1 variance might be different for each Level-2 unit and denoted σ_j^2, or it might be a function of some measured Level-1 characteristic. For example, Goldstein (1987, p. 33) describes a school-effects application where σ^2 takes on a different value for boys than for girls. Similarly at Level 2, a different covariance structure might exist for distinct subsets of Level-2 units. Lee and Bryk (1989) allude to this in their analysis of the social distribution of achievement in public and Catholic high schools. They discuss the possibility that different Level-2 **T** matrices be estimated for public and Catholic schools.

Choosing the Location of *X* and *W* (*Centering*)

In all quantitative research, it is essential that the variables under study have precise meaning so that statistical results can be related to the theoretical concerns that motivate the research. In the case of hierarchical linear models, the intercept and slopes in the Level-1 model become outcome variables at Level 2. It is vital that the meaning of these outcome variables be clearly understood.

The meaning of the intercept in the Level-1 model depends upon the location of the Level-1 predictor variables, the *X*s. We know, for example, that in the simple model

$$Y_{ij} = \beta_{0j} + \beta_{1j}X_{ij} + r_{ij}, \qquad [2.26]$$

the intercept, β_{0j}, is defined as the expected outcome for a student attending school j who has a value of zero on X_{ij}. If the researcher is to make sense of models that account for variation in β_{0j}, he or she must be clear about the meaning of $X_{ij} = 0$. In particular, if an X_{ij} value of 0 is not meaningful, then the researcher may want to transform X_{ij}, or "choose a location for X_{ij}" that will render β_{0j} more meaningful. In some cases, a proper choice of location will be required in order to insure numerical stability in estimating hierarchical linear models.

Similarly, interpretations regarding the intercepts in the Level-2 models (i.e., γ_{00} and γ_{10} in Equations 2.4a and 2.4b) depend on the location of the W_j variables. The numerical stability of estimation is not affected by the location for the *W*s, but a suitable choice will ease interpretation of results. We describe below some common choices for the location of the *X*s and *W*s.

Location of the ***X*****s**

We consider four possibilities for the location of X: the natural X metric, centering around the grand mean, centering around the group mean, and other locations for X. We assume that X is measured on an interval scale. The case of dummy variables is considered separately.

The Natural X *Metric.* Although the natural X metric may be quite appropriate in some applications, in others this may lead to nonsensical results. For example, suppose X is a score on the Scholastic Aptitude Test (SAT), which ranges from 200 to 800. Then the intercept, β_{0j}, will be the expected outcome for a student in school j who had an SAT of zero. The β_{0j} parameter is meaningless in this instance because the minimum score on the test is 200. In such cases, the correlation between the intercept and slope will tend to be near −1.0. As a result, the intercept is essentially determined by the slope. Schools with strong positive SAT-outcome slopes will tend to have very low intercepts. In contrast, schools where the SAT slope is negligible will tend to have much higher intercepts. In some applications, of course, an X value of zero will in fact be meaningful. For example, if X is the dosage of an experimental drug, $X_{ij} = 0$ implies that subject i in group j had no exposure to the drug. As a result, the intercept β_{0j} is the expected outcome for such a subject. That is, $\beta_{0j} = E(Y_{ij} \mid X_{ij} = 0)$. We wish to emphasize that it is always important to consider the meaning of $X_{ij} = 0$ because it determines the interpretation of β_{0j}.

Centering Around the Grand Mean. It is often useful to center the variable X around the grand mean, as discussed earlier (see "One-Way ANCOVA with Random Effects"). In this case, the Level-1 predictors are of the form

$$(X_{ij} - \bar{X}_{..}) . \qquad [2.27]$$

Now, the intercept, β_{0j}, is the expected outcome for a subject whose value on X_{ij} is equal to the grand-mean, $\bar{X}_{..}$. This is the standard location for X_{ij} in the classical ANCOVA model. As is the case in ANCOVA, grand-mean centering yields an intercept that can be interpreted as an adjusted mean for group j,

$$\beta_{0j} = \mu_{Y_j} + \beta_{1j}(X_{.j} - \bar{X}_{..}) .$$

Similarly, the $\text{Var}(\beta_{0j}) = \tau_{00}$ is the variance among the Level-2 units in the adjusted means. We illustrate grand-mean centering in Chapter 5.

Centering Around the Level-2 Mean (Group-Mean Centering). Another option is to center the original predictors around their corresponding Level-2 unit means:

$$(X_{ij} - \overline{X}_{\cdot j}) \, . \qquad [2.28]$$

In this case the intercept β_{0j} becomes the unadjusted mean for group j. That is,

$$\beta_{0j} = \mu_{Y_j} \qquad [2.29]$$

and $\text{Var}(\beta_{0j})$ is now just the variance among the Level-2 unit means, μ_{Y_j}. In Chapter 4, we present a set of analyses where student SES is centered around the school mean so that we can study the population distribution of school means, β_{0j}, and school slopes, β_{1j} .

Other Locations for X. Specialized choices of location for X are often sensible. In some cases the population mean for a predictor may be known and the investigator may wish to define the intercept β_{0j} as the expected outcome in group j for the "average person in the population" (Willms, 1986). In this case, the Level-1 predictor would be the original value of X_{ij} minus the population mean. In applications of two-level hierarchical linear models to the study of growth, the data involve time-series observations so that the Level-1 units are occasions and the Level-2 units are persons. The investigator may wish to define the metric of the Level-1 predictors such that the intercept is the expected outcome for person i at a specific time point of theoretical interest (e.g., entry to school). So long as the data encompass this time point, such a definition is quite appropriate. Examples of this sort are illustrated in Chapters 6 and 8.

In general, sensible choices of location depend upon the purposes of the research. No single rule covers all cases. It is important, however, that the researcher carefully consider choices of location in light of those purposes; and it is vital to keep the location in mind while interpreting results.

Dummy Variables. Consider the familiar Level-1 model,

$$Y_{ij} = \beta_{0j} + \beta_{1j} X_{ij} + r_{ij} \, , \qquad [2.30]$$

where X_{ij} is now an indicator or dummy variable. Suppose, for example, that X_{ij} takes on a value of 1 if subject i in school j is a female and 0 if not. In this case, the intercept β_{0j} is defined as the expected outcome for a male student in group j (i.e., the predicted value for student with $X_{ij} = 0$). We note in this case that $\text{Var}(\beta_{0j}) = \tau_{00}$ will be the variance in the male outcome means across schools.

Although it may seem strange at first to center a Level-1 dummy variable, this is appropriate and often quite useful. Suppose, for example, that the indicator variable for sex is centered around the grand mean, $\bar{X}_{..}$. This centered predictor can take on two values. If the subject is female, $X_{ij} - \bar{X}_{..}$ will equal the proportion of male students in the sample. If the subject is male, $X_{ij} - \bar{X}_{..}$ will be equal to minus the proportion of female students. As in the case of continuous Level-1 predictors centered around the respective grand means, the intercept, β_{0j}, is the adjusted mean outcome in unit j . In this case, it is adjusted for differences among units in the percentage of female students.

Alternatively, we might use group-mean centering. For females, $X_{ij} - \bar{X}_{.j}$ will take on the value equal to the proportion of male students in school j; for males, $X_{ij} - \bar{X}_{.j}$ will take on a value equal to minus the proportion of female students in school j . The fact that X_{ij} is a dummy variable does not change the interpretation given to β_{0j} when group-mean centering is employed. The intercept still represents the average outcome for unit j, μ_{Y_j}.

In sum, several locations of dichotomous predictors will produce meaningful intercepts. Again, it is incumbent on the researcher to take this location into account in interpreting results. Care is especially needed when there are multiple dummy variables. For example, in a school-effects study with indicators for whites, females, and students with preprimary education, the intercept for school j might be the expected outcome for a nonwhite male student with no preprimary experience. This may or may not be the intercept the investigator wants. Again the general caveat—be conscious of the choice of location for each Level-1 predictor because it has implications for interpretation of β_{0j}, $\text{Var}(\beta_{0j})$, and by implication, all of the covariances involving β_{0j} .

Location of *W*s

In general, the choice of location for the *W*s is not as critical as for the Level-1 predictors. Problems of numerical instability are less likely, except when cross-product terms are introduced at Level-2 (e.g., a predictor set of the form W_{1j}, W_{2j}, and $W_{1j}W_{2j}$). All of the γ coefficients can be easily interpreted whatever choice of metric (or nonchoice) is made for Level-2 predictors. Nevertheless, it is often convenient to center all of the Level-2 predictors around their corresponding grand means, for example $W_{1j} - \overline{W}_1$.

Summary of Terms and Notation Introduced in this Chapter

A Simple Two-Level Model

Hierarchical form:

Level 1 (e.g., students) $\quad Y_{ij} = \beta_{0j} + \beta_{1j}X_{ij} + r_{ij}$

Level 2 (e.g., schools) $\quad \beta_{0j} = \gamma_{00} + \gamma_{01}W_j + u_{0j}$

$$\beta_{1j} = \gamma_{10} + \gamma_{11}W_j + u_{ij}$$

Model in *combined form*:

$$Y_{ij} = \gamma_{00} + \gamma_{10}X_{ij} + \gamma_{01}W_j + \gamma_{11}X_{ij}W_j + u_{0j} + u_{1j}X_{ij} + r_{ij}$$

where we assume:

$$E(r_{ij}) = 0 \qquad \mathrm{Var}(r_{ij}) = \sigma^2$$

$$E\begin{bmatrix} u_{0j} \\ u_{1j} \end{bmatrix} = \begin{bmatrix} 0 \\ 0 \end{bmatrix} \qquad \mathrm{Var}\begin{bmatrix} u_{0j} \\ u_{1j} \end{bmatrix} = \begin{bmatrix} \tau_{00} & \tau_{01} \\ \tau_{10} & \tau_{11} \end{bmatrix} = \mathbf{T}$$

$$\mathrm{Cov}(u_{0j},\ r_{ij}) = \mathrm{Cov}(u_{1j},\ r_{ij}) = 0$$

Notation and Terminology Summary

There are $i = 1, \ldots, n_j$ Level-1 units nested with $j = 1, \ldots, J$ Level-2 units. We speak of student i nested within school j.

β_{0j}, β_{1j} are Level-1 coefficients. These can be of three forms:

fixed Level-1 coefficients (e.g., β_{1j} in the one-way random-effects ANCOVA model, Equation 2.14b)

nonrandomly varying Level-1 coefficients (e.g., β_{1j} in the nonrandomly varying slopes model, Equation 2.20) random Level-1 coefficients (e.g., β_{0j} and β_{1j} in the random-coefficient regression model [Equations 2.17a and 2.17b] and in the intercepts- and slopes-as-outcomes model [Equations 2.4a and 2.4b])

$\gamma_{00}, \ldots, \gamma_{11}$ are Level-2 coefficients and are also called fixed effects.

X_{ij} is a Level-1 predictor (e.g., student social class, race, and ability).

W_j is a Level-2 predictor (e.g., school size, sector, social composition).

r_{ij} is a Level-1 random effect.

u_{0j}, u_{1j} are Level-2 random effects.

σ^2 is the Level-1 variance.

τ_{00}, τ_{01}, τ_{11} are Level-2 variance-covariance components.

Some Definitions

Intraclass correlation coefficient (see "One-Way ANOVA with Random Effects"):

$$\rho = \tau_{00}/(\sigma^2 + \tau_{00}) .$$

This coefficient measures the proportion of variance in the outcome that is between groups (i.e., the Level-2 units). It is also sometimes called the *cluster effect.* It applies only to random-intercept models (i.e., $\tau_{11} = 0$).

Unconditional variance-covariance of β_{0j}, β_{1j} are the values of the Level-2 variances and covariances based on the random-coefficient regression model.

Conditional or residual variance-covariance of β_{0j}, β_{1j} are the values of the Level-2 variances and covariances after Level-2 predictors have been added for β_{0j} and β_{1j} (see, e.g., Equations 2.4a and 2.4b).

Submodel Types

One-way random-effects ANOVA model involves no Level-1 or Level-2 predictors. We call this a *fully unconditional* model.

Random-intercept model has only one random Level-1 coefficient, β_{0j}.

Means-as-outcomes regression model is one form of a random-intercept model.

One-way random-effects ANCOVA model is a classic ANCOVA model, except that the Level-2 effects are viewed as random.

Random-coefficients regression model allows all Level-1 coefficients to vary randomly. This model is *unconditional at level 2.*

Centering Definitions	**Implications for β_{0j}**
X_{ij} in the natural metric	$\beta_{0j} = E(Y_{ij} \mid X_{ij} = 0)$
$(X_{ij} - \overline{X}_{..})$ called grand-mean centering	$\beta_{0j} = \mu_{Y_j} - \beta_{1j}(X_{ij} - \overline{X}_{..})$ (i.e., adjusted Level-2 means)
$(X_{ij} - \overline{X}_{.j})$ called group-mean centering	$\beta_{0j} = \mu_{Y_j}$ (i.e., Level-2 means)
X_{ij} centered at some theoretically chosen location for X	$\beta_{0j} = E(Y_{ij} \mid X_{ij} =$ chosen centering location for X)

3 Principles of Estimation and Hypothesis Testing for Hierarchical Linear Models

Our goal in Chapter 2 was to clarify the meaning of the model parameters. In this chapter, we consider methods of estimation and hypothesis testing. These methods are illustrated in Chapter 4 using a sample of data on American high schools.

Estimation Theory

Three types of parameters can be estimated in a hierarchical analysis: fixed effects, random Level-1 coefficients, and variance-covariance components. In actuality, estimation of each of these depends on the others. To clarify basic principles, however, we consider first the estimation of the fixed effects and random coefficients in the case where the variance-covariance components are assumed known. We then consider the estimation of the variance-covariance components themselves. Chapter 10 presents a more rigorous account of the estimation theory and computational approaches used throughout this book.

Estimation of Fixed Effects

We consider fixed-effects estimation for three simple models. First is the one-way random-effects ANOVA model. This involves a single fixed effect, the overall mean, which is estimated as an optimally weighted average of the sample means from the J Level-2 units. Second, we examine the means-as-outcomes model, which includes a Level-2 regression coefficient. Again, the optimal weighting principle applies. Third, we consider the random coefficient regression model. Although the optimal weighting principle applies here too, the weighting is now multivariate and requires matrix notation. For those unfamiliar with such notation, the first two examples should suffice to convey the essential idea.

One-Way ANOVA: Point Estimation. As in Chapter 2, we begin with the one-way random-effects ANOVA. Recall from Equation 2.6 that the Level-1 model was

$$Y_{ij} = \beta_{0j} + r_{ij} \qquad [3.1]$$

for Level-1 units $i = 1, \ldots, n_j$ and Level-2 units $j = 1, \ldots, J$, where we assume $r_{ij} \sim \mathrm{N}(0, \sigma^2)$.

Averaging across the n_j observations within school j yields a Level-1 model with the sample mean as the outcome

$$\bar{Y}_{\cdot j} = \beta_{0j} + \bar{r}_{\cdot j} \qquad [3.2]$$

where

$$\bar{r}_{\cdot j} = \sum_{i=1}^{n_j} r_{ij}/n_j .$$

Equation 3.2 shows that the sample mean, $\bar{Y}_{\cdot j}$, is an estimate of true school mean, β_{0j}. The error of estimation is $\bar{r}_{\cdot j}$, which has a variance

$$\mathrm{Var}(\bar{r}_{\cdot j}) = \sigma^2/n_j = V_j . \qquad [3.3]$$

We refer to V_j as the *error variance,* that is, the variance of $\bar{Y}_{\cdot j}$ as an estimator of β_{0j}.

The Level-2 model is

$$\beta_{0j} = \gamma_{00} + u_{0j} \qquad [3.4]$$

where we assume $u_{0j} \sim \mathrm{N}(0, \tau_{00})$. Notice that τ_{00} is the variance of the true means, β_{0j}, about the grand mean, γ_{00}. We shall refer to τ_{00} as *parameter variance.*

Substituting Equation 3.4 into Equation 3.2 yields the combined model for $\bar{Y}_{\cdot j}$:

$$\bar{Y}_{\cdot j} = \gamma_{00} + u_{0j} + \bar{r}_{\cdot j} \ . \qquad [3.5]$$

The variance of $\bar{Y}_{\cdot j}$ has two components:

$$\begin{aligned} \mathrm{Var}(\bar{Y}_{\cdot j}) &= \mathrm{Var}(u_{0j}) + \mathrm{Var}(\bar{r}_{\cdot j}) \qquad [3.6] \\ &= \tau_{00} + V_j \\ &= \text{parameter variance} + \text{error variance} \\ &= \Delta_j \ . \end{aligned}$$

Notice that although the parameter variance, τ_{00}, is constant across Level-2 units, the error variance, $V_j = \sigma^2/n_j$, varies depending on the sample size, n_j, for each Level-2 unit.

If every Level-2 unit has the same sample size, every V_j will be equal to a common V and every Δ_j will be equal to a common Δ, that is, $\Delta = \tau_{00} + V$. Then the unique, minimum-variance, unbiased estimator of γ_{00} would be just the average value of $\bar{Y}_{\cdot j}$:

$$\tilde{\gamma}_{00} = \sum \bar{Y}_{\cdot j}/J \ . \qquad [3.7]$$

If the sample sizes are not equal, however, the statistics, $\bar{Y}_{\cdot j}$, have unequal variances $\Delta_j = \tau_{00} + V_j$. Viewing each $\bar{Y}_{\cdot j}$ as an independent, unbiased estimator of γ_{00} with variance Δ_j, we define the *precision* of $\bar{Y}_{\cdot j}$ as the reciprocal of its variance—that is,

$$\text{Precision } (\bar{Y}_{\cdot j}) = \Delta_j^{-1} \ . \qquad [3.8]$$

Then, assuming Δ_j is known, the unique, minimum-variance, unbiased estimator of γ_{00} is the *precision weighted average*:

$$\hat{\gamma}_{00} = \sum \Delta_j^{-1} \bar{Y}_{\cdot j} / \sum \Delta_j^{-1} \ . \qquad [3.9]$$

Equation 3.9 is commonly called the weighted least squares estimator of γ_{00} . Note that the values of Δ_j must be known (or estimated) to compute $\hat{\gamma}_{00}$, which was not true in the equal-sample-size case (see Equation 3.7). Clearly, the precision-weighted average applies generally. When all the precisions are equal, the precision weighted average (Equation 3.9) reduces to the simple average (Equation 3.7).

One-Way ANOVA: Interval Estimation. The precision of $\hat{\gamma}_{00}$ is the sum of the precisions, that is,

$$\text{Precision}\,(\hat{\gamma}_{00}) = \sum \Delta_j^{-1}\,. \qquad [3.10]$$

The variance of $\hat{\gamma}_{00}$ is the inverse of its precision:

$$\text{Var}(\hat{\gamma}_{00}) = \left(\sum \Delta_j^{-1}\right)^{-1}. \qquad [3.11]$$

Therefore, the 95% confidence interval for $\hat{\gamma}_{00}$ is given by

$$95\%\ \text{CI}(\gamma_{00}) = \hat{\gamma}_{00} \pm 1.96\left(\sum \Delta_j^{-1}\right)^{-1/2}. \qquad [3.12]$$

Regression with Means-as-Outcomes: Point Estimation. Again paralleling the presentation in Chapter 2, we now consider an analysis in which the Level-1 mean is predicted by a Level-2 variable. The combined model for the sample mean is now

$$\bar{Y}_{\cdot j} = \gamma_{00} + \gamma_{01}W_j + u_{0j} + \bar{r}_{\cdot j}\,, \qquad [3.13]$$

and the variance of $\bar{Y}_{\cdot j}$ given W_j is

$$\text{Var}(\bar{Y}_{\cdot j}) = \tau_{00} + V_j = \Delta_j\,, \qquad [3.14]$$

where $V_j = \sigma^2/n_j$. Note that Δ_j is now the residual variance of $\bar{Y}_{\cdot j}$, that is, the conditional variance of $\bar{Y}_{\cdot j}$ given W_j . Again, we assume that u_{0j} and r_{ij} are normally distributed.

If every group had the same sample size, Δ_j would be identical in each group and the unique, minimum-variance, unbiased estimator of γ_{01} would be the ordinary least squares (OLS) estimator

$$\tilde{\gamma}_{01} = \frac{\sum (W_j - \bar{W}_{\cdot})(\bar{Y}_{\cdot j} - \bar{Y}_{\cdot\cdot})}{\sum (W_j - \bar{W}_{\cdot})^2} \qquad [3.15]$$

where

$$\overline{W}. = \sum W_j/J \quad \text{and} \quad \overline{Y}.. = \sum \overline{Y}._j/J .$$

The OLS estimator of γ_{00} is

$$\tilde{\gamma}_{00} = \overline{Y}.. - \tilde{\gamma}_{01}\overline{W}. \quad . \qquad [3.16]$$

If the sample sizes n_j are unequal, however, the $\overline{Y}._j$s will have unequal variance $\Delta_j = \tau_{00} + V_j$. In this case, assuming every Δ_j is known, the unique, minimum variance, unbiased estimator of γ_{01} will be the weighted least squares estimator in which each group's data is weighted proportional to its precision, Δ_j^{-1}:

$$\hat{\gamma}_{01} = \frac{\sum \Delta_j^{-1} (W_j - \overline{W}.^*)(\overline{Y}._j - \overline{Y}.^*.)}{\sum \Delta_j^{-1} (W_j - \overline{W}.^*)^2} . \qquad [3.17]$$

where $\overline{W}.^*$ and $\overline{Y}.^*.$ are now also precision weighted averages:

$$\overline{W}.^* = \sum \Delta_j^{-1} W_j / \sum \Delta_j^{-1} \qquad [3.18a]$$

$$\overline{Y}.^*. = \sum \Delta_j^{-1} \overline{Y}._j / \sum \Delta_j^{-1} . \qquad [3.18b]$$

The weighted least squares estimator of γ_{00} is

$$\hat{\gamma}_{00} = \overline{Y}.^*. - \hat{\gamma}_{01}\overline{W}.^* . \qquad [3.19]$$

Regression with Means-as-Outcomes: Interval Estimation. The sampling variance of the statistic $\hat{\gamma}_{01}$, given Δ_j, is

$$\text{Var}(\hat{\gamma}_{01}) = \left[\sum \Delta_j^{-1}(W_j - \overline{W}.^*)^2\right]^{-1} . \qquad [3.20]$$

Thus a 95% confidence interval for $\hat{\gamma}_{01}$ is given by

$$95\%\ \text{CI}(\gamma_{01}) = \hat{\gamma}_{01} \pm 1.96[\text{Var}(\hat{\gamma}_{01})]^{1/2} , \qquad [3.21]$$

and a test of the null hypothesis H_0: $\gamma_{01} = 0$ is given by the statistic

$$z = \hat{\gamma}_{01}/[\text{Var}(\hat{\gamma}_{01})]^{1/2} , \qquad [3.22]$$

to be compared with the critical value of a unit normal variate.

More General Models: Point Estimation.[1] The extension of these basic principles to more general cases is straightforward. The general Level-1 model with Q predictor variables can be expressed in matrix notation as

$$\mathbf{Y}_j = \mathbf{X}_j \boldsymbol{\beta}_j + \mathbf{r}_j\,, \qquad \mathbf{r}_j \sim \mathrm{N}(\mathbf{0}\,,\ \sigma^2 \mathbf{I})\,, \tag{3.23}$$

where $\mathbf{Y}_j$ is an n_j by 1 vector of outcomes, $\mathbf{X}_j$ is an n_j by $(Q + 1)$ matrix of predictor variables, $\boldsymbol{\beta}_j$ is a $(Q + 1)$ by 1 vector of unknown parameters, $\mathbf{I}$ is an n_j by n_j identity matrix, and $\mathbf{r}_j$ is an n_j by 1 vector of random errors assumed normally distributed with a mean vector of $\mathbf{0}$ and a variance-covariance matrix in which all diagonal elements are equal to σ^2 and all off-diagonal elements are 0.

Assuming $\mathbf{X}_j$ to be of full column rank $Q + 1$, the OLS estimator of $\boldsymbol{\beta}_j$ is

$$\hat{\boldsymbol{\beta}}_j = (\mathbf{X}_j' \mathbf{X}_j)^{-1}\, \mathbf{X}_j' \mathbf{Y}_j\,, \tag{3.24}$$

and its dispersion matrix is given by

$$\mathrm{Var}(\hat{\boldsymbol{\beta}}_j) = \mathbf{V}_j = \sigma^2 (\mathbf{X}_j' \mathbf{X}_j)^{-1}\,. \tag{3.25}$$

Premultiplying Equation 3.23 by $(\mathbf{X}_j'\mathbf{X}_j)^{-1}\mathbf{X}_j'$ yields the model for $\hat{\boldsymbol{\beta}}_j$:

$$\hat{\boldsymbol{\beta}}_j = \boldsymbol{\beta}_j + \mathbf{e}_j\,, \quad \mathbf{e}_j \sim \mathrm{N}(\mathbf{0}\,,\ \mathbf{V}_j)\,, \tag{3.26}$$

where $\mathbf{V}_j$ is the error-variance matrix, indicating the error dispersion of the $\hat{\boldsymbol{\beta}}_j$ as an estimate of $\boldsymbol{\beta}_j$.

At Level 2, the general model for $\boldsymbol{\beta}_j$ is

$$\boldsymbol{\beta}_j = \mathbf{W}_j \boldsymbol{\gamma} + \mathbf{u}_j\,, \quad \mathbf{u}_j \sim \mathrm{N}(\mathbf{0}\,,\ \mathbf{T})\,, \tag{3.27}$$

where $\mathbf{W}_j$ is a $(Q + 1)$ by F matrix of predictors, $\boldsymbol{\gamma}$ is an F by 1 vector of fixed effects, $\mathbf{u}_j$ is a $(Q + 1)$ by 1 vector of Level-2 errors or random effects, and $\mathbf{T}$ is an arbitrary $(Q + 1)$ by $(Q + 1)$ variance-covariance matrix. Note that $\mathbf{T}$ is the residual variance-covariance matrix, indicating the dispersion of $\boldsymbol{\beta}_j$ about the expected value $\mathbf{W}_j\boldsymbol{\gamma}$. The $\mathbf{W}_j$ matrix involves a stacking of the $Q + 1$ row vectors of predictors in a block diagonal fashion. Each row in the matrix corresponds to one of the $Q + 1$ outcome variables, β_{qj}, in the Level-2 model. (For a simple illustration of this block diagonal $\mathbf{W}_j$ see Equation 3.68.)

Substituting Equation 3.27 into Equation 3.26 yields the single, combined model

$$\hat{\beta}_j = \mathbf{W}_j\gamma + \mathbf{u}_j + \mathbf{e}_j\,, \qquad [3.28]$$

where the dispersion of $\hat{\beta}_j$ given $\mathbf{W}_j$ is

$$\text{Var}(\hat{\beta}_j) = \text{Var}(\mathbf{u}_j + \mathbf{e}_j) = \mathbf{T} + \mathbf{V}_j = \Delta_j \qquad [3.29]$$

$$= \text{parameter dispersion} + \text{error dispersion}\,.$$

If the data were perfectly balanced such that each group had the same number of observations and the same values of the predictor matrix **X**, each $\hat{\beta}_j$ would have the same dispersion Δ, where

$$\Delta = \mathbf{T} + \mathbf{V} = \mathbf{T} + \sigma^2(\mathbf{X}'\mathbf{X})^{-1}\,. \qquad [3.30]$$

In this case, the unique, minimum-variance, unbiased estimator of γ would be the OLS regression estimator

$$\tilde{\gamma} = \left(\sum \mathbf{W}_j'\mathbf{W}_j\right)^{-1} \sum \mathbf{W}_j'\hat{\beta}_j\,. \qquad [3.31]$$

However, given that the data are not perfectly balanced, the Δ_j values will differ from group to group, and, assuming each Δ_j is known, the unique, minimum-variance, unbiased estimator of γ will be the *generalized least squares* (GLS) estimator

$$\hat{\gamma} = \left(\sum \mathbf{W}_j'\Delta_j^{-1}\mathbf{W}_j\right)^{-1} \sum \mathbf{W}_j'\Delta_j^{-1}\hat{\beta}_j\,. \qquad [3.32]$$

The GLS estimator weights each group's data by its precision matrix, that is, Δ_j^{-1}, which is the inverse of the variance-covariance matrix. Notice the close parallel between the GLS estimator and the weighted least squares estimator (Equation 3.17) in the case of means-as-outcomes.

More General Models: Interval Estimation. Confidence regions for γ are based on the diagonal elements of $\mathbf{V}_{\hat{\gamma}}$, the dispersion matrix of the estimates $\hat{\gamma}$, where

$$\mathbf{V}_{\hat{\gamma}} = \text{Var}(\hat{\gamma}) = \left(\sum \mathbf{W}_j\Delta_j^{-1}\mathbf{W}_j\right)^{-1}\,. \qquad [3.33]$$

For example, a 95% confidence interval for a particular element, say γ_h, is given by

$$95\%\ \text{CI}(\gamma_h) = \hat{\gamma}_h \pm 1.96(V_{hh})^{1/2} \qquad [3.34]$$

where V_{hh} is the hth diagonal element of $\mathbf{V}_{\hat{\gamma}}$.

Deficient Rank Data. The formulas for $\hat{\gamma}$ (Equation 3.32) and $\mathbf{V}_{\hat{\gamma}}$ (Equation 3.33) are useful for purposes of exposition but are rather limited in application. Specifically, they require (a) that all Level-1 coefficients are random, and (b) that every Level-2 unit contains an adequate sample to allow computation of the OLS estimate, $\hat{\beta}_j$ (Equation 3.24). More general formulas, which allow relaxation of both of these conditions, are presented in Chapter 10. These general formulas reduce to Equations 3.32 and 3.33 when the two restrictions apply.

Estimation of Random Level-1 Coefficients

In the examples provided thus far, we have formulated a Level-1 model in which the outcome depends on certain coefficients (e.g., a mean or a regression coefficient) that vary across Level-2 units. The question now arises: What is the "best estimate" of these Level-1 coefficients?

The One-Way ANOVA Case: Point Estimation. In our simplest example, we had the two-level model

$$\bar{Y}_{.j} = \beta_{0j} + \bar{r}_{.j}, \quad \bar{r}_{.j} \sim \text{N}(0,\ V_j)$$

$$\beta_{0j} = \gamma_{00} + u_{0j}, \quad u_{0j} \sim \text{N}(0,\ \tau_{00}).$$

This model suggests two alternative estimators of β_{0j}. First, based on the Level-1 model, we see that $\bar{Y}_{.j}$ is an unbiased estimator of β_{0j} with variance V_j. However, $\hat{\gamma}_{00} = \Sigma\Delta_j^{-1}\bar{Y}_{.j}/\Sigma\Delta_j^{-1}$ could also be viewed as a common estimator of each β_{0j}. A Bayes estimator (Lindley & Smith, 1972), call it β^*_{0j}, is in fact an "optimal" weighted combination of these two:

$$\beta^*_{0j} = \lambda_j \bar{Y}_{.j} + (1 - \lambda_j)\hat{\gamma}_{00}. \qquad [3.35]$$

The weight λ_j is equal to the reliability of $\bar{Y}_{.j}$ as an estimate of β_{0j} (Kelley, 1927)—that is,

$$\lambda_j = \text{Var}(\beta_{0j})/\text{Var}(\bar{Y}_{.j}) = \tau_{00}/(\tau_{00} + V_j). \qquad [3.36]$$

= (parameter variance)/(parameter variance + error variance).

In the language of classical test theory, $\bar{Y}_{.j}$ is a measure of the true, unknown parameter β_{0j}. We refer to λ_j as a reliability because it measures the ratio of the *true score* or parameter variance, relative to the *observed score* or total variance of the sample mean, $\bar{Y}_{.j}$. The reliability λ_j will be close to 1 when (a) the group means, β_{0j}, vary substantially across Level-2 units (holding constant the sample size per group); or (b) the sample size n_j is large.

When the sample mean is a highly reliable estimate, β^*_{0j} puts substantial weight on $\bar{Y}_{.j}$. However, if the sample mean is unreliable, the estimated grand mean $\hat{\gamma}_{00}$ will be given more weight in composing β^*_{0j}.[2]

The weighted average, β^*_{0j}, can also be understood by noting that

$$\lambda_j = V_j^{-1}/(V_j^{-1} + \tau_{00}^{-1}) \qquad [3.37a]$$

and

$$1 - \lambda_j = \tau_{00}^{-1}/(V_j^{-1} + \tau_{00}^{-1})^{-1} . \qquad [3.37b]$$

These expressions show that λ_j, the weight accorded to $\bar{Y}_{.j}$ in composing β^*_{0j}, is proportional to V_j^{-1}, which is the precision of $\bar{Y}_{.j}$ as an estimate of β_{0j}. The weight of $1 - \lambda_j$ accorded $\hat{\gamma}_{00}$ is proportional to τ_{00}^{-1}, which represents the concentration of the β_{0j} parameters around their central tendency γ_{00}. Thus, the more precise $\bar{Y}_{.j}$ is as an estimate of β_{0j}, the more weight it is accorded. Also, the more concentrated the β_{0j} values are around their central tendency γ_{00}, the more weight $\hat{\gamma}_{00}$ is accorded.

We say that the weighted average, β^*_{0j}, is optimal in that no other estimator of β_{0j} has a smaller expected mean-squared error (Lindley & Smith, 1972).[3] Actually, β^*_{0j} is biased toward γ_{00}. When the true value of β_{0j} is greater than γ_{00}, β^*_{0j} will be negatively biased; when β_{0j} is less than γ_{00}, β^*_{0j} will be positively biased. However, on average, β^*_{0j} will tend to be closer to β_{0j} than will any unbiased estimator (e.g., $\bar{Y}_{.j}$). The efficiency of $\bar{Y}_{.j}$ relative to β^*_{0j} is approximately λ_j, which cannot exceed unity (Raudenbush, 1988). Because β^*_{0j} "pulls" $\bar{Y}_{.j}$ toward γ_{00}, β^*_{0j} is called a *shrinkage estimator.* Similar shrinkage estimators were derived by James and Stein (1961), who proved their advantageous properties. Applications of shrinkage estimators are reviewed in detail by Efron and Morris (1975) and Morris (1983).

The estimate β^*_{0j} has often been labeled a Bayes estimate (Lindley & Smith, 1972). When the variances are unknown and β^*_{0j} is based on substituting an estimate of λ_j into Equation 3.35, the estimates have been termed *empirical Bayes estimates* (Morris, 1983).

One-Way ANOVA Case: Interval Estimation. A confidence interval for β_{0j} may be constructed based on V_j^* where[4]

$$V_j^* = (V_j^{-1} + \tau_{00}^{-1})^{-1} + (1 - \lambda_j)^2 \, \text{Var}(\hat{\gamma}_{00}) . \quad [3.38]$$

A 95% confidence interval for β_{0j} is therefore given by

$$95\% \ \text{CI}(\beta_{0j}) = \beta_{0j}^* \pm 1.96 V_j^{*1/2} . \quad [3.39]$$

This confidence interval is exact when the variances σ^2 and τ_{00} are known. However, it is only an approximation when these variances are unknown, and in this case, the confidence intervals will be shorter than they should be. Unless J is large, these intervals should be used with caution.[5]

Regression with Means-as-Outcomes: Point Estimation. Suppose now that we are interested in using information about a Level-2 variable, W_j, to predict β_{0j}. What is the "best" estimator of β_{0j}? Our Level-1 model remains as in Equation 3.2, but the Level-2 model becomes

$$\beta_{0j} = \gamma_{00} + \gamma_{01} W_j + u_{0j} , \quad u_{0j} \sim \text{N}(0 , \tau_{00}) . \quad [3.40]$$

Again we are confronted with two estimators of β_{0j}. First, we have the sample mean $\hat{\beta}_{0j} = \bar{Y}_{.j}$. Second, we have the predicted value of β_{0j} given W_j:

$$\hat{\beta}_{0j} = \hat{\gamma}_{00} + \hat{\gamma}_{01} W_j . \quad [3.41]$$

Again we can optimally combine these two estimators in a composite estimator

$$\beta_{0j}^* = \lambda_j \bar{Y}_{.j} + (1 - \lambda_j)(\hat{\gamma}_{00} + \hat{\gamma}_{01} W_j) . \quad [3.42]$$

This version of β_{0j}^* is again an empirical Bayes or shrinkage estimator. However, now $\bar{Y}_{.j}$ is shrunk toward a predicted value rather than toward the grand mean. We refer to this estimate as a *conditional shrinkage estimator* because the amount of shrinkage is now conditional on W_j. The weight accorded $\bar{Y}_{.j}$ is still proportional to its precision V_j^{-1}, but now the weight accorded the predicted value is proportional to τ_{00}^{-1}, which is the concentration of the β_{0j} values around the regression line, $\hat{\gamma}_{00} + \hat{\gamma}_{01} W_j$. This means that if a substantial proportion of the variation in β_{0j} is explained by W_j, the residual variance around the regression line, τ_{00}, will be small. As a result, the concentration, τ_{00}^{-1}, of the β_{0j} around the regression line will be large.

Corresponding to the empirical Bayes estimator β_{0j}^* is the *empirical Bayes residual,* u_{0j}^*. This is an estimate of the deviation of β_{0j}^* from its predicted value based on the Level-2 model. In terms of Equation 3.41,

$$u_{0j}^* = \beta_{0j}^* - \hat{\gamma}_{00} - \hat{\gamma}_{01} W_j . \qquad [3.43]$$

It is useful to compare these to the *least squares residual,* $\hat{u}_{0j}$. The latter is an estimate of the deviation of the OLS estimator of β_{0j} from its predicted value based on the Level-2 model. In this instance,

$$\hat{u}_{0j} = \bar{Y}_{\cdot j} - \hat{\gamma}_{00} - \hat{\gamma}_{01} W_j . \qquad [3.44]$$

It can be shown easily that u_{0j}^* is a value of $\hat{u}_{0j}$ "shrunk" toward zero:

$$u_{0j}^* = \lambda_j \hat{u}_{0j} . \qquad [3.45]$$

Thus, if the reliability λ_j is unity, no shrinkage occurs. In contrast, if $\lambda_j =$ 0, shrinkage toward the predicted value (e.g. Equation 3.41) is complete.

Regression with Means-as-Outcomes: Interval Estimation. A confidence interval for β_{0j} may be constructed based on V_j^* and the predictor W_j, where now

$$V_j^* = (V_j^{-1} + \tau_{00}^{-1})^{-1} + (1 - \lambda_j)^2 \,[\mathrm{Var}(\hat{\gamma}_{00} + \hat{\gamma}_{01} W_j)] . \qquad [3.46]$$

A 95% confidence interval for β_{0j} is therefore given by

$$95\%\ \mathrm{CI}(\beta_{0j}) = \beta_{0j}^* \pm 1.96 V_j^{*1/2} . \qquad [3.47]$$

As in the one-way ANOVA case, such confidence intervals will be spuriously short when J is small.

More General Models: Point Estimation.[6] Again we can extend the basic principle of shrinkage to the more general model represented by Equations 3.23 and 3.27. Our goal is to find the best estimator of β_j. Again we are confronted with two alternatives. The first estimator is simply the OLS regression estimator, $\hat{\beta}_j$, based on data from group *j:*

$$\hat{\beta}_j = (\mathbf{X}_j' \mathbf{X}_j)^{-1} \mathbf{X}_j' \mathbf{Y}_j . \qquad [3.48]$$

The second estimator is the predicted value of β_j given group characteristics captured in $\mathbf{W}_j$:

$$\hat{\hat{\beta}}_j = \mathbf{W}_j \hat{\gamma}, \qquad [3.49]$$

where $\hat{\gamma}$ is estimated by means of GLS as in Equation 3.32.

The optimal combination of these two estimators is

$$\beta_j^* = \Lambda_j \hat{\beta}_j + (\mathbf{I} - \Lambda_j) \mathbf{W}_j \hat{\gamma} \qquad [3.50]$$

where

$$\Lambda_j = \mathbf{T}(\mathbf{T} + \mathbf{V}_j)^{-1} \qquad [3.51]$$

is the ratio of the parameter dispersion matrix for β_j (i.e., $\mathbf{T}$) relative to the dispersion matrix for the $\hat{\beta}_j$, which contains both error dispersion and parameter dispersion (i.e., $\mathbf{T} + \mathbf{V}_j$). We may view Λ_j as a *multivariate reliability matrix.* In general, the more reliable $\hat{\beta}_j$ is as an estimate of β_j, the more weight it will be accorded in composing β_j^* . If the $\hat{\beta}_j$ values are unreliable, β_j^* will pull $\hat{\beta}_j$ toward $\mathbf{W}_j \hat{\gamma}$. The shrinkage formulas for the simple models (Equations 3.35 and 3.42) can be derived from Equation 3.50 after substitution and simplification.

Reliability of the OLS Level-1 Coefficients. The diagonal elements of $\mathbf{T}$ and $\mathbf{V}_j$, denoted by τ_{qq} and v_{qqj}, respectively, can be used to form reliability indices for each of the $Q + 1$ OLS Level-1 coefficients. Analogous to Equation 3.36,

$$\text{reliability of } (\hat{\beta}_{qj}) = \tau_{qq}/(\tau_{qq} + v_{qqj}) \text{ for each } q = 0, \ldots, Q\,. \qquad [3.52]$$

Because the sampling variance v_{qqj} of $\hat{\beta}_{qj}$ will in general be different among the J units, each Level-2 unit has a unique set of reliability indices. The overall reliability across the set of J Level-2 units can be summarized as

$$\text{reliability } (\hat{\beta}_q) = \frac{1}{J} \sum_{j=1}^{J} \tau_{qq}/(\tau_{qq} + v_{qqj}) \qquad [3.53]$$

$$\text{for each } q = 0, \ldots, Q\,.$$

We explicitly note that Equation 3.53 is not the same as the diagonal elements of Λ_j in Equation 3.51.

More General Models: Interval Estimation. A confidence interval for β_j may be constructed based on the conditional variance-covariance matrix, $\mathbf{V}_j^*$, given the data, where

$$\mathbf{V}_j^* = (\mathbf{V}_j^{-1} + \mathbf{T}^{-1})^{-1} + (\mathbf{I} - \Lambda_j)\,[\mathrm{Var}(\mathbf{W}_j\hat{\gamma})]\,(\mathbf{I} - \Lambda_j)'. \qquad [3.54]$$

For example, a 95% confidence interval for β_{qj} is given by

$$95\%\ \mathrm{CI}(\beta_{qj}) = \beta_{qj}^* \pm 1.96(V_{qqj}^*)^{1/2}, \qquad [3.55]$$

where V_{qqj}^* is the qth diagonal element of $\mathbf{V}_j^*$.

Deficient Rank Data. Equations 3.48 and 3.50 are useful for exposition, but they require that (a) all elements of β_j are random, and (b) every group j has sufficient data to allow computation of $\hat{\beta}_j$ by means of OLS. Chapter 10 presents general formulas that do not require these conditions (see especially Equations 10.31, 10.32, 10.33, and 10.34).

Estimation of Variance and Covariance Components

So far we have assumed that the variance and covariance components are known. Although this assumption clarifies understanding of estimation of the fixed and random effects, the variances and covariances must nearly always be estimated in practice.

Past use of hierarchical models has been limited by the fact that only in cases of perfectly balanced designs are closed-form mathematical formulas available to estimate the variance and covariance components. To achieve balance, not only must each Level-2 unit have the same sample size ($n_j = n$ for every j), but the distribution of predictors within each Level-2 unit must be identical ($\mathbf{X}_j = \mathbf{X}$ for every j). When designs are unbalanced (as is typically true), iterative numerical procedures must be used to obtain efficient estimates, usually via maximum likelihood. In recent years several computer algorithms have become available that economically provide estimates even for complex models.

Three conceptually distinct approaches to this problem have come into use. They are *full maximum likelihood* (Goldstein, 1986; Longford, 1987), *restricted maximum likelihood* (Mason et al. 1983; Raudenbush & Bryk, 1986), and *Bayes estimation.* Dempster et al. (1981) discuss the differences among these approaches. Details on maximum likelihood methods for estimating the variances and covariances are presented in Chapter 10. We limit our discussion here to a conceptual introduction.

Full Maximum Likelihood (MLF). For any set of possible values of the parameters γ, **T**, and σ^2 in Equations 3.23 and 3.27, there is some likelihood of observing a particular sample of data **Y**, where **Y** is an N by 1 vector containing the outcomes for the N Level-1 units of the study. (Note: $N = \Sigma n_j$ where n_j is the sample size per Level-2 unit.) The basic idea of maximum likelihood is to choose estimates of γ, **T**, and σ^2 for which the likelihood of observing the actual data **Y** is a maximum.

Estimates based on this approach have certain desirable properties. Under quite general assumptions, these estimates are *consistent* (i.e., they will be very near the true parameter with high probability if enough data are collected) and asymptotically *efficient* (i.e., given a large sample of data, the maximum likelihood estimators are approximately unbiased with minimum variance). Another advantage is that if one wants to estimate a function of parameters, one simply plugs in maximum likelihood estimates of the parameters. The resulting function will itself be a maximum likelihood estimator.

For example, we mentioned earlier that the estimator of γ_{00} in a one-way unbalanced ANOVA with random effects was

$$\hat{\gamma}_{00} = \sum \Delta_j^{-1}\bar{Y}_{\cdot j} / \sum \Delta_j^{-1} ,$$

under the assumption that Δ_j is known. If each Δ_j is not known, but a maximum likelihood estimate of Δ_j is substituted, the resulting estimator $\hat{\gamma}_{00}$ will itself be a maximum likelihood estimator with its desirable statistical properties.

Another useful feature of maximum likelihood estimators is that as sample sizes increase, their sampling distributions become approximately normal with a variance that can readily be estimated. Thus, even if the method for obtaining the MLF estimator is iterative (because no closed-form analytic expression is available), the large sample distribution of the estimator is well defined.

Restricted Maximum Likelihood (MLR). One shortcoming of MLF is that estimates of variances and covariances are conditional upon point estimates of the fixed effects. Consider a simple regression model

$$Y_i = \beta_0 + \beta_1 X_{1i} + \beta_2 X_{2i} + \ldots + \beta_Q X_{Qi} + r_i \qquad [3.56]$$

where the errors r_i, $i = 1, \ldots, n$, are normally distributed with a mean of zero and a constant variance, σ^2. Imagine for a moment that the $Q + 1$ regression coefficients $\beta_0, \beta_1, \ldots, \beta_Q$ were known. Then the maximum likelihood estimator of σ^2 would be

$$\hat{\sigma}^2 = \sum r_i^2/n\,. \qquad [3.57]$$

Now suppose that the regression parameters were unknown (which is typically the case) and therefore must be estimated. The residuals will be

$$\hat{r}_i = Y_i - \hat{\beta}_0 - \hat{\beta}_1 X_{1i} - \hat{\beta}_2 X_{2i} - \ldots - \hat{\beta}_Q X_{Qi}\,, \qquad [3.58]$$

where each $\hat{\beta}_q$ is the OLS estimate. In this case, the usual unbiased estimator of σ^2 will be

$$\hat{\sigma}^2 = \sum \hat{r}_i^2/(n - Q - 1)\,. \qquad [3.59]$$

Notice that the denominator, $(n - Q - 1)$, corrects for the degrees of freedom used in estimating the $Q + 1$ regression parameters. Often Q is small, so the correction will have little effect.[7] However, as Q increases, use of Equation 3.57 can lead to a serious bias in estimating σ^2. The bias will be negative, so the σ^2 estimate will typically be too small, leading to artificially short confidence intervals and overly liberal hypothesis tests. This distinction between Equations 3.57 and 3.59 is precisely the difference between MLF (Equation 3.57) and MLR (Equation 3.59).[8]

For hierarchical linear models, the difference between variance-covariance estimates based on MLF versus MLR is not expressible in simple algebraic form. However, the MLR estimates of variance components do adjust for the uncertainty about the fixed effects, and the MLF results do not. For the two-level model, MLF and MLR will generally produce very similar results for σ^2, but noticeable differences can occur in the estimation of $\mathbf{T}$. In cases where the number of Level-2 units, J, is large, the two methods will produce very similar results. However, when J is small the MLF variance estimates, $\hat{\tau}_{qq}$, will be smaller than MLR by a factor of approximately $(J - F)/J$, where F is the total number of elements in the fixed-effects vector, γ.

Confidence Intervals for Variance Components Based on Maximum Likelihood. It is possible to compute standard error estimates for each variance and covariance term contained in $\mathbf{T}$, as well as for σ^2. Longford (1987) provides formulas for these (in the case of MLF), and such estimates may also be computed as a by-product of the method of iterative GLS discussed by Goldstein (1987). Chapter 10 of this book presents formulas for both MLF and MLR cases.

Difficulties arise, however, in using such standard error estimates. The key problem is that the sampling distribution of the variance estimates, $\hat{\tau}_{qq}$, is skewed to a degree that is unknown. As a result, symmetrical confidence intervals and statistical tests based on these may be highly misleading. Alternative approaches to hypothesis testing are presented later in this chapter.

Bayes Estimation. Both MLF and MLR have a weakness that is corrected by a Bayesian approach to estimation of variances and covariances. Inferences about the fixed effects—that is, confidence intervals and hypothesis tests—are conditional on the accuracy of point estimates of the variance-covariance parameters. For example, the 95% confidence interval for $\hat{\gamma}_{01}$ in the means-as-outcomes example was

$$95\%\ \mathrm{CI}(\gamma_{01}) = \hat{\gamma}_{01} \pm 1.96(V_{\hat{\gamma}_{01}})^{1/2},$$

where

$$V_{\hat{\gamma}_{01}} = \mathrm{Var}(\hat{\gamma}_{01}) = \left[\sum \Delta_j^{-1}(W_j - \overline{W}.^*)^2\right]^{-1}.$$

Suppose that estimates of $\hat{\Delta}_j = \hat{\tau}_{00} + \hat{V}_j$ were substituted into this formula. If τ_{00} were poorly estimated, the confidence interval could be quite inaccurate. Note also that using 1.96, the critical value of a unit normal variate at the .025 level, would not be exact, because the sampling distribution of $(\hat{\gamma}_{01} - \gamma_{01})/(V_{\hat{\gamma}_{01}})^{1/2}$ is exactly normal only if $V_{\hat{\gamma}_{01}}$ is known.

Fotiu's (1989) simulation study found that more appropriate confidence intervals use the critical t value as the multiplier, yielding

$$95\%\ \mathrm{CI}(\hat{\gamma}_{01}) = \hat{\gamma}_{01} \pm t_{.025}(\hat{V}_{\hat{\gamma}_{01}})^{1/2},$$

where $\hat{V}_{\hat{\gamma}_{01}}$ is based on substituting estimates of τ_{00} and σ^2 into the formula for $V_{\hat{\gamma}_{01}}$.

Bayesian estimation allows the researcher to make inferences about γ that are not conditional on specific point estimates of $\mathbf{T}$ and σ^2. Using the Bayesian approach, inferences about γ are based on its posterior distribution given only the data.[9]

The comparative advantage of the Bayes approach is well known (see, e.g., Lindley & Smith, 1972). However, the Bayesian conceptualization until recently has been implemented only for very simple hierarchical linear models, because the numerical integrations required for more complex models have been difficult to program. Tanner and Wong (1987) have developed an alternative algorithm to numerical integration, known as *data augmentation,* that produces a Bayes estimate for σ^2 and **T**. Seltzer (1990) has developed this algorithm for a fairly general class of hierarchical models. One advantage of the data augmentation approach is that it can also provide a family of robust estimators for all model parameters: fixed effects, random Level-1 coefficients, and variance-covariance components. Because the algorithm involves an iterative simulation of the full posterior density, it is computationally very intensive, particularly with large data sets and complex models. Fortunately, MLF and MLR will usually work well in these "big" problems and a true Bayes solution is unnecessary. In "small" research problems, however, the data augmentation strategy can provide a significant improvement.

Hypothesis Testing

In the previous section, we discussed estimation of three kinds of parameters: the fixed effects, the random Level-1 coefficients, and the variance-covariance components. We now consider hypothesis tests.

To place our discussion in a reasonably general framework, let us consider a Level-1 regression model having the form

$$\begin{aligned} Y_{ij} &= \beta_{0j} + \beta_{1j}X_{1ij} + \beta_{2j}X_{2ij} + \ldots + \beta_{Qj}X_{Qij} + r_{ij} \\ &= \beta_{0j} + \sum_{q=1}^{Q} \beta_{qj}X_{qij} + r_{ij} \quad \text{where } r_{ij} \sim \mathrm{N}(0, \sigma^2) . \end{aligned} \qquad [3.60]$$

Equation 3.60 has $Q + 1$ coefficients, any one of which could be viewed as fixed, nonrandomly varying, or random. In the Level-2 model, each coefficient β_{qj} can be modeled as

$$\begin{aligned} \beta_{qj} &= \gamma_{q0} + \gamma_{q1}W_{1j} + \gamma_{q2}W_{2j} + \ldots + \gamma_{qS_q}W_{S_qj} + u_{qj} \\ &= \gamma_{q0} + \sum_{s=1}^{S_q} \gamma_{qs}W_{sj} + u_{qj} , \end{aligned} \qquad [3.61]$$

for some set of Level-2 predictors W_{sj}, $s = 1, \ldots, S_q$. Because each β_{qj} can have a unique set of predictors in Equation 3.61, there are $S_q + 1$ fixed

TABLE 3.1 Type of Hypothesis Testable in Hierarchical Models

Type of Hypothesis	*Fixed Effect*	*Random Level-1 Coefficient*	*Variance Component*
Single-parameter			
H_0	$\gamma_h = 0$	$\beta_{qj} = 0$	$\tau_{qq} = 0$
H_1	$\gamma_h \neq 0$	$\beta_{qj} \neq 0$	$\tau_{qq} > 0$
Multiparameter			
H_0	$\mathbf{C}'\gamma = 0$	$\mathbf{C}'\beta = 0$	$\mathbf{T} = \mathbf{T}_0$
H_1	$\mathbf{C}'\gamma \neq 0$	$\mathbf{C}'\beta \neq 0$	$\mathbf{T} = \mathbf{T}_1$

effects for each β_{qj}, and the total number of fixed effects in the Level-2 model, F, is equal to $\Sigma_q(S_q + 1)$. We assume that each random component, u_{qj}, is multivariate normally distributed, such that for any q

$$\text{Var}(u_{qj}) = \tau_{qq} \qquad [3.62]$$

and for any pair of random effects q and q'

$$\text{Cov}(u_{qj}, u_{q'j}) = \tau_{qq'} \,. \qquad [3.63]$$

Hypotheses may be formulated and tested about the fixed effects (each γ_{qs}), the random Level-1 coefficients (each β_{qj}), and the variance-covariance parameters. The tests may be either single-parameter tests or multiparameter tests. Hence, there are six types of hypotheses that can be tested, as displayed in Table 3.1. The corresponding test statistics commonly employed in these models are displayed in Table 3.2. Each is described and illustrated below.

Hypothesis Tests for Fixed Effects

Single-Parameter Tests. The typical null hypothesis here is

$$H_0: \gamma_{qs} = 0 \,, \qquad [3.64]$$

which implies that the effect of a Level-2 predictor, W_{sj}, on a particular Level-2 parameter, β_{qj}, is null. In Chapter 4, for example, we shall test the hypothesis that school sector (Catholic versus public) is unrelated to school mean achievement in U.S. high schools. The tests for such hypotheses have the form

TABLE 3.2 Common Hypothesis Tests for Hierarchical Models

Type of Hypothesis	*Fixed Effect*	*Random Level-1 Coefficient*	*Variance Component*
Single parameter	*t* ratio	*t* ratio	univariate χ^2 or *z* ratio
Multiparameter	general linear hypothesis test[a]	general linear hypothesis test	likelihood -ratio test (χ^2)

a. A likelihood-ratio test also may be used in the case of the MLF model.

$$z = \hat{\gamma}_{qs} / (\hat{V}_{\hat{\gamma}_{qs}})^{1/2}, \qquad [3.65]$$

where $\hat{\gamma}_{qs}$ is the maximum likelihood estimate of γ_{qs} and $\hat{V}_{\hat{\gamma}_{qs}}$ is the estimated sampling variance of $\hat{\gamma}_{qs}$. Formally the z statistic is asymptotically unit normal. It will often be the case, however, that a t statistic with degrees of freedom equal to $J - S_q - 1$ will provide a more accurate reference distribution for testing effects of Level-2 predictors.

Multiparameter Tests. Consider now a simple example that we shall elaborate in Chapter 4. Within each U.S. high school, we model student mathematics achievement as a function of student SES plus error:

$$Y_{ij} = \beta_{0j} + \beta_{1j}(\text{SES})_{ij} + r_{ij}, \qquad [3.66]$$

where Y_{ij} is the math achievement of student i in school j, $(\text{SES})_{ij}$ is the SES of that student, r_{ij} is random error, and β_{0j}, β_{1j} are the regression intercept and slope for school j . Suppose now that we wanted to test a composite null hypothesis that Catholic and public schools are similar both in their intercepts and slopes. This is a simultaneous test of two hypotheses. The Level-2 model might be written as

$$\beta_{0j} = \gamma_{00} + \gamma_{01}(\text{SECTOR})_j + u_{0j} \qquad [3.67a]$$

$$\beta_{1j} = \gamma_{10} + \gamma_{11}(\text{SECTOR})_j + u_{1j} \qquad [3.67b]$$

where $(\text{SECTOR})_j$ is an indicator variable (1 = Catholic, 0 = public). The hypothesis to be tested is that both γ_{01} and γ_{11} are null. If this composite hypothesis were retained, $(\text{SECTOR})_j$ might be dropped entirely from this model.

To understand our approach to such multiparameter tests requires a reformulation of Equation 3.67 in matrix notation:

$$\begin{pmatrix}\beta_{0j}\\ \beta_{1j}\end{pmatrix}=\begin{pmatrix}1 & (\text{SECTOR})_j & 0 & 0\\ 0 & 0 & 1 & (\text{SECTOR})_j\end{pmatrix}\begin{pmatrix}\gamma_{00}\\ \gamma_{01}\\ \gamma_{10}\\ \gamma_{11}\end{pmatrix}+\begin{pmatrix}u_{0j}\\ u_{1j}\end{pmatrix} \qquad [3.68]$$

That is,

$$\beta_j = \mathbf{W}_j\gamma + \mathbf{u}_j$$

The composite hypothesis could be written as

$$\text{H}_0: \ \mathbf{C}'\gamma = \mathbf{0}\,, \qquad [3.69]$$

where

$$\mathbf{C}' = \begin{pmatrix}0 & 1 & 0 & 0\\ 0 & 0 & 0 & 1\end{pmatrix},$$

so that according to the null hypothesis,

$$\mathbf{C}'\gamma = \begin{pmatrix}\gamma_{01}\\ \gamma_{11}\end{pmatrix} = \begin{pmatrix}0\\ 0\end{pmatrix}. \qquad [3.70]$$

This is an example of a general linear hypothesis (see, e.g., Anderson, 1984, chapter 8).

Given a known Δ_j, the sampling variance of $\hat{\gamma}$ is

$$\text{Var}(\hat{\gamma}) = \left(\sum \mathbf{W}_j' \Delta_j^{-1}\mathbf{W}_j\right)^{-1} = \mathbf{V}_{\hat{\gamma}}\,. \qquad [3.71]$$

Thus the *contrast vector,* $\mathbf{C}'\hat{\gamma}$, has variance

$$\text{Var}(\mathbf{C}'\hat{\gamma}) = \mathbf{C}'\mathbf{V}_{\hat{\gamma}}\mathbf{C} = \text{(say)}\ \mathbf{V}_c\,. \qquad [3.72]$$

When $\mathbf{V}_{\hat{\gamma}}$ is not known but is estimated by

$$\hat{V}_{\hat{\gamma}} = \left(\sum \mathbf{W}_j' \hat{\Delta}_j^{-1}\mathbf{W}_j\right)^{-1},$$

an approximate test statistic for the null hypothesis H_0: $\mathbf{C}'\boldsymbol{\gamma} = \mathbf{0}$ is given by

$$H = \hat{\boldsymbol{\gamma}}'\mathbf{C}\hat{\mathbf{V}}_c^{-1}\mathbf{C}'\hat{\boldsymbol{\gamma}}, \quad [3.73]$$

which has a large sample χ^2 distribution under H_0 with degrees of freedom equal to the number of contrasts to be tested (i.e., the number of rows in $\mathbf{C}'$). In the present example, $\mathbf{C}'$ has two rows so that the degrees of freedom are two.

Multiparameter tests regarding $\boldsymbol{\gamma}$ are useful for

omnibus tests of the relationship between a categorical Level-2 predictor and a β_{qj} parameter. (Example: Is school mean achievement related to region of the country, where five regions [Northeast, Southeast, Midwest, Southwest, and Pacific Coast] are represented by four dummy variables?)

contrasts between categories of a Level-2 predictor. (Example: Do students in the South achieve significantly more or less than students in the Midwest?)

examining whether a Level-2 characteristic interacts with any of several Level-1 predictors. (Example: Do the effects on achievement of student SES, minority group status, or academic background depend on sector?)

examining whether some subset of Level-2 predictors is needed in a particular β_{qj} model. (Example: Does overall school climate—academic, disciplinary, and social—predict school mean achievement?)

There are many possible uses for multiparameter tests, some of which are illustrated in future chapters. One benefit of multiparameter hypothesis tests is protection against the heightened probability of type I errors that arises from performing many univariate tests. One might employ the strategy of using post-hoc univariate tests only when the relevant omnibus (multiparameter) hypothesis has been rejected.

Another approach to multiparameter testing is a likelihood-ratio test. This approach is available using the MLF approach but not the MLR approach. We discuss this distinction further in the appendix to this chapter and in Chapter 10.

Hypothesis Tests for Random Level-1 Coefficients

Continuing with our example of research on high schools, a researcher may be interested in testing a hypothesis that a regression coefficient in a particular school is null or that a regression coefficient in one school is larger than the comparable coefficient in a second school. The first question is an example of a single-parameter hypothesis, and the second may be viewed as a multiparameter test, in that it is a comparison among two or more components of the random-coefficients vector.

Single-Parameter Tests. The hypothesis that a particular regression coefficient for an individual school is null may be formulated as

$$H_0:\ \beta_{qj} = 0\,. \qquad [3.74]$$

The appropriate test is directly analogous to the fixed-effects case; that is, we compute the ratio of the estimated coefficient to its estimated standard error. However, the researcher has a choice of using the empirical Bayes or OLS estimates.

In the empirical Bayes approach, the ratio may be denoted

$$z = \beta^*_{qj}/V^{*1/2}_{qqj}, \qquad [3.75]$$

where

β^*_{qj} is the empirical Bayes estimate;

V^*_{qqj} is the qth diagonal element of the posterior dispersion of the β_{qj} coefficients; and

z is distributed approximately as a unit normal variate when the null hypothesis is true.

General expressions for the posterior means and variances under MLF and MLR are derived in Chapter 10. We note, however, that the posterior variances will be larger—and more realistic—under MLR than under MLF. This will especially be true when the number of Level-2 units (e.g., schools) is small. Under MLF, the fixed effects are assumed known so that the posterior variance of β_{qj} does not reflect uncertainty about them. This assumption is realistic only when the number of Level-2 units, J, is large.

We strongly caution the reader that regardless of whether we use MLF or MLR, these tests will be too liberal, with actual significance values substantially exceeding the nominal values, unless J is large. Further, little is known about how large J must be or how liberal the tests are.

A much more conservative t test, but one that has an exact t distribution under the null hypothesis, is available when β estimates can be computed by means of ordinary least squares. One simply computes the regression for a particular Level-2 unit and tests the hypotheses in the standard manner. In many applications, where Level-1 sample sizes are small, this test will be too conservative to be of much use.

Multiparameter Tests. If we consider β to be the entire vector of random parameters—with dimension $J(Q+1)$ by 1 where the parameter vector for each Level-2 unit is stacked one on top of the other—then the general linear hypothesis associated with β is

$$\mathrm{H}_0: \ \mathbf{C}'\beta = \mathbf{0} . \quad [3.76]$$

If the empirical Bayes estimates β^* are used as the basis of the test, the test statistic will be

$$H_{\mathrm{EB}} = \beta^{*\prime}\mathbf{C}(\mathbf{C}'\mathbf{V}^*\mathbf{C})^{-1}\mathbf{C}'\beta^* \quad [3.77]$$

where $\mathbf{V}^*$ is the entire $J(Q+1)$ by $J(Q+1)$ variance-covariance matrix of the coefficients. Under MLR, $\mathbf{V}^*$ is a *full* matrix. That is, under MLR, the empirical Bayes estimates for different Level-2 units are mutually dependent because they all rely on the same estimates of the fixed effects. Under MLF, on the other hand, the empirical Bayes estimates for different Level-2 units are independent, but this independence is based on the unrealistic assumption that the fixed effects are known.

For a single Level-2 unit, it is straightforward to test hypotheses about components of β_j using either MLR or MLF empirical Bayes estimates. It is also relatively easy to compare coefficients from a small number of Level-2 units (i.e., when only a small submatrix of Equation 3.77 is needed). In general, both the MLR and MLF approaches will be too liberal unless J is large.

An alternative to the empirical Bayes approach provides exact but very conservative multivariate tests. If the entire vector of OLS estimates, say $\hat{\beta}$, can be computed, then the general linear hypothesis given by Equation 3.76 can be tested by means of the statistic

$$H_{\mathrm{OLS}} = \hat{\beta}'\mathbf{C}(\mathbf{C}'\hat{\mathbf{V}}\mathbf{C})^{-1}\mathbf{C}'\hat{\beta} \quad [3.78]$$

where $\hat{\mathbf{V}}$ is a block diagonal matrix with each $(Q+1)$ by $(Q+1)$ block equal to

$$\hat{\mathbf{V}}_j = \hat{\sigma}^2(\mathbf{X}_j'\mathbf{X}_j)^{-1} . \quad [3.79]$$

Hypothesis Testing for Variance and Covariance Components

Single-Parameter Tests. In nearly all applications of hierarchical analysis, investigators will need to decide whether Level-1 coefficients should be specified as fixed, random, or nonrandomly varying (see Chapter 2).

To ask whether random variation exists, we may test a null hypothesis

$$\mathrm{H}_0: \ \tau_{qq} = 0\,, \qquad [3.80]$$

where $\tau_{qq} = \mathrm{Var}(\beta_{qj})$. If this hypothesis is rejected, the investigator may conclude that there is random variation in β_q.

A simple and useful test of H_0: $\tau_{qq} = 0$ is possible if all (or at least most) groups have sufficient data to compute the OLS estimates. Let $\hat{V}_{qqj}$ represent the qth diagonal element of $\hat{V}_j = \hat{\sigma}^2(\mathbf{X}_j'\mathbf{X}_j)^{-1}$. Then, under the model

$$\beta_{qj} = \gamma_{q0} + \sum_{s=1}^{S_q} \gamma_{qs} W_{sj}\,, \qquad [3.81]$$

the statistic

$$\sum_j \left(\hat{\beta}_{qj} - \hat{\gamma}_{q0} - \sum_{s=1}^{S_q} \hat{\gamma}_{qs} W_{sj} \right)^2 \Big/ \hat{V}_{qqj} \qquad [3.82]$$

will be distributed approximately χ^2 with $J - S_q - 1$ degrees of freedom.

A second test of the hypothesis H_0: $\tau_{qq} = 0$ is based on the estimated standard error of $\hat{\tau}_{qq}$ computed from the inverse of the information matrix (Longford, 1987). The ratio

$$z = \hat{\tau}_{qq} / [\mathrm{Var}(\hat{\tau}_{qq})]^{1/2} \qquad [3.83]$$

is approximately normally distributed under the large sample theory of maximum likelihood estimates. In many cases, however, especially when τ_{qq} is near zero, the normality approximation will be extremely poor. Technically, the likelihood is unlikely to be symmetric about the mode (i.e., asymptotic normality has not yet been achieved), and a test based on a symmetric confidence interval for τ_{qq} may be highly misleading.

Multiparameter Tests. The most general form of hypothesis testing for variances and covariances is based on the likelihood-ratio test. A common use of this test is to examine the null hypothesis that

$$\mathrm{H}_0: \ \mathbf{T} = \mathbf{T}_0 \qquad [3.84]$$

versus the alternative

$$H_1: \mathbf{T} = \mathbf{T}_1 \qquad [3.85]$$

where $\mathbf{T}_0$ is a reduced form of $\mathbf{T}_1$. For example, the qth row and column (or some set of rows and columns) in $\mathbf{T}_1$ may be null. For any model the *deviance* is –2 times the value of the log-likelihood function evaluated at the maximum (see Chapter 10 for details). The deviance may be viewed as a measure of model fit: the higher the deviance, the poorer the fit. To test a composite hypothesis, one estimates the two models, computes deviances D_0 and D_1 associated with each model, and then computes the test statistic

$$H = D_0 - D_1 . \qquad [3.86]$$

This statistic has a χ^2 distribution with m degrees of freedom, where m is the difference in the number of unique variance and covariance components estimated in the two models. In using any likelihood-ratio test for variances or covariances, the models compared must be identical with respect to the specification of the fixed effects. Application of this test is illustrated in Chapter 4.

Summary of Terms Introduced in this Chapter

General two-level model:

$$Y_{ij} = \beta_{0j} + \beta_{1j}X_{1ij} + \beta_{2j}X_{2ij} + \ldots + \beta_{Qj}X_{Qij} + r_{ij}$$

$$= \beta_{0j} + \sum_{q=1}^{Q} \beta_{qj}X_{qij} + r_{ij} \quad \text{where } r_{ij} \sim \mathrm{N}(0, \sigma^2) .$$

$$\beta_{qj} = \gamma_{q0} + \gamma_{q1}W_{1j} + \gamma_{q2}W_{2j} + \ldots + \gamma_{qS_q}W_{S_qj} + u_{qj}$$

$$= \gamma_{q0} + \sum_{s=1}^{S_q} \gamma_{qs}W_{sj} + u_{qj} \quad \text{For each } q = 0, \ldots Q .$$

We assume that the random components, u_{qj}, $q = 0, \ldots, Q$, are multivariate normal, each with a mean of 0, and some variance, $\mathrm{Var}(u_{qj}) = \tau_{qq}$. For any pair of random effects q and q', $\mathrm{Cov}(u_{qj}, u_{q'j}) = \tau_{qq'}$. These variance and covariance components can be collected into a $(Q + 1)$ by $(Q + 1)$ dispersion matrix, $\mathbf{T}$.

Precision: Reciprocal of the error variance of a statistic.

Precision-weighted average: A weighted average of a set of statistics in which each statistic is weighted proportional to its precision (Equation 3.9).

Ordinary least squares (OLS) estimator: An estimator that minimizes a sum of squared residuals. In the case of a single predictor, the OLS slope estimate is a sum of cross-products divided by a sum of squares (Equation 3.15).

Weighted least squares (WLS) estimator: An estimator that minimizes a weighted sum of squared residuals. In the case of a single predictor, the WLS slope estimate is a weighted sum of cross-products divided by a weighted sum of squares (Equation 3.17).

Generalized least squares (GLS) estimator: An estimator that minimizes a weighted sum of squares and cross-products (Equation 3.32).

Error variance: The variance of a statistic (e.g., $\hat{\beta}_{qj}$) used to estimate an unknown Level-1 coefficient (e.g., β_{qj}). This variance includes several sources: sampling error, measurement error, and *model error* (e.g., incomplete specification of the Level-1 model).

Parameter variance: The variance of an unknown Level-1 coefficient (e.g., β_{qj}) across the population of Level-2 units.

Empirical Bayes estimate of a random Level-1 coefficient: An estimate of the unknown Level-1 coefficient for a particular unit, which utilizes not only the data from that unit but also the data from all other similar units (e.g., Equations 3.35, 3.42, and 3.50).

Reliability: In the case of a two-level hierarchical linear model, we refer to the reliability of $\hat{\beta}_{qj}$ as the precision of this statistic as a measure of an unknown Level-1 coefficient β_{qj}. Reliability indices can be computed for each Level-2 unit (see Equation 3.52) and an overall or average reliability for the set of J Level-2 units (see Equation 3.53).

Unconditional shrinkage: The principal of shrinking a least squares estimator of a random Level-1 coefficient toward the grand mean by a factor proportional to its unreliability.

Conditional shrinkage: The principal of shrinking a least squares estimator of a random Level-1 coefficient toward a predicted value rather than toward the grand mean.

Least squares residual ($\hat{u}_{qj}$): The deviation of a least squares estimate, $\hat{\beta}_{qj}$, from its predicted value based on the Level-2 model.

Empirical Bayes residual (u^*_{qj}): The deviation of an empirical Bayes estimate, β^*_{qj}, from its predicted value based on the Level-2 model.

Single-parameter test: A test of a null hypothesis regarding a single parameter.

Multiparameter test: A combined null hypothesis involving the testing of multiple parameters.

Appendix

MLF Versus MLR. Earlier we drew a distinction between the full and restricted likelihood, or MLF versus MLR (see "Estimation of Variance and Covariance Components"). The general linear hypothesis testing we have described for testing multiparameter hypotheses about the fixed effects γ can be carried out when using either MLF or MLR. However, an alternative approach, using a likelihood-ratio test, is available under MLF. This approach is based on estimating two models. The first or "null" model excludes the fixed effects hypothesized to be null. The second or "alternative" model estimates all effects—those hypothesized to be null along with any other effects in the model. For each model, a deviance statistic is computed and the difference between the deviance statistics is used to test the multivariate hypothesis.

Specifically, for the null model the deviance, D_0, is computed, which is twice the negative log-likelihood or

$$D_0 = -2\log(L_0)\,, \qquad [3.87]$$

where L_0 is the value of the likelihood associated with the maximum likelihood estimates under the null hypothesis. Similarly, D_1 is the deviance associated with the maximum likelihood estimates computed under the alternative model:

$$D_1 = -2\log(L_1)\,. \qquad [3.88]$$

In general, the larger the deviance, the poorer the fit to the data. Under the null hypothesis, the difference between deviances,

$$D_0 - D_1\,, \qquad [3.89]$$

has a large-sample χ^2 distribution with degrees of freedom equal to the difference in the number of parameters estimated. Large values of the statistic are taken as evidence that the null hypothesis is implausible and that the null model is therefore "too simple" a description of the data.

The likelihood-ratio test will produce results that are nearly identical to those of the general linear hypothesis test. There are three advantages of the latter, however. First, using the general linear hypothesis approach, any set of linear hypotheses can be tested after computing estimates for just one model (the alternative model). In contrast, the likelihood-ratio approach requires recomputation of the estimates for any null hypothesis to be tested. Second, the general linear hypothesis approach allows for arbitrary linear contrasts among the parameters. For example, one might want to test the difference between two fixed effects or a linear contrast in the fixed effects. To test such hypotheses using the likelihood-ratio approach would actually require reprogramming the estimation algorithm in order to introduce the needed constraints among the parameters. Third, the likelihood-ratio approach is unavailable under MLR, and as mentioned above, there are circumstances where MLR is advantageous.

We note that when using the likelihood-ratio approach to test hypotheses about fixed effects, the variance-covariance components specification must be identical for both the null and alternative models.

Notes

1. This section requires some basic knowledge of matrix algebra and is optional.

2. Technically, the estimate β^*_{0j} is the conditional posterior mean of the random parameter β_{0j} given the data and the variances σ^2 and τ_{00}. Lindley and Smith (1972) and Box and Tiao (1973) discuss the properties of such conditional means as point estimators of unknown parameters.

3. To be precise, this estimator is optimal in the specific sense that no other point estimator of β_{0j} has smaller expected-mean squared error, where the expectation is taken over the conditional distribution of β_{0j} given the data, σ^2, and τ_{00} .

4. Formally, V^*_j is the posterior variance of β_{0j} given the data and the variances σ^2 and τ_{00} .

5. The problem of spuriously short confidence intervals is exacerbated in the MLF case (see Chapter 3) in which γ_{00} is also assumed known and therefore $V^*_j = (V_j^{-1} + \tau_{00}^{-1})^{-1}$ fails to adjust for uncertainty in $\hat{\gamma}_{00}$ as an estimator of γ_{00} .

6. This section requires some knowledge of matrix algebra and is optional.

7. A better correction for minimizing mean squared error is $n - Q + 1$ rather than $n - Q - 1$.

8. The restricted likelihood requires integration of the full likelihood with respect to γ. This notion of "integrating the likelihood" is a Bayesian idea that makes sense if we view the likelihood as the joint posterior density of γ, σ^2, and **T** (see Dempster et al., 1981). The restricted likelihood can also be viewed in classical terms as the conditional density of Y given $\hat{\gamma}$.

9. This posterior distribution is calculated by "integrating out" σ^2 and **T** from the joint posterior distribution of γ, σ^2 and **T**. For any specific set of values of (σ^2, **T**), there is an estimate of γ and its standard error. The Bayesian approach essentially takes a weighted average of all possible estimates of this kind where the weight accorded any single estimate is proportional to the posterior probability of (σ^2, **T**).

4 An Illustration

- Introduction
- The One-Way ANOVA
- Regression with Means-as-Outcomes
- The Random-Coefficient Model
- An Intercept- and Slopes-as-Outcomes Model
- Estimating the Level-1 Coefficient for a Particular Unit

Introduction

The purpose of this chapter is to illustrate the use of the techniques of estimation and hypothesis testing presented in Chapter 3. We shall present a series of analyses based on the models introduced in Chapter 2. These analyses use data from a nationally representative sample of U.S. public and Catholic high schools. These data are a subsample from the 1982 High School and Beyond Survey,[1] and include information on 7,185 students nested within 160 schools: 90 public and 70 Catholic. Sample sizes averaged about 45 students per school.

Attention is restricted to two student-level variables: (a) the outcome, Y_{ij}, a standardized measure of math achievement; and (b) one predictor, $(\text{SES})_{ij}$, student socioeconomic status, which is a composite of parental education, parental occupation, and income. School-level variables include $(\text{SECTOR})_j$, an indicator variable taking on a value of one for Catholic schools and zero for public schools, and $(\text{MEAN SES})_j$, the average of the student SES values within each school. In the language introduced in Chapter 2, the Level-1 units are students and the Level-2 units are schools. $(\text{SES})_{ij}$

TABLE 4.1 Descriptive Statistics from American High School Data

	Variable Name	*Mean*	*sd*
Student-level variables			
Math achievement	Y_{ij}	12.75	6.88
Socioeconomic status	$(\text{SES})_{ij}$	0.00	0.78
School-level variables			
Sector	$(\text{SECTOR})_j$	0.44	0.50
School average SES	$(\text{MEAN SES})_j$	0.00	0.41

is a Level-1 predictor; $(\text{SECTOR})_j$ and $(\text{MEAN SES})_j$ are Level-2 predictors. Means and standard deviations of these variables are supplied in Table 4.1.

Questions motivating these analyses include the following:

1. How much do U.S. high schools vary in their mean mathematics achievement?
2. Do schools with high MEAN SES also have high math achievement?
3. Is the strength of association between student SES and math achievement similar across schools? Or is SES a more important predictor of achievement in some schools than in others?
4. How do public and Catholic schools compare in terms of mean math achievement and in terms of the strength of the SES-math achievement relationship, after we control for MEAN SES?

The purpose of these analyses is to illustrate estimation of hierarchical models and explain how the results can be interpreted. We have deliberately kept the examples simple to clarify the essential data analytic issues. We caution that no substantive conclusions should be drawn from these analyses. In Chapter 5 we summarize results from a more complex analysis aimed at comparing the distribution of math achievement within public and Catholic schools.

The One-Way ANOVA

The one-way ANOVA with random effects, described in Chapter 2, provides useful preliminary information about how much variation in the outcome lies within and between schools and about the reliability of each school's sample mean as an estimate of its true population mean.

TABLE 4.2 Results from One-Way ANOVA Model

Fixed Effect		*Coefficient*	*se*	
Average school mean, γ_{00}		12.64	0.24	

Random Effect	*Variance Component*	*df*	χ^2	*p value*
School mean, u_{0j}	8.62	159	1,660.2	.000
Level-1 effect, r_{ij}	39.15			

The Model

Level 1 or student level is

$$Y_{ij} = \beta_{0j} + r_{ij} \qquad [4.1]$$

where we assume $r_{ij} \sim N(0, \sigma^2)$ for $i = 1, \ldots, n_j$ students in school j, and $j = 1, \ldots, 160$ schools. We refer to σ^2 as the student-level variance. Notice that this model characterizes achievement in each school with just an intercept, β_{0j}, which in this case is the mean.

At Level 2 or the school level, each school's mean math achievement, β_{0j}, is represented as a function of the grand mean, γ_{00}, plus a random error, u_{0j} :

$$\beta_{0j} = \gamma_{00} + u_{0j} \qquad [4.2]$$

where we assume $u_{0j} \sim N(0, \tau_{00})$. We refer to τ_{00} as the school-level variance.

Results

Table 4.2 reports the results. The maximum likelihood point estimate for the grand-mean math achievement is 12.64 with a standard error of .24, indicating a 95% confidence interval of

$$12.64 \pm 1.96(.24) = (12.17, 13.11).$$

The table also lists maximum likelihood estimates of the variance components. At the student level

$$\hat{\mathrm{V}}\mathrm{ar}(r_{ij}) = \hat{\sigma}^2 = 39.15.$$

At the school level, τ_{00} is the variance of the true school means, β_{0j}, around the grand mean as indicated by Equation 4.2. The estimated variability in these school means is

$$\hat{\tau}_{00} = 8.62 .$$

These estimates indicate that most of the variation in the outcome is at the student level, although a substantial proportion is between schools. The intraclass correlation, which represents in this case the proportion of variance in Y between schools, is estimated by substituting the estimated variance components for their respective parameters in Equation 2.10:

$$\hat{\rho} = \hat{\tau}_{00}/(\hat{\tau}_{00} + \hat{\sigma}^2) = 8.62/(8.62 + 39.15) = 0.18 , \qquad [4.3]$$

indicating that about 18% of the variance in math achievement is between schools.

Similarly, an estimator of the reliability of the sample mean in any school j can also be derived by substituting the estimated variance components into Equation 3.36. That is,

$$\hat{\lambda}_j = \text{Reliability}(\bar{Y}_{\cdot j}) = \hat{\tau}_{00}/[\hat{\tau}_{00} + (\hat{\sigma}^2/n_j)] . \qquad [4.4]$$

In general, the reliability of the sample mean $\bar{Y}_{\cdot j}$ as an estimate of the true school mean, β_{0j}, will vary from school to school because the sample size, n_j, varies. However, an overall measure of the reliability is the average of the school reliabilities:

$$\hat{\lambda} = \sum \hat{\lambda}_j / J . \qquad [4.5]$$

For our data $\hat{\lambda}$ = .90, indicating that the sample means tend to be quite reliable as indicators of the true school means.

We may wonder whether the estimated value of τ_{00} is significantly greater than zero. If not, it may be sensible to assume that all schools have the same mean. Formally, this hypothesis is

$$H_0 : \tau_{00} = 0 .$$

This hypothesis may be tested using Equation 3.82, which reduces in a one-way random ANOVA model to

$$H = \sum n_j(\bar{Y}_{\cdot j} - \hat{\gamma}_{00})^2/\hat{\sigma}^2, \qquad [4.6]$$

which has a large-sample χ^2 distribution with $J - 1$ degrees of freedom under the null hypothesis. In our case, the test statistic takes on a value of 1,660.2 with 159 degrees of freedom ($J = 160$ schools), highly implausible ($p < .001$) under the null hypothesis. The evidence indicates significant variation among schools in their achievement.

In summary, this one-way ANOVA produces useful preliminary information in our study of math achievement in U.S. high schools. It provides an estimate of the grand mean; a partitioning of the total variation in math achievement into variation between and within schools; information on the degree of dependence of the observations within each school (the intraclass correlation); a measure of the reliability of each school's sample average math achievement as an estimate of its true mean; and a test of the hypothesis that all schools have the same mean math achievement.

Regression with Means-as-Outcomes

The Model

The student-level model of Equation 4.1 remains unchanged: Student math achievement scores are viewed as varying around their school means. The school-level model of Equation 4.2 is now elaborated, however, so that each school's mean is now predicted by the MEAN SES of the school:

$$\beta_{0j} = \gamma_{00} + \gamma_{01}(\text{MEAN SES})_j + u_{0j}, \qquad [4.7]$$

where γ_{00} is the intercept, γ_{01} is the effect of MEAN SES on β_{0j}, and we assume $u_{0j} \sim N(0, \tau_{00})$.

Notice that the symbols u_{0j} and τ_{00} have different meanings than they had in Equation 4.2. Whereas the random variable u_{0j} had been the deviation of school j's mean from the grand mean, it now represents the residual $\beta_{0j} - \gamma_{00} - \gamma_{01}(\text{MEAN SES})_j$. Correspondingly, the variance τ_{00} is now a residual or conditional variance, that is, $\text{Var}(\beta_{0j} \mid \text{MEAN SES})$, the school-level variance in β_{0j} after controlling for school MEAN SES.

Results

Table 4.3 provides estimates and hypothesis tests for the fixed effects and the variances of the random effects. The results indicate a highly significant association between school MEAN SES and mean achievement ($\hat{\gamma}_{01} = 5.86$, $t = 16.22$). The t ratio employed for hypothesis testing of an

TABLE 4.3 Results from the Means-as-Outcomes Model

Fixed Effect	*Coefficient*	*se*	*t ratio*	
Model for school means				
INTERCEPT, γ_{00}	12.65	0.15	—	
MEAN SES, γ_{01}	5.86	0.36	16.22	
Random Effect	*Variance Component*	*df*	χ^2	*p value*
School mean, u_{0j}	2.64	158	633.52	0.000
Level-1 effect, r_{ij}	39.16			

individual fixed effect is simply the ratio of the estimated coefficient to its standard error and follows a unit normal distribution when J is large (see Chapter 3). The residual variance between schools, $\hat{\tau}_{00} = 2.64$, is substantially smaller than the original $\hat{\tau}_{00} = 8.62$ estimated in the context of the random ANOVA model and presented in Table 4.2.

Variance Explained at Level 2. By comparing the τ_{00} estimates across the two models, we can develop an index of the proportion reduction in variance or, loosely speaking, the variance explained by the Level-2 predictor, in this case MEAN SES. In this application,

$$\text{Proportion variance explained in } \beta_{0j} = \frac{\hat{\tau}_{00}(\text{random ANOVA}) - \hat{\tau}_{00}(\text{MEAN SES})}{\hat{\tau}_{00}(\text{random ANOVA})} \qquad [4.8]$$

where $\hat{\tau}_{00}$ (random ANOVA) = Var(β_{0j}) and $\hat{\tau}_{00}$(MEAN SES) = Var(β_{0j} | MEAN SES) refer to the estimates of τ_{00} under the alternative Level-2 models specified by Equations 4.2 and 4.7, respectively. Note the $\hat{\tau}_{00}$ (random ANOVA) provides the base in this application, because it represents the total parameter variance in the school means that is potentially explainable by alternative Level-2 models for β_{0j}. The estimated proportion of variance between schools explained by the model with MEAN SES is

$$(8.62 - 2.64)/8.62 = 0.69.$$

That is, 69% of the true between-school variance in math achievement is accounted for by MEAN SES.

Conditional Intraclass Correlation and Reliability. After removing the effect of school MEAN SES, the correlation between pairs of scores in the same school, which had been .18, is now reduced:

$$\hat{\rho} = \hat{\tau}_{00}/(\hat{\tau}_{00} + \hat{\sigma}^2)$$

$$= 2.64/(2.64 + 39.16) = .06\,.$$

The estimated ρ is now a *conditional intraclass correlation* and measures the degree of dependence among observations within schools that are of the same MEAN SES.

Similarly, we can calculate the reliability of the least squares residuals, $\hat{u}_{0j}$,

$$\hat{u}_{0j} = \bar{Y}_{\cdot j} - \hat{\gamma}_{00} - \hat{\gamma}_{01}(\text{MEAN SES})_j\,. \qquad [4.9]$$

This reliability is a *conditional reliability,* that is, the reliability with which one can discriminate among schools that are identical on MEAN SES. Substituting our new estimates of $\hat{\tau}_{00}$ and $\hat{\sigma}^2$ into Equations 4.4 and 4.5 yields a reliability of .74. As one might expect, the reliability of the residuals is less than the reliability of the sample means.

Homogeneity of Residual School Means. Do school achievement means vary significantly once mean SES is controlled? Here the null hypothesis that $\tau_{00} = 0$, where τ_{00} is now a residual variance, is tested by means of the statistic

$$\sum n_j[\bar{Y}_{\cdot j} - \hat{\gamma}_{00} - \hat{\gamma}_{01}(\text{MEAN SES})_j]^2/\hat{\sigma}^2, \qquad [4.10]$$

which, under the null hypothesis, has a χ^2 distribution with $J - 2 = 158$ degrees of freedom. In our case, the statistic has a value of 633.52, $p < .001$, indicating that the null hypothesis is easily rejected; after controlling for MEAN SES, significant variation among school mean math achievement remains to be explained.

The Random-Coefficient Model

We now consider an analysis of the SES-math achievement relationship within the 160 schools. We conceive therefore of each school as having "its own" regression equation with an intercept and a slope, and we shall ask the following:

1. What is the average of the 160 regression equations (i.e., what are the average intercept and slope)?
2. How much do the regression equations vary from school to school? Specifically, how much do the intercepts vary and how much do the slopes vary?
3. What is the correlation between the intercepts and the slopes? (Do schools with large intercepts [e.g., high mean achievement] also have large slopes [strong relationships between SES and achievement]?)

The Model

To answer these questions, we use the random-coefficient regression model introduced in Chapter 2. Specifically, we formulate the student-level model

$$Y_{ij} = \beta_{0j} + \beta_{1j}(X_{ij} - \overline{X}_{.j}) + r_{ij}. \quad [4.11]$$

Each school's distribution of math achievement is characterized by two parameters: the intercept, β_{0j}, and the slope, β_{1j}. Because the student-level predictor is centered around its school mean, the intercept, β_{0j}, is the school-mean outcome (see Equation 2.29). Again we assume $r_{ij} \sim N(0, \sigma^2)$, where now σ^2 is the residual variance at Level 1 after controlling for student SES.

These parameters, β_{0j} and β_{1j}, vary across schools in the Level-2 model as a function of a grand mean and a random error:

$$\beta_{0j} = \gamma_{00} + u_{0j}, \quad [4.12a]$$

$$\beta_{1j} = \gamma_{10} + u_{1j}, \quad [4.12b]$$

where

γ_{00} is the average of the school means on math achievement across the population of schools;

γ_{10} is the average SES-math regression slope across those schools;

u_{0j} is the unique increment to the intercept associated with school j; and

u_{1j} is the unique increment to the slope associated with school j.

We assume that u_{0j} and u_{1j} are multivariate normally distributed, both with expected values of 0. We label the variances in these school effects as

$$\text{Var}(u_{0j}) = \tau_{00}$$

$$\text{Var}(u_{1j}) = \tau_{11}$$

and the covariance between them as

$$\text{Cov}(u_{0j}, u_{1j}) = \tau_{01} .$$

Collecting these terms into a variance-covariance matrix,

$$\text{Var}\begin{bmatrix} u_{0j} \\ u_{1j} \end{bmatrix} = \begin{bmatrix} \tau_{00} & \tau_{01} \\ \tau_{10} & \tau_{11} \end{bmatrix} = \mathbf{T}$$

Because the Level-2 model is unconditional for both β_{0j} and β_{1j} (i.e., no predictors are included in Equations 4.12a and 4.12b), *in this case*

$$\text{Var}(\beta_{0j}) = \text{Var}(\beta_{0j} - \gamma_{00}) \qquad [4.13]$$

$$\text{Var}(\beta_{1j}) = \text{Var}(\beta_{1j} - \gamma_{10}) .$$

Thus, the random-coefficient regression model provides estimates for the unconditional parameter variability in the random intercepts and slopes.

Results

The Average Regression Equation Within Schools. Table 4.4 provides the results of the analysis. The average of the school means, γ_{00}, is estimated to be 12.64 with a standard error of .24. The average of the SES-achievement slopes is estimated to be 2.19 with a standard error of .13 and a t ratio of 17.26. This indicates that, *on average*, student SES is significantly positively related to math achievement within schools.

Variability Among the Regression Equations. Table 4.4 also provides estimates of the variances of the random effects and tests of the hypothesis that these variances are null. Specifically, the estimated variance among the means is $\hat{\tau}_{00} = 8.68$, with a χ^2 statistic of 1,770.5, to be compared to the critical value of χ^2 with $J - 1 = 159$ degrees of freedom. We infer that

TABLE 4.4 Results from the Random-Coefficient Model[a]

Fixed Effect	*Coefficient*	*se*	*t ratio*
Overall mean achievement, γ_{00}	12.64	0.24	—
Mean SES-achievement slope, γ_{10}[a]	2.19	0.13	17.26

Random Effect	*Variance*	*df*	χ^2	*p value*
School mean, u_{0j}	8.68	159	1,770.5	0.000
SES-achievement slope, u_{1j}	0.65	159	213.4	0.003
Level-1 effect, r_{ij}	36.71			

a. This is the estimated pooled-within-school regression coefficient.

highly significant differences exist among the 160 school means, a result quite similar to that encountered in the one-way ANOVA with random effects.

The estimated variance of the slopes is $\hat{\tau}_{11} = 0.65$ with a χ^2 statistic of 213.4 and 159 degrees of freedom, $p < .003$. Again, we reject the null hypothesis, in this case that $\tau_{11} = 0$, and infer that the relationship between SES and math achievement within schools does indeed vary significantly across the population of schools.

Associated with β_{0j} and β_{1j} is also a reliability estimate (see Equation 3.53). These indices provide answers to the question "How reliable, on average, are estimates of each school's intercept and slope based on computing the OLS regression separately for each school?" These reliabilities depend on two factors: the degree to which the true underlying parameters vary from school to school and the precision with which each school's regression equation is estimated.

The precision of estimation of the intercept (which in this application is a school mean) depends on the sample size within each school. The precision of estimation of the slope depends both on the sample size and on the variability of SES within that school. Schools that are homogeneous with respect to SES will exhibit slope estimation with poor precision.

The results indicate that the intercepts are quite reliable (.91) based on an average of 50 students per school. The slope estimates are far less reliable (.23). The primary reason for the lack of reliability of the slopes is that the true slope variance across schools is much smaller than the variance of the true means. Also, the slopes are estimated with less precision than are the means because many schools are relatively homogeneous on SES.

Variance Explained at Level 1. Notice that the estimate of the student-level variance $\hat{\sigma}^2$ is now 36.71. By comparison, the estimated variance in the one-way random ANOVA model, which did not include SES as a Level-1 predictor, was 39.15. Analogous to Equation 4.8, we can develop an index of the proportion of reduction in variance or "variance explained" at Level 1 by comparing the σ^2 estimates from these two alternative models. In this case,

$$\text{Proportion variance explained at Level 1} = \frac{\hat{\sigma}^2(\text{random ANOVA}) - \hat{\sigma}^2(\text{SES})}{\hat{\sigma}^2(\text{random ANOVA})} \quad [4.14]$$

where $\hat{\sigma}^2$(random ANOVA) and $\hat{\sigma}^2$(SES) refer to estimates of σ^2 based on the Level-1 models specified by Equations 4.1 and 4.11, respectively. Note that σ^2(random ANOVA) provides the appropriate base in this application because it represents the total within-school-variance that can be explained by any Level-1 model.

Using Equation 4.14 we see that adding SES as a predictor of math achievement reduced the within-school variance by 6.2%. Hence we can conclude that SES accounts for about 6% of the student-level variance in the outcome. When we recall that MEAN SES accounted for better than 60% of the between-school variance in the outcome, it is clear that the association between these two variables is far stronger at the school level than at the student level.

The Correlation Between the Intercept and the Slope. The model also produces a maximum likelihood estimate of the covariance between the intercept and the slope. When combined with the estimates of the intercept and slope variances, we can estimate the correlation between the intercept and slope using Equation 2.3. In this case, the correlation of slope and intercept is .02, indicating that there is little association between school means and school SES effects.

An Intercept- and Slopes-as-Outcomes Model

Having estimated the variability of the regression equations across schools, we now seek to build an explanatory model to account for this variability. That is, we seek to understand *why* some schools have higher means than others and why in some schools the association between SES and achievement is stronger than in others.

The Model

The student-level model remains the same as in Equation 4.11. However, we now expand the school-level model to incorporate two predictors: SECTOR and MEAN SES. The resulting school-level model can be written as

$$\beta_{0j} = \gamma_{00} + \gamma_{01}(\text{MEAN SES})_j + \gamma_{02}(\text{SECTOR})_j + u_{0j}, \qquad [4.15a]$$

$$\beta_{1j} = \gamma_{10} + \gamma_{11}(\text{MEAN SES})_j + \gamma_{12}(\text{SECTOR})_j + u_{1j}, \qquad [4.15b]$$

where u_{0j} and u_{1j} are again multivariate normally distributed with means of zero and variance-covariance matrix **T**. The elements of **T** are now residual or conditional variance-covariance components. That is, they represent residual dispersion in β_{0j} and β_{1j} after controlling for MEAN SES and SECTOR.

Combining the school-level model (Equation 4.15) and the student-level model (Equation 4.11) yields the combined model

$$Y_{ij} = \gamma_{00} + \gamma_{01}(\text{MEAN SES})_j + \gamma_{02}(\text{SECTOR})_j + \gamma_{10}(X_{ij} - \overline{X}_{\cdot j}) \qquad [4.16]$$

$$+ \gamma_{11}(\text{MEAN SES})_j(X_{ij} - \overline{X}_{\cdot j}) + \gamma_{12}(\text{SECTOR})_j(X_{ij} - \overline{X}_{\cdot j})$$

$$+ u_{0j} + u_{1j}(X_{ij} - \overline{X}_{\cdot j}) + r_{ij},$$

which illustrates that the outcome may be viewed as a function of the overall intercept (γ_{00}), the main effect of MEAN SES (γ_{01}), the main effect of SECTOR (γ_{02}), the main effect of SES (γ_{10}), and two cross-level interactions involving SECTOR with student SES (γ_{12}) and MEAN SES with student SES (γ_{11}), plus a random error

$$u_{0j} + u_{1j}(X_{ij} - \overline{X}_{\cdot j}) + r_{ij}.$$

Four questions motivate the analysis:

1. Do MEAN SES and SECTOR significantly predict the intercept? We estimate γ_{01} to study whether high-SES schools differ from low-SES schools in mean achievement (controlling for SECTOR). Similarly, we estimate γ_{02} to learn whether Catholic schools differ from public schools in terms of the mean achievement once MEAN SES is controlled.
2. Do MEAN SES and SECTOR significantly predict the within-school slopes? We estimate γ_{11} to discover whether high-SES schools differ from low-SES

TABLE 4.5 Results from Intercept- and Slopes-as-Outcomes Model

Fixed Effects	*Coefficient*	*se*	*t ratio*
Model for school means			
INTERCEPT, γ_{00}	12.10	0.20	—
MEAN SES, γ_{01}	5.33	0.37	14.45
SECTOR, γ_{02}	1.23	0.31	4.00
Model for SES-achievement slopes			
INTERCEPT, γ_{10}	2.94	0.16	—
MEAN SES, γ_{11}	1.03	0.31	3.35
SECTOR, γ_{12}	−1.64	0.25	−6.64

Random Effects	*Variance Component*	*df*	χ^2	*p value*
School mean, u_{0j}	2.38	157	605.64	0.000
SES-achievement slope, u_{1j}	0.21	157	162.40	0 .367
Level-1 effect, r_{ij}	36.68			

schools in terms of the strength of association between student SES and achievement within them (controlling for SECTOR). We estimate γ_{12} to examine whether Catholic schools differ from public schools in terms of the strength of association between student SES and achievement.

3. How much variation in the intercepts and the slopes is explained by using SECTOR and MEAN SES as predictors? To answer these questions, we estimate $\text{Var}(u_{0j}) = \tau_{00}$ and $\text{Var}(u_{1j}) = \tau_{11}$ and compare these with the estimates presented above from the random-coefficient regression model.
4. After taking into account SECTOR and MEAN SES, what is the correlation between the unique school contributions to the intercept and the slope respectively? To answer this question, we estimate $\text{Cor}(u_{0j}, u_{1j})$.

Results

SECTOR and MEAN SES as Predictors. Table 4.5 displays the results. We see, first, that MEAN SES is positively related to school mean math achievement, $\hat{\gamma}_{01} = 5.33$, $t = 14.45$. Also, Catholic schools have significantly higher mean achievement than do public schools, controlling for the effect of MEAN SES, $\hat{\gamma}_{02} = 1.23$, $t = 4.00$.

With regard to the slopes, there is a tendency for schools of high MEAN SES to have larger slopes than do schools with low MEAN SES, $\hat{\gamma}_{11} =$

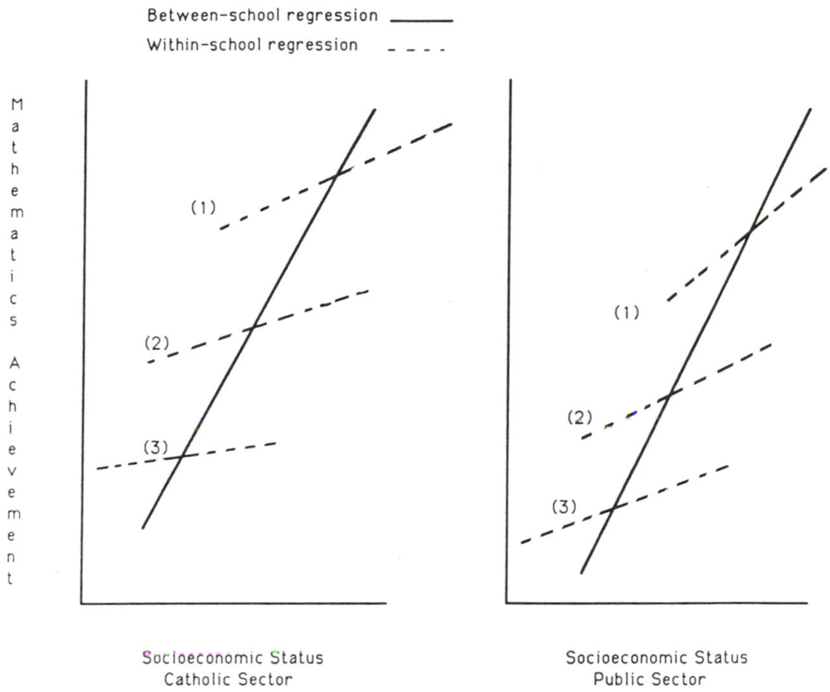

Figure 4.1. Regressions of Mathematics Achievement as a Function of Student and School SES Within Catholic and Public Sectors

NOTE: Schools 1, 2, and 3 are of high, medium, and low SES, respectively.

1.03, $t = 3.35$. Catholic schools have significantly weaker SES slopes, on average, than do public schools, $\hat{\gamma}_{12} = -1.64$, $t = -6.64$.

These results are depicted graphically in Figure 4.1. The fitted relationship between SES and math achievement is displayed for the Catholic and public sectors. Within each sector, results are displayed for (1) a high-SES school (one standard deviation above the mean), (2) a medium-SES school, and (3) a low-SES school (one standard deviation below the mean). Perhaps the most notable feature of the figure is that the within-school math-SES slopes are substantially less steep in the Catholic sector than in the public sector. This sector effect holds for schools at each level of MEAN SES. There is also a tendency for high-SES schools to have steeper slopes than do low-SES schools. This tendency is evident in both sectors. Main effects of MEAN SES and SECTOR are also evident. The MEAN SES effect is manifest by the solid lines that in both plots have positive slopes.

Variation Explained at Level 2. Table 4.5 also presents estimates and test statistics for residual variances of the intercepts and slopes. Analogous to Equation 4.8, we can develop a proportion reduction in variance or variance-explained statistic for each of the random coefficients (intercepts and slopes) in the Level-1 model. The variance estimate from the random-coefficient regression model estimated earlier provides the base for these statistics:

$$\begin{array}{c}\text{Proportion}\\ \text{variance explained}\\ \text{in } \beta_{qj}\end{array} = \frac{\hat{\tau}_{qq}(\text{random regression}) - \hat{\tau}_{qq}(\text{fitted model})}{\hat{\tau}_{qq}(\text{random regression})} \qquad [4.17]$$

where $\hat{\tau}_{qq}$(random regression) denotes the qth diagonal element of **T** estimated under the random-regression model (Equations 4.11 and 4.12) and $\hat{\tau}_{qq}$(fitted model) denotes the corresponding element in the **T** matrix estimated under an intercept- and slopes-as-outcomes model (in this case Equations 4.11 and 4.15).

In this application, we see a substantial reduction in variance of the school means once MEAN SES and SECTOR are controlled. Specifically, whereas the unconditional variance of intercepts had been 8.68, the residual variance is now $\hat{\tau}_{00} = 2.38$. This means that 73% of the parameter variation in mean achievement, Var(β_{0j}), has been explained by MEAN SES and SECTOR [i.e., (8.68 – 2.38)/8.68 = 0.73]. A test of the null hypothesis that no residual variance remains to be explained is rejected. The χ^2 statistic is 605.64 with $\text{df} = J - S_q - 1 = 157$, $p < .001$. Hence, the results encourage a search for further school-level variables that might help account for the remaining variation in the intercepts.

The residual variance of the slopes is $\hat{\tau}_{11} = .21$, which, when compared to the unconditional variance of .65, implies a reduction of 68%. A test of the null hypothesis that the residual variance of the true slopes is zero yields a χ^2 statistic of 162.40, which, when compared to the critical chi-square value with df = 157, implies there is no statistically significant residual variance in the slopes.

Multiparameter Hypothesis Tests

Fixed Effects. Chapter 3 discusses a procedure for testing multiparameter hypotheses regarding the fixed effects. We illustrate application of this procedure with respect to the cross-level interaction effects. One may wonder whether the variable SECTOR is needed in the model. Perhaps no distinction is justified between Catholic and public schools in terms of effectiveness or equity. The null hypothesis may be written as

$$H_0: \gamma_{02} = 0$$

$$\gamma_{12} = 0\,.$$

If $\gamma_{02} = 0$, Catholic and public schools do not differ in mean achievement after controlling for MEAN SES. If $\gamma_{12} = 0$, Catholic and public schools do not differ with respect to their average SES-math achievement relationships with schools. If both null hypotheses are true, the variable SECTOR may be dropped from the model. Using Equation 3.73, we obtain a χ^2 statistic of 64.38, df = 2, $p < .001$, indicating that one or both of the null hypotheses is false.

We may, of course, also test each individual null hypothesis. We see from Table 4.5 that $\hat{\gamma}_{02} = 1.23$, $t = 4.00$; also $\hat{\gamma}_{12} = -1.64$, $t = -6.64$. It is clear that both null hypotheses must be rejected, and we infer, after adjusting for MEAN SES, that Catholic schools have higher average achievement and weaker SES math relationships than do public schools.

Variance-Covariance Components. Our model included four unique variance and covariance parameters: (a) the student-level variance, σ^2; (b) the residual variance of the school means, τ_{00}; (c) the residual variance of the SES-math slopes, τ_{11}; and (d) the residual covariance between the means and the slopes, τ_{01}. In general, the number of variance-covariance parameters estimated in a two-level model is $[r(r + 1)/2] + 1$, where r is the number of random effects in the Level-2 model. In our case $r = 2$.

One might wonder whether a simpler model for the variance-covariance components is justified. If the residual slope variance were constrained to zero, the number of Level-2 random effects would be $r = 1$, so that two variance-covariance components would be estimated: σ^2 and τ_{00}. Chapter 3 described a likelihood-ratio test of the composite null hypothesis

$$H_0: \begin{pmatrix} \tau_{11} = 0 \\ \tau_{01} = 0 \end{pmatrix}.$$

One first estimates the full model with four variance-covariance parameters, and then one estimates a reduced model with just two parameters (σ^2 and τ_{00})—that is, where τ_{11} and τ_{01} have been constrained to zero. One then compares the deviance associated with the two models and asks whether the reduction in deviance associated with the more complex model is justified.

In our case, the results are

model	number of parameters	Deviance
restricted	2	46,514.0
unrestricted	4	46,513.1

The reduction in deviance is 0.9, which is not significant when compared against chi-square distribution with 2 df. Hence, the simpler model seems justified. We infer that explanatory power is not significantly enhanced by specifying the residual SES-achievement slopes as random. The reduced model with β_{1j} specified as nonrandomly varying appears sufficient.

Estimating the Level-1 Coefficients for a Particular Unit

In this chapter, we have characterized the distribution of achievement in each high school in terms of two school-specific parameters: a school's mean math achievement and a regression coefficient describing the relationship between SES and math achievement. We have viewed these Level-1 coefficients as "random parameters" varying over the population of schools as a function of certain fixed effects. Our object has been to estimate these fixed effects as well as the variances and covariances of the Level-1 coefficients.

As mentioned in Chapter 3, the empirical Bayes approach provides shrinkage estimators of each Level-1 coefficient. These shrinkage estimators may be subdivided into two categories: *unconditional* and *conditional* shrinkage estimators. We illustrate each approach and compare these with the OLS estimates.

Ordinary Least Squares

The most obvious strategy for estimating the regression equation for a particular school is simply to fit a separate model to each school's data by ordinary least squares (OLS). The model for each school might simply be Equation 4.11. Recall that with SES centered around the school mean, the intercept β_{0j} is the mean outcome for that school, and the regression coefficient β_{1j} represents the expected difference in achievement per unit difference in SES within that school. OLS will produce unbiased estimates of these parameters for any school that has at least two cases. Indeed, if the errors of the model are normally distributed, the OLS estimates are the unique, minimum-variance, unbiased estimators of these parameters.

Nevertheless, the OLS estimates of each school's regression may be very poor. Especially if a particular school has a small sample or a restricted range on SES, the slope estimates will tend to be imprecise. The collection of OLS estimates from the 160 schools will appear far more variable than the true parameters are.

Figure 4.2a shows the OLS estimates for each of the 160 schools. The intercept estimates (vertical axis) are plotted against the slope estimates (horizontal axis). Quite a few schools yield negative estimates of the SES-achievement relationship. Moreover, the apparent dispersion of the OLS estimates greatly exceeds the maximum likelihood estimate of the variance of the true slopes. Earlier, we estimated the variance of the true slope parameters to be .65. Yet the sample variance of the OLS slope estimates depicted in Figure 4.2a is 2.66. If we were to define effective and equitable schools as those with large means and small SES-math achievement slopes, we might identify many schools simply because of chance differences in their OLS slope estimates.

Unconditional Shrinkage

The empirical Bayes estimates of each school's regression line take into account the precision of its estimation (as described in Chapter 3). This principle is illustrated in Figure 4.2b, which displays the empirical Bayes estimates of the intercepts (vertical axis) and the math-SES slopes (horizontal axis) for the 160 schools. Notice that the empirical Bayes slope estimates are much more concentrated around the sample average than are the OLS estimates in Figure 4.2a. Unlike the collection of OLS slope estimates, none of the empirical Bayes estimates is negative. Also, the sample variance of the empirical Bayes slope estimates is only .14, much smaller than the sample variance of the the OLS slope estimates (2.66). In fact, the sample variance of the empirical Bayes slope estimates is smaller than the maximum likelihood estimate of the variance of the true slopes (.65). The fact that the empirical Bayes estimates have less variance than the estimated true variance is an expected result. In general, the shrinkage is slightly exaggerated; empirical Bayes tends to pull the estimates "too far" toward the sample average.

It is interesting to contrast the slope shrinkage in Figure 4.2 with the results for the achievement intercepts. Recall that the intercepts are just the mean achievement in each school and are much more reliably estimated than are the slopes (.91 versus .23). Given the greater precision of the intercept estimates, we would expect that the empirical Bayes estimator would rely more heavily on this component, and less shrinkage should

```
(a) Ordinary Least Squares

           -
           -                      *          *  *
      18.0+                          2     ***
           -                         2*****2 * *                 *
  OLS      -                      *     ********2 *        *
  Intercept -                       * 22 *33*424* *  **
           -                        ** *2***  6*424**
      12.0+                               22 *3  *2*2**2     *
           -                       2 *   2*22 * **2** **  2
           -                  *     2*   * 22 2 * *2
           -                        *    **   **   *
           -                        *    **    *2 *
       6.0+                              **
           -                       *   *    *
            +---------+---------+---------+---------+--
          -6.0      -3.0       0.0       3.0       6.0

                               OLS Slope

(b) Empirical Bayes[a]

           -
           -                             * *
      18.0+                               *4*
           -                              *3* *
  EB       -                             *483 *
Intercept  -                             *66+2
           -                             *34+6
      12.0+                                7373
           -                            **3654**
           -                           * 3242*
           -                             *3*32
           -                             * **
       6.0+                               2*
           -                              **
            +---------+---------+---------+---------+--
          -6.0      -3.0       0.0       3.0       6.0

                              EB Slope
```

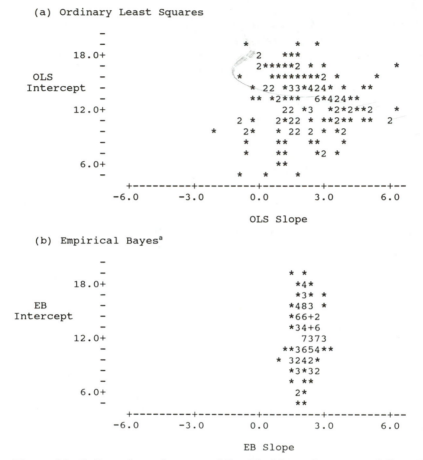

Figure 4.2. Ordinary Least Squares and Empirical Bayes Intercept and Slope Estimates for 160 High Schools

NOTE: Intercept estimates are plotted on the vertical axis, slope estimates on the horizontal axis.
a. A "+" indicates the presence of more than nine observations.

occur. This result is displayed in Figure 4.2 (compare the vertical axes of Figures 4.2a and 4.2b). Unlike the slopes, where the shrinkage is substantial, the difference between the OLS and empirical Bayes estimates for the intercepts is only modest.

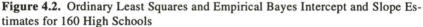

In general, the behavior of the empirical Bayes estimator is simpler in the case of random-intercept models than in models that also have random slopes. For example, consider the present case, in which we focus on each school's SES-achievement slope and its intercept. The empirical Bayes slope estimate will depend not only upon the OLS slope estimate and its reliability, but also upon the OLS intercept estimate, its reliability, and the correlation between the slopes and the intercepts. For example, if the intercept and slope are highly correlated, the empirical Bayes estimate of school *j*'s slope will be influenced not only by the OLS slope estimate, but also by the OLS intercept estimate. Because the intercept and slope are correlated, each contains information about the other. Further, because the intercepts are also estimated more reliably than the slopes, in some cases a school's empirical Bayes slope estimate may depend as much upon its OLS intercept estimate as it does its own OLS slope. Paterson (1990) provides an excellent discussion of this principle, which he terms *multivariate shrinkage*. In our case, the intercept-slope correlation is near zero, so the slope shrinkage is nearly independent of the shrinkage for the intercept.

Conditional Shrinkage

Unconditional shrinkage pulls each OLS regression line toward the grand average of the regression lines. This method is based on the assumption of "exchangeability" of the regression equations (Lindley & Smith, 1972): The regression equations are exchangeable in the sense that there is no a priori reason to believe that any school will have a larger intercept or slope than will any other school. However, when this assumption is untenable, unconditional shrinkage becomes indefensible.

For example, the results of our last analysis tell us that Catholic schools, on average, have substantially flatter slopes than do public schools. This means that, using unconditional shrinkage, a Catholic school with a slope estimate that is typically flat for Catholic schools will have its slope estimate increased—pulled toward the grand mean that is itself made steeper by the presence of the public schools in the sample. Similarly, a public school with a slope characteristic of public schools will see its slope estimate pulled down toward the sample average that is influenced by the presence of the Catholic schools.

A remedy for this problem is conditional shrinkage. Rather than pulling each OLS regression line toward the grand mean regression line, the OLS regression lines will now be pulled toward a *predicted value* based on the school-level model (see Chapter 3 for actual estimation formulas).

We illustrate conditional shrinkage based on the model where each school's mean and slope are predicted by its MEAN SES and SECTOR. Using the Level-2 model of Equation 4.15, it is possible to predict the value of each school's mean and slope. The empirical Bayes estimate for each school's regression equation will then be a weighted average of the OLS estimate and the value predicted by this model. Notice that the more powerful the explanatory model, the more severe will be the shrinkage. The extreme case would occur if the variability of the true school parameters were completely explained by their respective Level-2 models. In that case, shrinkage would be total and the predicted values based in the school-level model and the empirical Bayes estimates would coincide.

In order to discern the effects of conditional shrinkage, we use the idea of OLS and empirical Bayes residuals introduced in Chapter 3. The OLS residuals for the intercepts and slopes in Equation 4.15 are

$$\hat{u}_{0j} = \hat{\beta}_{0j} - [\hat{\gamma}_{00} + \hat{\gamma}_{01}(\text{MEAN SES})_j + \hat{\gamma}_{02}(\text{SECTOR})_j]\,, \quad [4.18a]$$

$$\hat{u}_{1j} = \hat{\beta}_{1j} - [\hat{\gamma}_{10} + \hat{\gamma}_{11}(\text{MEAN SES})_j + \hat{\gamma}_{12}(\text{SECTOR})_j]\,. \quad [4.18b]$$

The corresponding empirical Bayes residuals are

$$u^*_{0j} = \beta^*_{0j} - [\hat{\gamma}_{00} + \hat{\gamma}_{01}(\text{MEAN SES})_j + \hat{\gamma}_{02}(\text{SECTOR})_j]\,, \quad [4.19a]$$

$$u^*_{1j} = \beta^*_{1j} - [\hat{\gamma}_{10} + \hat{\gamma}_{11}(\text{MEAN SES})_j + \hat{\gamma}_{12}(\text{SECTOR})_j]\,. \quad [4.19b]$$

Figure 4.3 displays the results. The intercept residuals are plotted on the vertical axis and the slope residuals on the horizontal axis. The OLS slope residuals are highly misleading. They suggest considerable unexplained variability in the SES-achievement relationships. In contrast, the empirical Bayes residuals are tightly clumped around zero with even less dispersion than in Figure 4.2. This result is consistent with the results in Table 4.5, where 68% of the variability in β_{1j} was accounted for by MEAN SES and SECTOR.

In contrast, the empirical Bayes and OLS residuals for the intercept are much more similar. These residuals, however, are less dispersed than in the unconditional model (Figure 4.2), which is consistent with the fact that Equation 4.15a accounts for about 73% of the variance in β_{0j} .

Cautionary Note

The conditional shrinkage estimators will be substantially more accurate than the OLS estimators *when the school-level model is appropriately specified.* That is, the underlying assumption of empirical Bayes conditional shrinkage is that given the predictors in the Level-2 model, the regression lines are "conditionally exchangeable." This means, in the case of Equation 4.15, that once MEAN SES and SECTOR have been taken

(a) Ordinary Least Squares Residuals

```
            -
            -
         6.0+                              **
            -                      *
  OLS       -                        *        *  *  *
Intercept   -                 *      3 2 3*3***
            -                  **    *22263433233**   *
         0.0+                 ** 2*23323232262**    2 *
            -                 * * 2*4*4***232* 4    *
            -                  *     2323* *22* 2
            -                        *  **
            -                           * *   **
        -6.0+
            -                     *
            -
            -
              --------+---------+---------+---------+---------+----
                    -6.0      -3.0       0.0       3.0       6.0

                                        OLS Slope
```

(b) Empirical Bayes Residuals[a]

```
            -
            -
         6.0+
            -                              2
  EB        -                             2*
Intercept   -                             6**
            -                            2++
         0.0+                            9+72
            -                            ++4
            -                            54
            -                            24
            -
        -6.0+
            -
              --------+---------+---------+---------+---------+----
                    -6.0      -3.0       0.0       3.0       6.0

                                       EB Slope
```

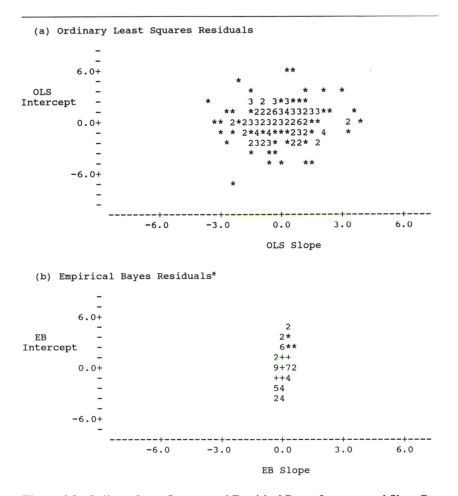

Figure 4.3. Ordinary Least Squares and Empirical Bayes Intercept and Slope Residuals for 160 High Schools

NOTE: Intercept residuals are plotted on the vertical axis, slope residuals on the horizontal axis.
a. A "+"indicates the presence of more than nine observations.

into account, there is no reason to believe that the deviation of any school's regression line from its predicted value is larger or smaller than that of any other school. This assumption depends strongly upon the validity of the Level-2 model. If that model is misspecified, the empirical Bayes estimates will also be misspecified: The predicted values of the γ parameters will be biased and the empirical Bayes shrinkage will lead to distortion in each group's estimated equation. We shall return to this concern in Chapter 5 when we consider the problem of estimating the effectiveness of individual organizations.

Note

1. Data tapes and a user's manual are available from the Office of Educational Research and Improvement, U.S. Department of Education, 55 New Jersey Avenue, Washington, DC 20208-1327.

5 Applications in Organizational Research

- Background Issues in Research on Organizational Effects
- Formulating Models
- Case 1: Modeling the Common Effects of Organizations via Random-Intercept Models
- Case 2: Explaining the Differentiating Effects of Organizations via Intercepts- and Slopes-as-Outcomes Models
- Special Topics
- Estimating the Effects of Individual Organizations

Background Issues in Research on Organizational Effects

A number of conceptual and technical difficulties have plagued past analyses of multilevel data in organizational research. Among the most commonly encountered difficulties have been aggregation bias, misestimated standard errors, and heterogeneity of regression.

In brief, aggregation bias can occur when a variable takes on different meanings and therefore may have different effects at different organizational levels. In educational research, for example, the average social class of a school may have an effect on student achievement above and beyond the effect of the individual child's social class. At the student level, social class provides a measure of the intellectual and tangible resources in a child's home environment. At the school level, it is a proxy measure of a school's resources and normative environment. Hierarchical linear models help resolve this confounding by facilitating a decomposition of any observed relationship between variables, such as achievement and social class, into separate Level-1 and Level-2 components.

Misestimated standard errors occur with multilevel data when we fail to take into account the dependence among individual responses within the same organization. This dependence may arise because of shared experiences within the organization or because of the ways in which individuals were initially drawn into the organization. Hierarchical linear models resolve this problem by incorporating into the statistical model a unique random effect for each organizational unit. The variability in these random effects is taken into account in estimating standard errors. In the terminology of survey research, these standard error estimates adjust for the intraclass correlation (or related to it, the design effect) that occurs as a result of cluster sampling.

Heterogeneity of regression occurs when the relationships between individual characteristics and outcomes vary across organizations. Although this phenomenon has often been viewed as a methodological nuisance, the causes of heterogeneity of regression are often of substantive interest. Hierarchical linear models enable the investigator to estimate a separate set of regression coefficients for each organizational unit, and then to model variation among the organizations in their sets of coefficients as multivariate outcomes to be explained by organizational factors. Burstein (1980) provides an excellent review of this idea of slopes-as-outcomes.

Formulating Models

Many questions about how organizations affect the individuals within them can be formulated as two-level hierarchical linear models. At Level 1, the units are persons and each person's outcome is represented as a function of a set of individual characteristics. At Level 2, the units are organizations. The regression coefficients in the Level-1 model for each organization are conceived as outcome variables that are hypothesized to depend on specific organizational characteristics.

Person-Level Model (Level 1)

We denote the outcome for person i in organization j as Y_{ij}. This outcome is represented as a function of individual characteristics, X_{qij}, and a model error r_{ij}:

$$Y_{ij} = \beta_{0j} + \beta_{1j}X_{1ij} + \beta_{2j}X_{2ij} + \ldots + \beta_{Qj}X_{Qij} + r_{ij}, \qquad [5.1]$$

where we will generally assume throughout this chapter that $r_{ij} \sim N(0, \sigma^2)$.

The regression coefficients β_{qj}, $q = 0, \ldots, Q$, indicate how the outcome is distributed in organization j as a function of the measured person characteristics. We therefore term these coefficients *distributive effects.* Equation 5.1 is sometimes referred to as the *microlevel* model in organizational research (Mason et al., 1983).

Organization-Level Model (Level 2)

The effects for each organization, captured in the set of β_{qj}s in Equation 5.1, are presumed to vary across units. This variation is in turn modeled in a set of Q+1 Level-2 equations—one for each of the regression coefficients from the Level-1 model. Each β_{qj} is conceived as an outcome variable that depends on a set of organization-level variables, W_{sj}, and a unique organization effect, u_{qj} . Each β_{qj} has a model of the form

$$\beta_{qj} = \gamma_{q0} + \gamma_{q1} W_{1j} + \gamma_{q2} W_{2j} + \ldots + \gamma_{qS_q} W_{S_q j} + u_{qj} . \qquad [5.2]$$

distributive effects in organization j	=	effects of organizational characteristics on the distribution of outcomes within the organization	+	unique effect associated with organization j

where a unique set of W_s ($s = 1, \ldots, S_q$) may be specified for each β_q .

Equation 5.2 is sometimes referred to as the *macrolevel* model (Mason et al., 1983). The γ_{qs} coefficients capture the influence of organizational variables, W_{sj}, on the within-organizational relationships represented by β_{qj} . We generally assume throughout this chapter that the set of $Q + 1$ Level-2 random effects is multivariate normally distributed. Each u_{qj} has a mean of 0, some variance, τ_{qq}, and covariances, $\tau_{qq'}$, between any two random effects q and q'. These are the standard Level-2 model assumptions introduced in Chapter 3 and discussed in more detail in Chapter 9.

In this chapter, we demonstrate how this model can be applied to investigate two broad classes of organizational effects. In "Case 1," some aspect of the organization such as its technology, structure, or climate exerts a common influence on each person within it. Such organization effects modify only the mean level of the outcome for the organization. They leave unchanged the distribution of effects among persons within the organization. In statistical terms, only the intercept, β_{0j}, varies across organizations; all other Level-1 coefficients remain constant. As discussed in this section, such problems involve the use of random-intercept models.

In "Case 2," organization effects may modify both the mean level of outcomes and how effects are distributed among individuals. In statistical terms, both the intercept and regression slopes vary among the units. This section details this application of the full hierarchical linear model with both intercepts and slopes-as-outcomes.

The following section of this chapter ("Special Topics") considers some special issues that arise in organizational research applications. We illustrate and explain why hierarchical analyses can produce different results from an ordinary Level-1 regression. We also demonstrate how the two-level model affords a decomposition of person-level effects and compositional (or contextual) effects. The final section of the chapter considers how hierarchical estimators can be used to evaluate the performance of specific organizational units. Such applications of hierarchical linear models draw on the empirical Bayes estimates of the Level-1 coefficients. This chapter concludes with a discussion of some validity issues that arise using the shrunken estimates.

Case 1: Modeling the Common Effects of Organizations via Random-Intercept Models

The basic problem in this case is that the key predictors are measured at the organization level, but the outcome variable is measured at the person level. Historically, such data have raised questions about the appropriate unit of analysis (organization or person) and the problems associated with either choice. If the data are analyzed at the person level, thereby ignoring the nesting of individuals within organizational units, the estimated standard errors will be too small, and the risk of type I errors inflated (see Aitkin, Anderson, & Hinde, 1981; Burstein, 1980; and Haney, 1980 for a review). Alternatively, if the data are analyzed at the organization level, using the means of the person responses as the outcome, it becomes problematic to incorporate other Level-1 predictors into the analysis. In addition, inefficient and biased estimates of organizational effects can result.

As Burstein (1980) pointed out, posing the problem as the "choice of an appropriate unit of analysis" is misguided. The key fact is that random variation and structural effects may exist at both levels, and a multilevel modeling framework is required to explicitly represent these features.

A Simple Random-Intercept Model

The basic idea of the random-intercept model was previously introduced in Chapter 2. The key feature of such models is that only the intercept parameter in the Level-1 model, β_{0j}, in Equation 5.1, is assumed to vary at Level 2. Specifically, the organization model at Level 2 consists of

$$\begin{aligned} \beta_{0j} &= \gamma_{00} + \gamma_{01}W_{1j} + \gamma_{02}W_{2j} + \ldots + \gamma_{0S}W_{Sj} + u_{0j} \\ \beta_{1j} &= \gamma_{10} \\ \beta_{2j} &= \gamma_{20} \\ &\vdots \\ \beta_{QJ} &= \gamma_{Q0}. \end{aligned} \quad [5.3]$$

Example: Examining School Effects on Teacher Efficacy

Bryk and Driscoll (1988) used the Administrator and Teacher Supplement of the High School and Beyond Survey to investigate how characteristics of school organization were related to teachers' sense of efficacy in their work. Specifically, they hypothesized that teachers' efficacy would be higher in schools with a communal, rather than a bureaucratic, organizational form. The data consisted of responses from over 8,000 teachers nested within 357 schools. The average school sample size was 22 teachers.

The teacher-level model specified that the sense of efficacy varied among teachers within a school. Because no teacher variables were considered as Level-1 predictors, Equation 5.1 reduced to

$$Y_{ij} = \beta_{0j} + r_{ij}, \quad [5.4]$$

where Y_{ij} was the reported efficacy for teacher i in school j, and β_{0j} was the true mean level of efficacy in school j.

Three school-level models were estimated. The first was an unconditional model for β_{0j}. This results in a one-way random-effects ANOVA model, which partitions the total variance in Y_{ij} into its within- and between-school components. These estimates of σ^2 and τ_{00}, respectively, prove helpful in evaluating the results of subsequent models. The second model examined the effects of several measures of school composition and size on teacher efficacy (see Table 5.1 for description of variables). Formally,

$$\begin{aligned} \beta_{0j} = \gamma_{00} &+ \gamma_{01}(\text{MEAN BACKGROUND})_j + \gamma_{02}(\text{MEAN SES})_j \\ &+ \gamma_{03}(\text{HI MINORITY})_j + \gamma_{04}(\text{SIZE})_j + \gamma_{05}(\text{ETHNIC MIX})_j \\ &+ \gamma_{06}(\text{SES MIX})_j + u_{0j}. \end{aligned} \quad [5.5]$$

TABLE 5.1 Description of Variables Used in the Study of the Effects of School Organization on Teacher Efficacy

Variable Name	*Description*
TEACHER EFFICACY	A factor composite of five teacher responses about their sense of satisfaction in their work. It is a standardized measure (i.e. mean = 0; sd = 1.0).
MEAN BACKGROUND	A factor composite of four items about students' academic experiences prior to high school (e.g. retained in grade) and initial placement (e.g. remedial English or math). It is a standardized variable (mean = 0; sd = 1.0) with positive scores indicating a stronger background.
MEAN SES	Average social class of students in the school. It is a standardized variable with positive values indicating more affluent schools.
HI MINORITY	A dummy variable indicating schools with minority enrollment in excess of 40%.
SIZE	The natural log of number of students enrolled in the school.
ETHNIC MIX	A standardized measure of the diversity in students' ethnicity within the school. Low values imply a single ethnic group. High positive values indicate significant student representation in several ethnic groups.
SES MIX	Like ethnic mix, this is a standardized measure of the social class diversity within the school. Positive values indicate a socially heterogeneous school.
COMMUNAL	A composite measure based on 23 separate indices of the extent to which a school has a communal organization. It is a standardized measure with positive values indicating a greater frequency of shared activities, consensus on common beliefs, teacher collegiality, and a broader teacher role. Low values indicate a more segmented, specialized, bureaucratic organization.

NOTE: For a further discussion of the measures, see Bryk and Driscoll (1988).

The third model added a measure of the degree of communal organization in the school, COMMUNAL, to Equation 5.5. In both models, the residual school-specific effects, u_{0j}, were assumed normally distributed with mean 0 and variance τ_{00} .

One-Way Random-Effects ANOVA Model. The analysis began with fitting an unconditional model for β_{0j} at Level 2. The estimate for the within-school or Level-1 variance (i.e., $\mathrm{Var}(r_{ij}) = \sigma^2$) was 0.915. This estimate remains the same for the three analyses discussed here, because the Level-1 model (Equation 5.4) is identical for all three. The overall variability among the true school means on teacher efficacy [i.e., Var(β_{0j}) = τ_{00}] was 0.084. This resulted in an intraclass correlation of 0.092 (see Equation 4.3), and an estimated reliability for the school means on teacher efficacy of 0.669 (see Equations 4.4 and 4.5).

Two Explanatory Models at Level 2. The first set of columns in Table 5.2 presents the results of two hierarchical linear model analyses. In the top panel are the estimates for the compositional model and in the bottom panel are the results after the COMMUNAL variable was added. In the compositional model (top panel) students' MEAN BACKGROUND ($\hat{\gamma}_{01}$ = 0.044, se = 0.020) and the school's MEAN SES ($\hat{\gamma}_{02}$ = 0.133, se = 0.023) were positively related to teachers' sense of efficacy. School SIZE had a significant negative effect ($\hat{\gamma}_{04}$ = −0.066, se = 0.027). The effects of the other three Level-2 predictors were small both in absolute terms and in comparison to their estimated standard errors.

The results for the communal organization model were quite startling. The estimated effect of COMMUNAL ($\hat{\gamma}_{07}$ = 0.504, se = 0.045) was by far the largest—almost an order of magnitude bigger than all the others. (Note: this interpretation depends on the fact that all of the Level-2 predictors, except the dummy variable HI MINORITY, were standardized to mean = 0, sd = 1.0.) This means that teacher efficacy was substantially higher in schools with a communal organization, even after controlling for compositional differences among schools. We also note that the effects of MEAN SES found in the composition model have largely disappeared (0.015 versus 0.133). This suggests that the positive levels of teacher efficacy found in high social-class schools may reflect the greater prevalance of communal organizational features in these schools. Notice also that the school-size effect has become positive, implying somewhat higher levels of teacher efficacy in larger schools *after* controlling for communal organization. As Bryk and Driscoll (1988) explain, teacher efficacy tends to be lower in large schools because these schools are less likely to be communal. Once this effect is controlled for, however, large schools appear to promote somewhat greater efficacy presumably by virtue of the greater resources and expanded professional opportunities typically found there.

After controlling for composition effects, as specified in Equation 5.5, the residual variability at Level 2, $\hat{\tau}_{00}$, was 0.055. We refer to this as $\hat{\tau}_{00}$(compositional model). The model accounted for 34.5% of the total parameter variance among schools in mean levels of teacher efficacy. This proportion reduction in variance statistic was computed using the procedure introduced in Chapter 4. Specifically,

TABLE 5.2 Effects of School Organization on Teacher Efficacy

	Hierarchical Analysis Coefficient	*se*	*Teacher-Level Analysis* Coefficient	*se*	*School-Level Analysis* Coefficient	*se*
Compositional model						
MEAN BACKGROUND, γ_{01}	0.044	0.020	0.046	0.014	0.040	0.021
MEAN SES, γ_{02}	0.133	0.023	0.132	0.015	0.137	0.023
HI MINORITY, γ_{03}	0.031	0.046	0.028	0.031	0.035	0.047
SIZE, γ_{04}	–0.066	0.027	–0.066	0.019	–0.068	0.026
ETHNIC MIX, γ_{05}	–0.014	0.019	–0.014	0.013	–0.013	0.019
SES MIX, γ_{06}	–0.028	0.023	–0.029	0.016	–0.025	0.023
Proportion of variance accounted for	0.345		0.029		0.234	
Communal model						
MEAN BACKGROUND, γ_{01}	0.038	0.017	0.040	0.013	0.033	0.018
MEAN SES, γ_{02}	0.015	0.022	0.015	0.017	0.019	0.023
HI MINORITY, γ_{03}	–0.055	0.040	–0.056	0.031	–0.051	0.041
SIZE, γ_{04}	0.061	0.026	0.062	0.021	0.060	0.025
ETHNIC MIX, γ_{05}	–0.014	0.016	–0.014	0.013	–0.014	0.017
SES MIX, γ_{06}	0.001	0.020	0.002	0.016	–0.000	0.020
COMMUNAL, γ_{07}	0.504	0.045	0.507	0.035	0.493	0.045
Proportion of variance accounted for	0.631		0.054		0.426	
Incremental variance	0.286		0.025		0.192	

Note: Residual variance estimates for hierarchical analyses: τ_{00} (compositional model) = 0.055; τ_{00} (communal model) = 0.031.

$$\text{Proportion variance explained} = \frac{\hat{\tau}_{00}(\text{unconditional}) - \hat{\tau}_{00}(\text{compositional model})}{\hat{\tau}_{00}(\text{unconditional})} \qquad [5.6]$$

$$= \frac{0.084 - 0.055}{0.084} = 0.345$$

where $\hat{\tau}_{00}$(unconditional) is the overall variability in the true school means as estimated from the one-way random-effects ANOVA model.

The percentage of variance explained jumped to 63.1% after COMMUNAL was entered into the model. That is, the residual variance in β_{0j}, $\hat{\tau}_{00}$(communal model), was 0.031. Replacing $\hat{\tau}_{00}$(compositional model) in Equation 5.6 with $\hat{\tau}_{00}$(communal model) yields a proportion of variance explained as

$$\frac{0.084 - 0.031}{0.084} = 0.631\,. \qquad [5.7]$$

The incremental variance explained by adding COMMUNAL to the model was 28.6%. This statistic is just the difference between the proportion reduction in variance statistics calculated in Equations 5.6 and 5.7.

Comparison of Results with Conventional Teacher-Level and School-Level Analyses

Table 5.2 also presents results from teacher (Level-1) and school (Level-2) analyses. A comparison of these conventional alternatives to the multi-level results helps to clarify some of the basic features of estimates in random-intercept models. We compare below the fixed-effect estimates, the standard errors of these estimates, and the variance-explained statistics typically reported with such analyses.

Fixed Effects. Notice in Table 5.2 that the estimates for the regression coefficents are quite similar across the three analyses. The hierarchical estimates, however, are somewhat closer to the results from the teacher analysis, which will generally be the case.

As presented in Chapter 3, the estimators for the Level-2 coefficients in a hierarchical linear model can be viewed as weighted least squares estimators where the the weights are of the form

$$\Delta_j^{-1} = (V_j + \tau_{00})^{-1} . \qquad [5.8]$$

Assuming a homogeneous Level-1 variance (i.e., $\sigma_j^2 = \sigma^2$ for all J), then $V_j = \sigma^2/n_j$ and the variation in the weights depends strictly on n_j.

In comparison, the typical OLS Level-1 analysis of these data is also weighted, but the weights are just n_j. Specifically, suppose a simple univariate model where the teacher outcome, Y_{ij}, depends on one school characteristic, W_j:

$$Y_{ij} = \gamma_0 + \gamma_1 W_j + e_{ij} . \qquad [5.9]$$

It can be shown easily that the estimator for γ_1 based on an OLS Level-1 analysis is simply

$$\hat{\gamma}_1 = \frac{\sum_j n_j(W_j - \overline{W}.)(\overline{Y}._j - \overline{Y}..)}{\sum_j n_j(W_j - \overline{W}.)^2} . \qquad [5.10]$$

Notice that the numerator and denominator are sums of squares and cross-products, weighted by n_j instead of Δ_j^{-1}.

In contrast, the Level-2 analysis is unweighted. The comparable univariate model would be

$$\bar{Y}_{\cdot j} = \gamma_0 + \gamma_1 W_j + \bar{r}_{\cdot j} \qquad [5.11]$$

and the corresponding estimator for γ_1 is

$$\hat{\gamma}_1 = \frac{\sum_j (W_j - \bar{W}_\cdot)(\bar{Y}_{\cdot j} - \tilde{Y}_{\cdot\cdot})}{\sum_j (W_j - \bar{W}_\cdot)^2}, \qquad [5.12]$$

where

$$\tilde{Y}_{\cdot\cdot} = \sum \bar{Y}_{\cdot j}/J \quad \text{and} \quad \bar{W}_\cdot = \sum W_j/J .$$

All three estimators are unbiased, but the hierarchical estimator is the most efficient. Variations in results among the three analyses will depend on the degree of unbalance in the n_j. (If the sample sizes n_j are identical for each of the J organizations, the three estimators are the same.) In the Bryk and Driscoll (1988) application, the n_j were not grossly different. No school with less than five teachers was included in the analysis, and the vast majority of schools had between 20 and 30 cases. Thus, the Level-2 results were quite similar in this application.

In general, an issue of robustness is the primary concern when estimating the fixed effects with a Level-2 analysis in the presence of unbalanced data. A unit with a very small sample size can easily become an outlier or leverage point because of the instability associated with the limited amount of information about that unit. The weighting employed in the hierarchical and Level-1 analyses protect against this.

Standard Errors of the Fixed Effects. As noted in the introduction to this chapter, the standard errors produced by a Level-1 analysis will generally be too small, because this analysis fails to take into account the fact that Level-1 units are not independent but rather are actually clustered within Level-2 units. In the compositional analysis, for example, the Level-1 estimates are about a third smaller than those provided by the hierarchical and Level-2 analyses.

A direct comparison of the formulas for the three different standard errors is difficult when sample sizes are unequal. Some basic features can be ascertained, however, if we consider the balanced data case with a single W_j predictor. It can readily be shown that the expected values of the estimators for the sampling variance for γ_1 from the hierarchical linear model and Level-2 analyses are identical:

$$E[\mathrm{Var}(\hat{\gamma}_1)]_{\text{hierarchical}} = \frac{V + \tau_{00}}{\sum_j (W_j - \overline{W}.)^2} \qquad [5.13]$$

As for the Level-1 analysis, the expected value of the sampling variance estimator is

$$E[\mathrm{Var}(\hat{\gamma}_1)]_{\text{level 1}} = \frac{J(n-1)\sigma^2 + (J-2)n(V + \tau_{00})}{(Jn-2)n\sum_j (W_j - \overline{W}.)^2}. \qquad [5.14]$$

When the Level-1 and Level-2 samples (n and J, respectively) are large, the ratio of the expected sampling variance form a Level-1 analysis, Equation 5.14, to that from a hierarchical analysis (or equivalently a Level-2 analysis), Equation 5.13, is approximately

$$\frac{E[\mathrm{Var}(\hat{\gamma}_1)]_{\text{level 1}}}{E[\mathrm{Var}(\hat{\gamma}_1)]_{\text{hierarchical}}} \approx 1 - \lambda \qquad [5.15]$$

where from Equation 3.36, $\lambda = \tau_{00}/[(\sigma^2/n) + \tau_{00}]$, and is the reliability of the OLS estimated school means, $\hat{\beta}_{0j}$.

Equation 5.15 closely approximates the empirical results reported in Table 5.2. With an average Level-1 sample size of 22 teachers per school, a Level-1 variance estimate, $\hat{\sigma}^2 = 0.915$, and an estimate of τ_{00} for the compositional model of 0.055,

$$1 - \lambda = 1 - \frac{0.055}{(0.915/22) + 0.055} = 0.431.$$

As for the relative size of the standard errors, their ratio is simply $(1 - \lambda)^{1/2}$, which, for the compositional model, yields a value of 0.657. This ratio closely corresponds to the results reported in the top panel of Table 5.2. Visual inspection indicates that the Level-1 standard errors are approximately two thirds of the more appropriate values reported by the hierarchical and Level-2 analyses.

In sum, the hierarchical analysis captures the best features of both the Level-1 and Level-2 analyses. It provides unbiased and efficient estimates of the fixed effects, which are more closely approximated by the Level-1 analysis, and provides proper standard error estimates, regardless of the degree of within-unit clustering, that are more closely approximated by the Level-2 analysis.

The results obtained above are typical of what one might routinely encounter in this type of analysis. The fixed-effects estimates will often be similar across the three analyses; however, the estimated standard errors will not.

Variance-Explained Statistics. The estimates of the proportion of variance explained from a hierarchical analysis may be quite different from those generated in conventional Level-1 or Level-2 analyses and may lead to different conclusions. In the Bryk and Driscoll (1988) study, for example, a judgment about the importance of communal organization depended considerably on the analysis considered (bottom panel in Table 5.2). The incremental reduction in variance associated with COMMUNAL was 28.6% in the hierarchical linear model analysis. The comparable statistics from the teacher and school-level analyses were 2.5% and 19.2% respectively. Although most analysts would probably judge 28.6% sufficiently substantial to merit further consideration of the construct under study, the 2.5% statistic could easily lead to the opposite inference.

To understand why the proportion of variance accounted for by COMMUNAL is so different requires a closer consideration of how the total outcome variability is partitioned in the three analyses. In a random-intercept problem, Level-2 variables such as COMMUNAL can only account for variation among the true school means, β_{0j}. That is, only the parameter variation, τ_{00}, is explainable. (This is why we use τ_{00} from the unconditional model as the denominator in the proportion reduction in variance statistic.) The 28.6% variance explained by COMMUNAL implies that a substantial portion of the variation among the true school means is associated with variation in school organization. Relative to all other school-level sources of variation, communal organization is indeed important.

In comparison, the Level-1 analysis employs the total outcome variability in Y_{ij}, $\tau_{00} + \sigma^2$, as the denominator for the variance-explained statistics. The within-unit variation, σ^2, however, reflects individual effects and errors of measurement in the outcome variable, both of which are unexplainable by organizational features. Judged against this standard, some researchers might erroneously conclude that the COMMUNAL effect is trivially small.

In general, the relative variance explained by a hierarchical versus a Level-1 analysis depends on the ratio

$$\frac{\text{Variance explained (level 1)}}{\text{Variance explained (hierarchical)}} \approx \frac{\tau_{00}}{\tau_{00}+\sigma^2} = \rho \qquad [5.16]$$

where ρ is the intraclass correlation coefficient (see Equation 2.10). Note that the intraclass correlation represents the theoretically maximal amount of the total variance in the outcome Y_{ij} that is explainable by all school factors. As noted earlier, the estimated intraclass correlation was 0.092 for the teacher-efficacy data. We can use $\hat{\rho}$ to relate the variance-explained statistics from the Level-1 and hierarchical analyses. For example,

$$\hat{\rho} \times \begin{bmatrix} \text{Incremental variance} \\ \text{explained (hierarchical)} \end{bmatrix} \approx \begin{bmatrix} \text{Incremental variance} \\ \text{explained (level 1)} \end{bmatrix}$$

$$0.092 \times [0.286] \approx 0.025$$

A similar formula can be derived for comparing the variance-explained statistics from the hierarchical and Level-2 analyses. The denominator for the variance-explained statistic in a Level-2 analyses is $\tau_{00} + (\sigma^2/n_j)$, which is just the total variance of the *sample* means. Thus, the relative variance explained by a hierarchical versus Level-2 analysis is approximately

$$\frac{\text{Variance explained (level 2)}}{\text{Variance explained (hierarchical)}} \approx \frac{\tau_{00}}{\tau_{00}+(\sigma^2/\bar{n}.)} = \bar{\lambda} \qquad [5.17]$$

where $\bar{\lambda}$ is the average reliability of the $\bar{Y}_{.j}$ as estimates of μ_{Y_j} (see Equation 3.36) based on an average Level-1 sample size of $\bar{n}.$. For the teacher-efficacy data, $\hat{\lambda}$ was 0.669, and the variances explained by the Level-2 analyses were approximately two thirds of those represented in the corresponding hierarchical analyses.

In sum, the variance-explained statistic from the hierarchical analysis provides the clearest evidence for making judgments about the importance of Level-2 predictors. They are not affected by the degree of clustering as the Level-1 statistics are (i.e., the dependence on ρ), nor they are affected by the unreliability of $\bar{Y}_{.j}$ as the Level-2 statistics are. Further, because good estimates of λ and ρ are not generally available with conventional analyses, the analyst has no way to assess the explanatory power of a set of Level-2 predictors relative to the maximum amount explainable by *any* model. Intuitively, this is what variance-explained statistics should tell us.

A Random-Intercept Model with Level-1 Covariates

In the previous example, we estimated the relationship between organizational characteristics and mean outcomes. We made no attempt to adjust the Level-2 effect estimates for the different characteristics of the individuals in the various organizations.

In general, statistical adjustments for individual background are important for two reasons. First, because persons are not usually assigned at random to organizations, failure to control for background may bias the estimates of organization effects. Second, if these Level-1 predictors (or covariates) are strongly related to the outcome of interest, controlling for them will increase the precision of any estimates of organizational effects and the power of hypothesis tests by reducing unexplained Level-1 error variance, σ^2.

The formal model for this type of analysis was introduced in Chapter 2. At Level 1,

$$Y_{ij} = \beta_{0j} + \beta_{1j}(X_{1ij} - \bar{X}_{1..}) + \beta_{2j}(X_{2ij} - \bar{X}_{2..}) + \dots \qquad [5.18]$$
$$+ \beta_{Qj}(X_{Qij} - \bar{X}_{Q..}) + r_{ij}.$$

The Level-2 model is Equation 5.3. Because each covariate is centered around its respective grand mean, the random intercept, β_{0j}, is now the adjusted mean rather than the raw mean. As in ANCOVA models, Equation 5.18 assumes homogeneous Level-1 coefficients for $\beta_{1j}, \dots, \beta_{Qj}$. The validity of this assumption can be easily tested using the methods described in Chapter 3. If needed, any Level-1 coefficient can be specified as either nonrandomly varying or as a random effect.

Example: Evaluating Program Effects on Writing

This example uses data from the Cognitive Strategies in Writing Project (Englert et al., 1988). The project sought to improve childrens' writing and to enhance childrens' self-perceptions of academic competence through a variety of strategies. The outcome variable was a measure of perceived academic self-competence (mean = 2.918; sd = 0.580) for which a pretest, denoted X_{ij}, served as the covariate. The study involved 256 children in 22 classrooms in a standard two-group design, with 15 experimental classrooms and 7 control classrooms. Because classroom teachers administered the treatments to intact classrooms, we have, in classical terms, a nested or hierarchical design: Students are nested within classrooms and classrooms are nested within two treatment groups. As in the previous example, we first present the results of a hierarchical analysis. We then compare these results to conventional alternatives: an ANCOVA at the student level ignoring classes, and an ANCOVA based on class means.

For the hierarchical analysis, the Level-1 model was

$$Y_{ij} = \beta_{0j} + \beta_{1j}(X_{ij} - \overline{X}_{..}) + r_{ij}, \qquad [5.19]$$

where

Y_{ij} is the self-perceived competence of child i in class j ($j = 1, \ldots, 22$ classrooms);

β_{0j} is the *adjusted* mean outcome in class j after controlling for differences in pretest status; and

β_{1j} is the fixed Level-1 covariate effect.

A preliminary analysis specified a model where both β_{0j} and β_{1j} were random and tested the homogeneity hypothesis for the covariate effect (H_0: $\text{Var}(\beta_{1j}) = 0$). Because the null hypothesis was retained for β_{1j}, it was appropriate to assume a fixed effect for the pretest covariate. The final Level-2 model was

$$\beta_{0j} = \gamma_{00} + \gamma_{01} W_j + u_{0j}, \qquad [5.20]$$

$$\beta_{1j} = \gamma_{10},$$

where

W_j is a treatment-indicator variable (1 = experimental; 0 = control);

γ_{00} is the adjusted mean achievement in the control-group classrooms;

γ_{01} is the treatment effect; and

γ_{10} is the pooled within-classroom regression coefficient for the Level-1 covariate.

The results of this analysis appear in Table 5.3. The estimated difference between experimental and control means adjusted for the pretest, was .188 ($t = 1.87$, df = 20, p [one tail] $< .04$). The estimated pooled within-classroom regression slope for the posttest on the pretest was 0.396 ($t = 7.02$, $p < .001$).

TABLE 5.3 Effects of Experimental Instruction on Self-Perceived Competence in Writing

	Hierarchical Analysis[a]		*Student-Level Analysis*[b]		*Classroom-Level Analysis*[c]	
	Coefficcient	*se*	*Coefficient*	*se*	*Coefficient*	*se*
Intercept, γ_{00}	2.774	0.084	2.802	0.063	2.763	0.112
Treatment indicator, γ_{01}	0.188	0.100	0.160	0.074	0.209	0.135
Pretest, γ_{10}	0.396	0.056	0.406	0.056	0.649	0.223

a. Residual variance estimates: $\hat{\sigma}^2 = 0.258$;
$\hat{\tau}_{00} = 0.019$.
b. Estimated residual variance = 0.273 .
c. Estimated residual variance = 0.087 .

Comparison of Results with Conventional Student- and Classroom-Level Analyses

The model for the student-level analyses was

$$Y_i = \gamma_{00} + \gamma_{01} W_i + \gamma_{10}(X_i - \bar{X}.) + r_i, \qquad [5.21]$$

where the parameters γ_{00}, γ_{01}, and γ_{10} represent the intercept, the treatment effect, and the covariate effect, respectively, and $\bar{X}.$ is the mean pretest score (i.e., $\Sigma_{i=1}^{N} X_i / N$). Notice that the j subscript has disappeared because class membership is ignored, as is the effect associated with classrooms (i.e., u_{0j}) in Equation 5.20.

The results for this analysis appear in the second column of Table 5.3. They indicate that experimental children developed a significantly higher perceived self-competence than did the control children ($\hat{\gamma}_{01} = .160$, $t = 2.17$, p [one-tail] $< .02$). The estimated pooled within-treatment groups regression slope for the posttest on the pretest was 0.406 ($t = 7.25$, $p < .001$).

As for the classroom-level analyses, the model was

$$\bar{Y}._j = \gamma_{00} + \gamma_{01} W_j + \gamma_{10}(\bar{X}._j - \tilde{X}..) + u_{0j} \qquad [5.22]$$

where $j = 1, \ldots, 22$ classrooms. Here $\bar{X}._j$ is the pretest mean for class j; $\bar{Y}._j$ is the posttest class mean. The grand mean for the pretest, $\tilde{X}..$, is the mean of the classroom means (i.e., $\tilde{X}.. = \Sigma\bar{X}._j / J$). These results appear in the third column of Table 5.3. Although the estimated treatment-effect size ($\hat{\gamma}_{01} = 0.209$) is actually larger than the hierarchical and classroom-level estimates, it is not statistically significant due to the substantially larger standard error [se ($\hat{\gamma}_{01}$) = 0.135]. The estimated covariate effect, $\hat{\gamma}_{10} =$ 0.649, is also substantially larger, as is its standard error of .223.

TABLE 5.4 Treatment Effect Estimates: Hierarchical, Student-Level, and Classroom-Level Analyses

	Hierarchical Analysis	*Student-Level Analysis*	*Class-Level Analysis*
$\bar{Y}_E$	2.968	2.980	2.964
$\bar{Y}_C$	2.742	2.754	2.980
$\bar{X}_E$	2.895	2.921	2.855
$\bar{X}_C$	2.797	2.759	2.893
$\hat{\beta}_{Y \cdot X}$	0.396	0.406	0.649
$\bar{Y}_E - \bar{Y}_C - \hat{\beta}_{Y \cdot X}(\bar{X}_E - \bar{X}_C)$	0.188	0.160	0.209

It may seen surprising that the hierarchical analysis produced inferences similar to those of the student-level analysis and different from the class-level analysis. In each case, the test statistic for the effect of innovative instruction depends on a ratio of two quantities: the fixed effect size estimate and the standard error of this estimate. A comparison of each is offered below.

Fixed Effects. The estimate for the treatment effect is quite similar in all three analyses, with the student-level analysis producing the smallest effect (.160), the classroom-level analysis the largest (.209), and the hierarchical estimate falling in between (.188). In all three analyses, the treatment-effect estimator is of the general form

$$\hat{\gamma}_{10} = \hat{\mu}_{Y_T} - \hat{\mu}_{Y_C} - \hat{\beta}_{Y \cdot X}(\hat{\mu}_{X_T} - \hat{\mu}_{X_C}) \,. \qquad [5.23]$$

The key differences among the analyses are in the way $\beta_{Y \cdot X}$ and the pre- and posttest means are estimated. Table 5.4 presents the relevant statistics from each analysis.

For the student-level analysis, $\beta_{Y \cdot X}$ is the regression of the posttest on the pretest, pooled within the treatment and control groups. The hierarchical analysis is similar, except $\beta_{Y \cdot X}$ is pooled within each of the 22 classrooms. In contrast, the school-level analysis regresses the posttest means for the 22 classes on their corresponding pretest means. As Table 5.4 shows, the $\beta_{Y \cdot X}$ are quite similar in the hierarchical ($\hat{\beta}_{Y \cdot X}$ = .396) and the student-level analyses ($\hat{\beta}_{Y \cdot X}$ = .406). The classroom-level estimate, however, is quite discrepant ($\hat{\beta}_{Y \cdot X}$ = .649).

The three alternative methods also employ different estimators of the pre- and posttest means for each treatment group. Consider, for example, the experimental posttest mean. The hierarchical-analysis estimator is a weighted average,

$$\bar{Y}_{\mathrm{E}}(\text{hierarchical}) = \sum_{j}^{J_{\mathrm{E}}} \Delta_{j\mathrm{E}}^{-1} \bar{Y}_{\cdot j\mathrm{E}} / \sum_{j} \Delta_{j\mathrm{E}} , \qquad [5.24]$$

where $\bar{Y}_{\cdot j\mathrm{E}}$ is the mean of the *j*th classroom in the experimental group. The weight, $\Delta_{j\mathrm{E}}^{-1}$, is the precision of the corresponding sample mean. Thus, the hierarchical estimates are precision-weighted averages.

The student-level estimators weight by sample sizes:

$$\bar{Y}_{\mathrm{E}j}(\text{student level}) = \sum_{j}^{J_{\mathrm{E}}} n_{j\mathrm{E}} \bar{Y}_{\cdot j\mathrm{E}} / \sum_{j} n_{j\mathrm{E}} , \qquad [5.25]$$

where $n_{j\mathrm{E}}$ is the sample size of the *j*th classroom in the experimental group.

In contrast, the classroom-level analysis uses an unweighted average:

$$\bar{Y}_{\mathrm{E}j}(\text{classroom level}) = \sum_{j} \bar{Y}_{\cdot j\mathrm{E}} / J_{\mathrm{E}} , \qquad [5.26]$$

where J_{E} is the number of classrooms in the experimental group.

When the reliability of individual classroom means varies significantly, the classroom-level estimate is likely to be inaccurate because it will be strongly influenced by the extreme classroom means, which result from unreliability. This is not true of the student-level or hierarchical estimators. In fact, when the precisions Δ_j^{-1} are known or estimated accurately, the hierarchical weighting scheme is optimal. The classroom-level estimate is only defensible if the sample means are equally reliable.

Standard Errors. The standard errors of the treatment effect estimates are also different across the three analyses. The value of 0.074 for the student-level analysis is clearly misleading because, as noted earlier, the model for this analysis fails to take into account the dependence among the observations within classrooms. In essence, the student-level analysis assumes more information is present than is actually the case (i.e., it assumes that each individual response within a classroom provides an additional independent piece of information). But why is the standard error estimated under the hierarchical model (0.100) smaller than the estimate based on the class-level analysis (0.135)?

Apart from sample size, the standard error of the difference between two treatment groups in an ANCOVA depends on three factors: (a) the unexplained variance in the outcome, (b) the precision of the estimated regression coefficient for the covariate, and (c) the magnitude of the difference between the groups on the covariate. The hierarchical analysis is generally more powerful than the class-level analysis because factors a and b work in its favor.

In terms of factor a, the unexplained variance in the outcome is smaller in the hierarchical analysis. The variance of $\bar{Y}_{\cdot j}$, classroom *j*'s sample mean, is $\Delta_j = \tau_{00} + \sigma^2/n_j$. In a class-level analysis, only τ_{00} is potentially explainable by the covariate. In the hierarchical analysis, both τ_{00} and σ^2 may be explained. The reduction in σ^2 can be substantial if the Level-1 covariate is strongly related to the outcome within classrooms, yielding a potentially substantial advantage in power over the class-level analysis.

In terms of factor b, the precision of the estimated covariate effect in the hierarchical analysis is greater than in the class-level analysis, because the hierarchical analysis uses all of the data to estimate the covariate effect. In contrast, the class-level analysis uses only information about the covariation between the class means on the pre- and posttest.

Specifically, the se $(\hat{\beta}_{Y \cdot X})$ for the hierarchical analysis will generally be smaller than se $(\hat{\beta}_{Y \cdot X})$ from the class-level analysis, as is demonstrated in Table 5.3. This is significant because the standard error of the treatment effect, se $(\hat{\gamma}_{10})$, depends on the se $(\hat{\beta}_{Y \cdot X})$, which is obvious from an inspection of Equation 5.23.

In sum, the hierarchical analysis offers several advantages in this application. First, it is an *honest* model. Rather than erroneously assuming independent responses within classes, the hierarchical model takes into account the dependence among responses within classrooms.

Second, it provides efficient estimates of treatment effects in unbalanced, nested designs. Traditionally, the class-level analysis has been recommended as the preferred alternative to the student-level analysis because of the untenability of the assumption of independent errors. Researchers have lamented, however, that such analyses, although perhaps more appropriate, have low power to detect effects, and for this reason, researchers have tended to ignore this advice. The key point is that researchers no longer have to make a choice between a clearly untenable model (i.e., student-level analysis) and an honest but low-power alternative (class-level analysis). The hierarchical linear model properly represents the sources of variation in nested designs and provides efficient parameter estimates.

Finally, the hierarchical model enables a test for homogeneity of regression and provides a sensible way to proceed, regardless of the outcome. In this application, the regression of posttest on pretest was homogeneous with regard to classrooms, so we treated the covariate as a fixed effect. However, if the regression coefficients had been found to vary across classrooms, we could have built a model to predict such variation. Any unexplained variation in this Level-1 coefficient would then be incorporated into inference about treatments.

Case 2: Explaining the Differentiating Effects of Organizations via Intercepts- and Slopes-as-Outcomes Models

In the applications discussed above, organizational characteristics exercised a common influence on all individuals within the organization. The sole effect of the organizational variable under study was to shift the mean level of the outcomes, leaving the distribution of outcomes otherwise unaffected. In this section we consider situations where organizational features affect Level-1 relationships, either amplifying or attenuating them. The corresponding statistical model for such phenomena is the full hierarchical model represented in Equations 5.1 and 5.2. The within-organization relations are represented by the regression coefficients in the Level-1 model. The effects of organization variables on each of these relationships is represented in the corresponding Level-2 model.

Difficulties Encountered in Past Efforts at Modeling Regression Slopes-as-Outcomes

The use of regression coefficients or slopes-as-outcomes is appealing because it extends substantially the kinds of questions that organizational research can examine. Unfortunately, a number of technical difficulties have inhibited past use of models that incorporate slopes-as-outcomes.

First, as a general rule, regression coefficients have considerably greater sampling variability than do sample means. If the sample within a unit is small, the regression coefficients will be estimated with large error. The resultant unreliability in slopes weakens our power to detect relationships in the Level-2 model. This imprecision is exacerbated when the dispersion in the Level-1 predictors is constrained. For example, students tend to be more homogeneous in social class within schools than they are in a true random sample. As a result, the sampling variability of the estimated within-schools SES-achievement slope is increased. The analysis can produce negative slope estimates for individual schools even when the structural parameter is clearly positive (see Chapter 4, "Ordinary Least Squares"). This is particularly problematic because such outliers can exert undue influence on the Level-2 results.

Second, the sampling precision of the estimated slopes varies across units depending on the data-collection design used within each unit. But ordinary least squares, the estimation method typically used for the Level-2 analysis, assumes equal variances across units on the dependent variable. Ignoring the variation in sampling precision across units results in a weakened efficiency in parameter estimation that further limits our ability to detect relationships between slopes and the Level-2 variables hypothesized to account for them.

Third, the total variability in the estimated slopes consists of two components. First, there may be real differences across organizations in the slope parameters. It is essential, however, to distinguish between this parameter variance and the error variance in the slope estimates. This distinction becomes especially important when we attempt to interpret the results from the Level-2 model. As noted earlier in this chapter, only parameter variance in the Level-1 coefficients is potentially explainable by Level-2 predictors. In many applications, much of the observed variance in the slopes is error variance for the reasons noted above. A Level-2 model that explains only a small percentage of the observed variance in a regression slope might be discounted, when in fact it is explaining a very large portion of what can, in principle, be explained. Unfortunately, the simple slopes-as-outcomes model provides little guidance in this regard.

Finally, to include multiple slopes-as-outcomes in the Level-2 model requires us to take into account the special covariance structure that exists among the multiple-regression coefficients estimated for each Level-2 unit. In the absence of such a model, further weakened precision is a likely result.

Example: The Social Distribution of Achievement in Public and Catholic High Schools

This application was motivated by earlier research findings of Coleman et al. (1982), which suggested that academic achievement had a more equitable social distribution in the Catholic than in the public sector. Lee and Bryk (1989) used hierarchical analyses on a subset data from the High School and Beyond Survey, similar to that used in Chapter 4, to further explore this hypothesis. Specifically, they drew a sample of 74 Catholic high schools and a random subsample of 86 public high schools. Data were combined from two cohorts of students to increase the Level-1 sample sizes, n_j, to yield a total sample size, N, of 10,999 students. Table 5.5 describes selected variables used in their analyses. We discuss below some of their analyses and comment on the logic involved in using an intercepts- and slopes-as-outcomes model to explain the social distribution of achievement in Catholic and public high schools.

TABLE 5.5 Description of Variables from a Study of the Social Distribution of Math Achievement in Public and Catholic High Schools (Lee & Bryk, 1989)

Variable Name	*Description*
Student-level	
MATH ACHIEVEMENT	A mathematics test in senior year (mean = 12.92, sd = 6.70).
SES	A composite measure of social class provided by High School and Beyond. For the analytic sample it had a mean of approximately zero and standard deviation of 0.8.
MINORITY	A dummy variable (1 = black or Hispanic; 0 = other).
BACKGROUND	A composite measure of students' academic background up to high school entry. It includes information on retention in elementary school, assignment to remedial classes in 9th grade, and educational expectation at high school entry. It is a standardized measure (mean = 0; sd = 1.0).
School-level	
SECTOR	An effects-coded variable (1 = Catholic; -1 = public).
AVSES	Average social class of students within a school (i.e. school mean for SES).
HIMNRTY	An effects-coded variable (1 = school enrollment exceeds 40% minority; -1 = otherwise).
AVBACKGRD	Average academic background of students within a school (i.e. school mean for BACKGROUND).

NOTE: AVSES and AVBACKGRD were contructed from a larger sample of students than those in the analytic sample and so differ from MEAN SES and MEAN BACKGROUND used in examples in Chapter 4 of this volume.

A Random-Effects ANOVA Model. The analysis began with fitting a one-way random-effects ANOVA model in order to determine the total amount of variability in the outcome (senior-year mathematics achievement) within and between schools. The average school mean, γ_{00}, was estimated as 12.125. The pooled within-school or Level-1 variance, $\hat{\sigma}^2$, was 39.927, and the variance among the J school means, $\hat{\tau}_{00}$, was 9.335. Using these results and Equation 2.10, we can estimate the proportion of variance between schools (i.e., the intraclass correlation) as 0.189. We note that the estimate of σ^2 from the random-effects ANOVA model represents the total Level-1 variance. As we will see below, some of this variance is explained as predictors are introduced into the Level-1 model.

A Random-Coefficient Regression Model. The next step in the analysis involved posing a model to represent the social distribution of achievement in each of the J schools. Specifically, at Level 1 (the student model), the mathematics achievement for student i in school j (Y_{ij}) was regressed on minority status (MINORITY), social class (SES), and academic background (BACKGROUND):

$$Y_{ij} = \beta_{0j} + \beta_{1j}(\text{MINORITY})_{ij} + \beta_{2j}(\text{SES})_{ij} \qquad [5.27]$$

$$+ \beta_{3j}(\text{BACKGROUND})_{ij} + r_{ij}\,.$$

Note that the variance of r_{ij}, σ^2, now represents the residual variance at Level 1 that remains unexplained after taking into account students' minority status, social status, and academic background.

Each school's distribution of achievement is characterized in terms of four parameters: an intercept and three regression coefficients. The MINORITY, SES, and BACKGROUND variables were all group-mean centered (see Chapter 2). As a result, the four parameters can be interpreted as follows:

β_{0j} is the mean achievement in school j;

β_{1j} is the "minority" gap in school j (i.e., the mean difference between the achievement of white and minority students);

β_{2j} is the differentiating effect of social class in school j (i.e., the degree to which SES differences among students relate to senior-year achievement);

β_{3j} is the differentiating effect of academic background in school j (i.e., the degree to which differences in students' academic BACKGROUND eventuate in senior-year achievement differences).

Each of the distributive effects, β_{0j}, β_{1j}, β_{2j}, and β_{3j}, are net of the others. For example, the minority gap in school j, β_{1j}, is the adjusted mean achievement difference between white and minority students in school j after controlling for the effects of individual student's SES and BACKGROUND.

In terms of this model, an effective and equitable school would be characterized by a high level of mean achievement (i.e., a large positive value for β_{0j}), a small minority gap (i.e., a small negative value for β_{1j}), and weak differentiating effects for social class and academic background (i.e., small positive values for β_{2j} and β_{3j}, respectively).

Each of the four coefficients in Equation 5.27 was specified as random in the Level-2 model. Specifically,

$$\beta_{qj} = \gamma_{q0} + u_{qj} \quad \text{for } q = 0, 1, 2, 3 \qquad [5.28]$$

where γ_{q0} is the mean value for each school effect. Because there are four Level-2 random effects, the variances and covariances among them now form a 4 by 4 matrix:

$$\begin{bmatrix} \mathrm{Var}(u_{0j}) & & \text{Symmetric} & \\ \mathrm{Cov}(u_{1j}, u_{0j}) & \mathrm{Var}(u_{1j}) & & \\ \mathrm{Cov}(u_{2j}, u_{0j}) & \mathrm{Cov}(u_{2j}, u_{1j}) & \mathrm{Var}(u_{2j}) & \\ \mathrm{Cov}(u_{3j}, u_{0j}) & \mathrm{Cov}(u_{3j}, u_{1j}) & \mathrm{Cov}(u_{3j}, u_{2j}) & \mathrm{Var}(u_{3j}) \end{bmatrix}$$

$$= \begin{bmatrix} \tau_{00} & & \text{Symmetric} & \\ \tau_{10} & \tau_{11} & & \\ \tau_{20} & \tau_{21} & \tau_{22} & \\ \tau_{30} & \tau_{31} & \tau_{32} & \tau_{33} \end{bmatrix}$$

The random-coefficient regression model specified by Equations 5.27 and 5.28 formally represents the hypothesis that the social distribution of achievement, as defined here, varies across the J schools. As shown below, the diagonal elements of the **T** matrix provides empirical evidence for examining this hypothesis.

In general, estimation of a random-coefficient regression model is an important early step in an hierarchical analysis. The results from this model guide the final specification of the Level-1 equation and provide a range of useful statistics for subsequent model building at Level 2.

Table 5.6 presents the results reported by Lee and Bryk (1989). As in the random-effects ANOVA, the average school achievement was estimated as 12.125. The average minority gap, $\hat{\gamma}_{10}$, was −2.78 points. This means that in a typical school, minority students were scoring 2.78 points behind white schoolmates with academic and social backgrounds like their own. Similarly, student SES and BACKGROUND ($\hat{\gamma}_{20}$ and $\hat{\gamma}_{30}$, respectively) were positively related to achievement. This means that in the average high school, more affluent students and those who enter better prepared had higher math achievement in their senior year. The reported t ratios are quite large, indicating that each of the Level-1 predictors was statistically significant.

The estimated variances of the random effects at Level 1 and 2 (σ^2 and τ_{qq}, respectively) are reported in the second panel of Table 5.6. Note that the Level-1 variance has been reduced from 39.927 in the random-effects ANOVA model to 31.771 after taking into account students' minority status,

TABLE 5.6 Random Coefficient Regression Model of the Social Distribution of Mathematics Achievement

Fixed Effect	*Coefficient*	*se*	*t ratio*	
School mean achievement, γ_{00}	12.125	0.252	48.207	
Minority gap, γ_{10}	– 2.780	0.242	–11.515	
SES differentiation, γ_{20}	1.135	0.104	10.882	
Academic differentiation, γ_{30}	2.582	0.093	27.631	
Random Effect	*Variance Component*	*df*	χ^2	*p value*
Mean achievement, u_{0j}	9.325	137	1,770.70	0.000
Minority gap, u_{1j}	1.367	137	161.01	0.079
SES differentiation, u_{2j}	0.360	137	173.39	0.019
Academic differentiation, u_{3j}	0.496	137	219.02	0.000
Level-1 effect, r_{ij}	31.771			
Correlation Among School Effects	*Mean Achievement*	*Minority Gap*	*SES Differentiation*	
Minority gap	0.397			
SES differentiation	0.182	–0.109		
Academic differentiation	0.327	0.085	0.652	
Reliability of OLS Regression-Coefficient Estimates				
Mean achievement	0.922			
Minority gap	0.098			
SES differentiation	0.167			
Academic differentiation	0.330			

social class, and academic background. The proportion of variance explained by this Level-1 model is

$$(39.927 - 31.771)/39.927 = 0.204.$$

The estimated Level-2 variances for the random-coefficient regression model provide empirical evidence about the variability in the social distribution of achievement across schools. The homogeneity of variance tests for these Level-2 random effects (see Chapter 3) can be used to test whether the structure of the social distribution achievement differs across schools. That is, rejecting the hypotheses that

$$H_0: \ \text{Var}(u_{qj}) = \text{Var}(\beta_{qj}) = 0 \quad \text{for } q = 0, 1, 2, 3 \qquad [5.29]$$

implies variation among schools in their social distribution of achievement.

In terms of the univariate χ^2 tests, the probability of the estimated variability in the β_{qj} coefficients, under a homogeneity hypothesis, is less than .001 for average achievement and academic differentiation, and less than .02 for the SES differentiation. The p value associated with the hypothesis of slope homogeneity for the minority gap coefficients is marginal (.079). Because substantial differences between sectors in minority achievement had been previously reported, however, this effect was maintained as random.

We note that these χ^2 tests provide only approximate probability values for two reasons. First, they are simple univariate tests that do not take into account the other random effects in the model. Second, they are estimated on the basis of only those schools that have sufficient data to compute a separate OLS regressions. In this particular application, only 138 of the total of 160 schools could be used, because the remaining 22 schools had no variation on minority status.

When in doubt, the results of these univariate homogeneity tests can be cross-checked through the use of a multivariate likelihood-ratio test (see Chapter 3), which uses all of the data available. Specifically, the deviance statistic from the full random-coefficient regression model can be compared with the corresponding statistic from a restricted model, say for example, a model with only a random intercept:

$$\beta_{0j} = \gamma_{00} + u_{0j} \qquad [5.30]$$

$$\beta_{qj} = \gamma_{qj} \quad \text{for } q = 1, 2, 3 .$$

In the Lee and Bryk (1989) data, the deviance statistic for the full random-coefficient regression model was 58,248.4 with 11 df. For the restricted model (which specified all regression slopes as fixed), it was 58,283.6 with 2 df. As a result, the likelihood-ratio test statistic was 35.2 with 9 df, which offers confirming evidence that schools do vary in their distributive effects.

The point estimates for the Level-2 variance components from the random-coefficient regression model provide useful descriptive statistics of how much schools really vary in terms of mean achievement, size of the minority gaps, and social- and academic-differentiation effects. Under the normality assumption, we would expect the effects for most schools to be captured within the 95% confidence band of

$$\hat{\gamma}_{q0} \pm 1.96 (\hat{\tau}_{qq})^{1/2} . \qquad [5.31]$$

Thus, in this High School and Beyond Survey data, school means (β_{0j}) would be expected in the range of (6.140, 18.110). Minority gaps (β_{1j}) of (−5.072, −0.488) are quite plausible, as are social- and academic-differentiation effects of (−0.041, 2.311) and (1.202, 3.962), respectively. Clearly, these results suggest considerable variation among schools on each effect. Interestingly, we could expect to find some schools where minority performance approximates white achievement and where social-class differences are inconsequential because values near zero are plausible for both β_{1j} and β_{2j}. However, all schools appear to engage in some degree of academic differentiation in that values of zero for β_{3j} do not appear plausible. We note that the ranges estimated using Equation 5.31 are for the true school parameters, β_{qj}, and not the separate OLS estimates of these parameters, $\hat{\beta}_{qj}$. The OLS estimates, especially of the regression slopes, would be far more variable because of the unreliability of sample estimates of these individual school parameters.

Another useful set of descriptive statistics that can be computed from the Level-2 variance-covariance components are the correlations among the school effects. Generalizing from Equation 2.3, for any two random effects u_{qj} and $u_{q'j}$ (or, equivalently, in the random-coefficient regression model β_{qj} and $\beta_{q'j}$, respectively),

$$\hat{\rho}(u_{qj}, u_{q'j}) = \hat{\tau}_{qq'}/(\hat{\tau}_{qq}\hat{\tau}_{q'q'})^{1/2}. \qquad [5.32]$$

These results are reported in the third panel of Table 5.6. Schools displaying high levels of achievement tended to have small minority gaps ($\hat{\rho}_{01} =$ 0.397) but were somewhat more differentiating with regard to social class ($\hat{\rho}_{02} = 0.182$) and academic background ($\hat{\rho}_{03} = 0.327$) than schools with lower achievement levels. Interestingly, the social- and academic-differentiation effects were correlated 0.652, suggesting that these two school effects may share some common causes.

In general, it is important to inspect the correlations estimated from the random-coefficient regression model. Although social and academic differentiation were moderately to strongly correlated in this application, there was still sufficient independent variation to treat each of them as separate school effects. In applications discussed later in this book correlations of .90 and higher were found. In such cases, the two random effects are carrying essentially the same variation across the Level-2 units. A reduction of the model to specify one of these Level-1 effects as fixed or nonrandomly varying would be warranted. Theory and research purposes should dictate which of the two is more important to treat as a random effect.

Table 5.6 also reports the reliabilities for each of the Level-2 random effects. In the random-coefficient regression model these are equivalent to the reliabilities of the OLS estimates, $\hat{\beta}_{qj}$, as measures of the true parameters, β_{qj}. These reliabilities were computed by substituting the estimated values for the Level-1 and Level-2 variance components into Equation 3.53. We note that these statistics, like the χ^2 homogeneity statistics, use the separate OLS estimates for each Level-2 unit. Thus, they are based on 138 schools in this application.

The reliability estimates from the random-coefficient regression model are helpful in that they provide additional guidance on appropriate specification of the Level-1 coefficients (i.e., as fixed, random, or nonrandomly varying). Because the metric of τ_{qq} depends on the metric of the corresponding X_q and Y_{ij}, interpreting the absolute values of τ_{qq} takes some care. The reliability provides an alternative indicator of amount of signal present in these data. That is, it tells us how much of the observed variation in the $\hat{\beta}_{qj}$ is potentially explainable. Past experiences working with these methods suggest that whenever the reliability of a random Level-1 coefficient drops below 0.05, that coefficient is a candidate for treatment either as fixed or nonrandomly varying.

These statistics also offer insight into the power of a particular data set to detect hypothesized structural effects. We have considerable power in the High School and Beyond data for examining hypotheses about effects of school characteristics on school mean achievement since the intercept estimates are highly reliable. In contrast, the data set is only marginally useful for studying how school characteristics influence the relative achievement of majority and minority children. As noted above, 22 schools have no information on this effect and some of the others have only limited information. This suggests caution in inferring that "school characteristics don't seem to matter" in terms of influencing the relative achievement levels of majority and minority group children. The reliability coefficients tell us that these data provide little evidence for making such assertions. In short, they caution us against overzealous interpretation of a null hypothesis affirmed.

An Intercept- and Slopes-as-Outcomes Model: The Effects of Sector and Context. The results from the random-coefficient regression model indicated that each of the Level-1 predictors had, on average, a significant relationship with math achievement. (This judgement is based on the fixed-effect estimates, their standard errors, and *t* ratios.) Thus, each of these predictors should remain at least as a fixed effect in the student-level model. Further, the statistical evidence provided by the τ_{qq} point estimates, the χ^2 homogeneity tests, the likelihood-ratio test, and the reliability statistics indicated that there was sufficient variability among schools in each of the Level-1 regression coefficents to treat these coefficients, at least initially, as random.

Lee and Bryk (1989) next sought to develop explanatory models to illuminate how differences among schools in their organizational characteristics might influence the social distribution of achievement within schools. One model hypothesized differential effects of sector and composition. The investigators noted that the student composition in both Catholic and public schools varied considerably and that these contextual differences might affect outcomes, even after adjusting for the individual student characteristics already included in the Level-1 model. (This idea of compositional effects in organizational research is discussed more fully later.) Thus, they modeled the joint effects of SECTOR and context (as measured by AVSES, HIMNRTY, AVBACKGRD from Table 5.5) on mean achievement, minority gap, social differentiation, and academic differentiation. They also hypothesized that these context effects might be different in the two sectors. Therefore, they included the interactions between SECTOR and each of the context measures as predictors in the Level-2 models.

The investigators allowed the Level-1 model to remain as in Equation 5.27. They posed the following Level-2 model:

$$\begin{aligned}\beta_{0j} = \gamma_{00} &+ \gamma_{01}(\text{AVSES})_j + \gamma_{02}(\text{HIMNRTY})_j + \gamma_{03}(\text{AVBACKGRD})_j \\ &+ \gamma_{04}(\text{SECTOR})_j + \gamma_{05}(\text{SECTOR} \times \text{AVSES})_j \\ &+ \gamma_{06}(\text{SECTOR} \times \text{HIMNRTY})_j \\ &+ \gamma_{07}(\text{SECTOR} \times \text{AVBACKGRD})_j + u_{0j} \\ \beta_{1j} = \gamma_{10} &+ \gamma_{11}(\text{HIMNRTY})_j + \gamma_{12}(\text{SECTOR})_j \\ &+ \gamma_{13}(\text{SECTOR} \times \text{HIMNRTY})_j + u_{1j} \\ \beta_{2j} = \gamma_{20} &+ \gamma_{21}(\text{AVSES})_j + \gamma_{22}(\text{SECTOR})_j \\ &+ \gamma_{23}(\text{SECTOR} \times \text{AVSES})_j + u_{2j} \\ \beta_{3j} = \gamma_{30} &+ \gamma_{31}(\text{AVBACKGRD})_j + \gamma_{32}(\text{SECTOR})_j \\ &+ \gamma_{33}(\text{SECTOR} \times \text{AVBACKGRD})_j + u_{3j}\end{aligned} \qquad [5.33]$$

TABLE 5.7 Estimated Effects of Sector and Control on the Social Distribution of Achievement

Fixed Effect	*Coefficients*	*se*	*t–ratio*	
School mean achievement				
BASE, γ_{00}	13.678	0.186	73.393	
AVSES, γ_{01}	4.106	0.493	8.327	
HIMNRTY, γ_{02}	–1.488	0.551	–2.699	
AVBACKGD, γ_{03}	1.301	0.517	2.514	
SECTOR, γ_{04}	0.716	0.194	3.700	
SECTOR×AVSES, γ_{05}	–1.572	0.432	–3.642	
Minority Gap				
BASE, γ_{10}	–2.894	0.256	–11.300	
SECTOR, γ_{12}	0.721	0.256	2.816	
Social class differentiation				
BASE, γ_{20}	1.381	0.141	9.819	
AVSES, γ_{21}	0.131	0.325	0.402	
SECTOR, γ_{22}	–0.362	0.141	–2.571	
SECTOR×AVSES, γ_{23}	–0.869	0.325	–2.671	
Academic differentiation				
BASE, γ_{30}	2.482	0.093	26.650	
SECTOR, γ_{32}	0.072	0.093	0.778	
Random Effect	*Variance Component*	*df*	χ^2	*p–value*
Mean achievement	2.681	132	631.19	0.000
Minority gap	0.624	136	151.04	0.179
SES differentiation	0.218	134	159.94	0.063
Academic differentiation	0.475	136	221.70	0.000
Level–1 effect, r_{ij}	31.778			

In their first analysis using this model, several of the estimated coefficients were trivially small (γ_{06}, γ_{07}, γ_{11}, γ_{13}, γ_{31}, γ_{33}). Each of the corresponding Level-2 predictors were deleted and a reduced model estimated. The results for this are presented in Table 5.7 and discussed below.

School Mean Achievement. The average academic background of students (AVBACKGRD) was positively related to school mean achievement ($\hat{\gamma}_{03} = 1.301$, $t = 2.514$). Mean achievement was lower in schools with high minority concentrations ($\hat{\gamma}_{02} = -1.488$, $t = -2.699$). The effect of average social class (AVSES) on school mean achievement varied across the two sectors. That is, a significant interaction effect was detected ($\hat{\gamma}_{05} = -1.572$, $t = -3.642$). In the Catholic sector, the relationship of AVSES with school mean achievement was 2.544 [i.e., $\hat{\gamma}_{01}$ + (1)$\hat{\gamma}_{05}$ = 4.106 − 1.572]. In the public sector, the relationship was much stronger, at 5.678 [i.e., $\hat{\gamma}_{01}$ + (−1)$\hat{\gamma}_{05}$ = 4.106 + 1.572].

The presence of such an interaction effect means that the magnitude of the sector effect depends upon the social class of the schools compared. In general, the sector effect on mean achievement was

$$\text{Catholic prediction} - \text{public prediction}$$

$$= (1)\hat{\gamma}_{04} + (1)(\text{AVSES})(\hat{\gamma}_{05}) - [(-1)\hat{\gamma}_{04} + (-1)(\text{AVSES})(\hat{\gamma}_{05})]$$

$$= 2[\hat{\gamma}_{04} + (\text{AVSES})_j(\hat{\gamma}_{05})] \,.$$

For schools of average social class (AVSES = 0), the sector effect was 1.432 points, or 2[$\hat{\gamma}_{04}$ + (0)$\hat{\gamma}_{05}$]. The Catholic advantage was greater for low social-class schools. For example, if AVSES = −1.0, the sector effect was 4.576 points, or 2[$\hat{\gamma}_{04}$ + (−1) $\hat{\gamma}_{05}$]. For affluent schools, however (AVSES > 1), average mathematic achievement was actually higher in public schools.

Minority Gap. The minority gap was also different in the two sectors ($\hat{\gamma}_{12} = 0.721$, $t = 2.816$). In the average Catholic school, minority students scored 2.173 points behind their white classmates [$\hat{\gamma}_{10}$ + (1)$\hat{\gamma}_{12}$]. (This is a net effect after controlling for students' SES and BACKGROUND.) In the average public school, the minority gap was 3.615 points [$\hat{\gamma}_{10}$ + (−1)$\hat{\gamma}_{12}$].

Social Class Differentiation. The differentiating effect of social class within a school depended jointly on the AVSES and SECTOR. The estimated interaction effect, $\hat{\gamma}_{23}$, was larger in magnitude than either of the main effects, $\hat{\gamma}_{21}$ and $\hat{\gamma}_{22}$. In the public sector, high social-class schools were more differentiating with regard to student social class than were low social-class schools. In the Catholic sector the opposite was true: high social-class schools were *less* socially differentiating than were low social-class schools. This can be seen by computing the effect of AVSES on social-class differentiation separately for the Catholic and public schools based on $\hat{\gamma}_{21}$ + (SECTOR)$\hat{\gamma}_{23}$. For public schools, the effect of AVSES is .131 + (−1)(−.869) = 1.000. For Catholic schools, the effect of AVSES is .131 + (1)(−.869) = −.738.

Academic Differentiation. With regard to academic differentiation, there was no evidence of context, sector, or sector-by-context effects.

The bottom panel of Table 5.6 reports the estimated-variance components at Level 1 and Level 2 for the sector-context effects model. The Level-1 variance estimate, $\hat{\sigma}^2$, was virtually identical to that reported for the random-coefficient regression model, an expected result because the Level-1 models are the same. In general, some slight variation in the estimation of $\hat{\sigma}^2$ may occur, because all fixed and random effects are estimated jointly and each parameter estimate depends on all of the others.

At Level 2, each $\hat{\tau}_{qq}$ estimate is now a conditional or residual variance. That is, u_{qj} is a residual school effect unexplained by the Level-2 predictors included in the model. In contrast, each $\hat{\tau}_{qq}$ associated with the random-coefficient model was an unconditional variance. Comparison of these conditional variances (Table 5.7) with the unconditional variances (Table 5.6) indicates a substantial reduction in variation once sector and context are taken into account. The proportion variance explained by the sector-context model at Level 2, using Equation 4.17, was

$$\begin{matrix}\text{Proportion}\\ \text{variation}\\ \text{explained}\\ \text{in } \beta_q\end{matrix} = \frac{\hat{\tau}_{qq}(\text{unconditional}) - \hat{\tau}_{qq}(\text{conditional})}{\hat{\tau}_{qq}(\text{unconditional})}.$$

These statistics are reported in Table 5.8. Substantial proportions of the variance in average achievement, minority gap, and social differentiation have been explained. Variation among schools in academic differentiation remains virtually unexplained. Because the reliability of the academic-differentiation effects was relatively high (0.330 in Table 5.6), we can be reasonably confident that the substantial differences observed in academic differentiation were probably not related to sector or context, but rather to other factors. In fact, subsequent analysis reported by Lee and Bryk (1989) explained a substantial variation in β_{3j} as a function of differences in the academic organization and normative environments of schools.

Returning to Table 5.7, we note that the χ^2 statistics for both the minority gap and SES differentiation effect were consistent with the hypothesis that the residual variation in these two school effects is zero. These results, of course, do not mean that this null hypothesis is actually true. Because the researchers had theoretical reasons to investigate whether these distributive effects also varied as a function of school organization and normative environments, they proceeded to estimate additional models with an expanded set of Level-2 predictors for each of the four random school effects. Many hypothesized organizational relations were detected. The point is that the homogeneity tests for intercepts and slopes are only a guide and should *not* substitute for informed judgment.

TABLE 5.8 Proportion of Variance Explained by Final Model

Model	*Average Achievement* $Var(\beta_{0j})$	*Minority Status* $Var(\beta_{1j})$	*Social Class* $Var(\beta_{2j})$	*Academic Background* $Var(\beta_{3j})$
Unconditional model	9.325	1.367	0.360	0.496
Conditional model	2.681	0.624	0.218	0.475
Proportion of variance explained (in percentage)	71.2	54.4	39.4	4.2

Applications with Both Random and Fixed Level-1 Slopes

In the interest of clarity of exposition, we have organized this chapter around two distinct classes of applications. In Case 1, only the intercept parameter varied across organizations, with the effects of Level-1 predictors, if included, treated as fixed coefficients. In Case 2 just discussed, all Level-1 coefficients were treated as random. In fact, many applications are well suited for a model with both random and fixed Level-1 coefficients. For example, suppose we had one randomly varying Level-1 slope, β_{1j}, and a series of other Level-1 predictors that we sought to introduce as covariates:

$$Y_{ij} = \beta_{0j} + \beta_{1j}(X_{1ij} - \bar{X}_{1\cdot j}) + \sum_{q=2}^{Q} \beta_{qj}(\bar{X}_{q\cdot j} - \bar{X}_{q\cdot\cdot}) + r_{ij}. \qquad [5.34]$$

At Level 2,

$$\beta_{qj} = \gamma_{q0} + \sum_{s=1}^{S_q} \gamma_{qs} W_{sj} + u_{qj} \quad \text{for } q = 0, 1 \qquad [5.35a]$$

and

$$\beta_{qj} = \gamma_{q0} \quad \text{for } q = 2, \ldots, Q \qquad [5.35b]$$

where u_{q0} and u_{q1} are assumed bivariate normal with means of 0, variances τ_{00} and τ_{11}, respectively, and covariances τ_{01}.

In this model, two random effects, an intercept and one slope, are hypothesized for each organization. The intercept, β_{0j}, is an adjusted mean taking into account differences among the individuals in these organizations with regard to $X_2, \ldots, X_Q$. Similarly, the slope β_{1j} is net of any fixed effects associated with $X_2, \ldots, X_Q$. At Level 2, β_{0j} and β_{1j} are hypothesized to vary as a function of measured organizational features, W_{sj}.

A diverse array of studies of schooling have employed this model (Raudenbush & Willms, 1991). Zuzovsky and Aitken (1991) used a similar model to study the effect of curriculum change and science achievement in Israel. The Level-1 random effects were adjusted mean-achievement differences among schools and a student social-class differentiation effect (i.e., the coefficient for the regression of science achievement on student social class was allowed to vary among schools). Fixed Level-1 covariates included national origin, sex, and reading level. Key Level-2 predictors were measures of school social composition and the degree of implementation of the new curriculum.

Raffe (1991) used this model in an evaluation of innovative technical and vocational education projects in the United Kingdom. The experiment was implemented in 19 sites with individuals nonrandomly assigned to treatment and control groups at each site. A number of Level-1 covariates were included to compensate for the nonrandom assignment within sites. The random Level-1 effects were an adjusted mean outcome and a treatment effect estimate for each site. Significant parameter variation was found for both the site means and treatment effects across the 19 sites with compositional variables linked to both β_{0j} and β_{1j} .

Lee and Smith (1991) employed a similar model in a study of sex discrimination in teacher salaries. Their data consisted of information from over 7,000 teachers nested within 309 American high schools. The fixed Level-1 covariates included measures of professional education and experience. The adjusted mean salary levels, β_{0j}, and the female salary differential, β_{1j}, varied significantly across schools. Of special importance to this study was that the hierarchical model afforded an estimate of the female salary differential that was both net of experience and professional training differences within schools and also net of possible market differences among schools.

In general, any combination of random, nonrandomly varying, and fixed coefficients can be employed in the Level-1 model. Theoretical considerations are primary in whether a Level-1 coefficient should be conceived as random. In the specific applications mentioned above, the researchers had reason to suspect that social-class differentiation, the treatment-effect size, or the salary differential, respectively, would vary across the Level-2 units. Interestingly, some of the other estimated Level-1 effects were also initially hypothesized as random in these studies, but no evidence was found to sustain this and the coefficients were eventually treated as fixed. For an application that involves fixed, random, and nonrandomly varying slopes, see Bryk and Frank (1991).

Special Topics

We now consider a somewhat special and interrelated set of statistical and conceptual issues that frequently arise in the analysis of multilevel organizational data.

The Estimation of Person-Level Effects

In addition to estimating how organizational factors influence person-level outcomes, multilevel data are often also used to estimate person-level effects. For example, in the High School and Beyond data, a primary analytic concern was the relationship between student social class and math achievement. The fact that students were nested within schools represented a nuisance consideration in an effort to obtain an appropriate estimate of this Level-1 relationship. Burstein (1980) provides an extensive review of the modeling issues that arise in such applications. We provide below a brief account of these concerns and show how they can be resolved through the formulation of hierarchical models that explictly represent the nesting structure. These methods are illustrated using the High School and Beyond data.

We begin by considering the most commonly employed technique for analyzing multilevel data—an OLS regression analysis at Level-1, which simply ignores the nesting of persons within groups. The first column of Table 5.9 presents the model for this analysis, and the results from a regression of math achievement on student SES. The estimated regression coefficient for SES was 3.184, with a standard error of 0.097. For reasons that will become clear below, we refer to the regression coefficient in this model as β_t .

For comparison, we present in the second column of Table 5.9 the corresponding model for a Level-2 or between-group analysis. When person-level data are not available, this regression coefficient, referred to as β_b, has often been used as an estimator of the person-level relationship. (Burstein [1980] and Aitkin and Longford [1986] discuss the conditions under which such use is appropriate.) In this particular application, however, the estimated β_b of 5.909 is almost twice as large as $\hat{\beta}_t$. Clearly, these two analyses provide very different answers about the magnitude of the relationship between individual social class and math achievement. Notice also that the standard error is considerably larger in this case (0.371 versus 0.097), primarily reflecting the fact that the degrees of freedom in the Level-2 analysis are 158, compared with 7,183 in the Level-1 analysis. Even when it

TABLE 5.9 Comparison of Alternative Estimators of Level-1 Regression Coefficient

Alternative Statistical Models			
OLS Regression at Level-1 (an ungrouped analysis)	*OLS Regression at Level-2 (a between-group analysis)*	*Hierarchical Linear Model (group-mean centering)*	*Hierarchical Linear Model (grand-mean centering)*
$Y_i = \beta_0 + \beta_1 X_i + r_i$ $i = 1, \ldots, N$ persons (note nesting of persons within organizations is ignored)	$\bar{Y}_{.j} = \beta_0 + \beta_1 \bar{X}_{.j} + u_j$ $j = 1, \ldots, J$ organizations	$Y_{ij} = \beta_{0j} + \beta_{1j}(X_{ij} - \bar{X}_{.j}) + r_{ij}$ $\beta_{0j} = \gamma_{00} + u_{0j}$ $\beta_{1j} = \gamma_{10}$	$Y_{ij} = \beta_{0j} + \beta_{1j}(X_{ij} - \bar{X}_{..}) + r_{ij}$ $\beta_{0j} = \gamma_{00} + u_{0j}$ $\beta_{1j} = \gamma_{10}$
$\beta_1 = \beta_t$	$\beta_1 = \beta_b$	$\gamma_{10} = \beta_w$	$\gamma_{10} = \dfrac{W_1\beta_w + W_2\beta_b}{W_1 + W_2}$

Estimates using High School and Beyond data

$\hat{\beta}_t = 3.184$	$\hat{\beta}_b = 5.909$	$\hat{\beta}_w = 2.191$	$\hat{\gamma}_{10} = 2.391$
$se(\hat{\beta}_t) = 0.097$	$se(\hat{\beta}_b) = 0.371$	$se(\hat{\beta}_w) = 0.109^*$	$se(\hat{\gamma}_{10}) = 0.106$

NOTE: For the illustrative purposes of this section, we have specified the SES coefficient as fixed. Results presented in Chapter 4, however, indicate that there is considerable variability among schools in β_{1j}. Estimation of this model with β_{1j} specified as a random coefficient did not substantially change the γ_{10} estimates (2.193 vs. 2.191). The standard error, however, increased from 0.109 to 0.125. By assuming a fixed Level-1 coefficient for SES, we constrained the $\text{Var}(\beta_{1j}) = \tau_{11} = 0$. Because τ_{11} is a component of the standard error of γ_{10} (see Chapter 3), setting it to zero when it is not at least close to zero will result in an underestimate of the standard error.

is appropriate to use $\hat{\beta}_b$ as an estimator of the person-level relationship (which does not appear to be the case here), the estimate will generally be less precise than an estimate based on a Level-1 analysis. Typically, there is just less information available in the unit means than in the full individual data.

It is frequently argued (see, e.g., Firebaugh, 1978) that the person-level coefficient really of interest is the pooled-within-organization relationship between math achievement and student SES. That is, we want to estimate the Level-1 relationship net of any group membership effects. This coefficient is typicially referred to as β_w and can be obtained with OLS methods by estimating the equation

$$Y_{ij} - \bar{Y}_{\cdot j} = \beta_w(X_{ij} - \bar{X}_{\cdot j}) + r_{ij}\,. \qquad [5.36]$$

Column 3 of Table 5.9 presents the equivalent hierarchical linear model. For the High School and Beyond data, $\hat{\beta}_w$ was 2.191 with a standard error of 0.109. Although the estimated standard error for $\hat{\beta}_w$ was quite similar to the standard error for $\hat{\beta}_t$ (which will typically be the case), $\hat{\beta}_t$ was actually partway between $\hat{\beta}_w$ and $\hat{\beta}_b$. It can readily be shown that $\hat{\beta}_t$ is formally a weighted combination of β_w and β_b :

$$\hat{\beta}_t = \eta^2\hat{\beta}_b + (1 - \eta^2)\hat{\beta}_w \qquad [5.37]$$

where η^2 is the ratio of the between-schools sum of squares on SES to the total sum of squares on SES.

Thus, ignoring the nested structure of the data can lead to misleading results when person-level effect estimates are desired. As Cronbach (1976) has noted, $\hat{\beta}_t$ is generally an uninterpretable blend of $\hat{\beta}_w$ and $\hat{\beta}_b$. We agree with Firebaugh (1978) that in most research applications that desire a person-level effect estimate, the coefficient of interest is $\hat{\beta}_w$ and not $\hat{\beta}_t$.

In estimating β_w based on a hierarchical analysis, the group-mean centering of X_{ij} plays a critical role. By contrast, if the data are grand-mean centered, as in the fourth column of Table 5.9, the resulting estimator is a mix of β_w and β_b . The weights, W_1 and W_2, are quite complex for the general case. Note that the coefficients estimate for the High School and Beyond data with grand-mean centering was 2.391.

This result derives from the fact that the model with grand-mean centering actually involves both X_{ij} and $\bar{X}_{\cdot j}$, but the analysis is constrained to estimate only one parameter rather than separate estimates for β_w and β_b (a hierarchical model for the joint estimator of β_w and β_b is presented in the next section).

However, if in a particular application it is reasonable to assume that β_b and β_w are identical, then the estimated model with grand-mean centering would in fact be efficient. Under the hypothesis that $\beta_b = \beta_w = \beta$, $\hat{\beta}_b$ and β_w are independent, unbiased estimators of β. In a balanced design, the sampling variances of each of these OLS estimates, respectively, is

$$\mathrm{Var}(\hat{\beta}_b) = \Delta / \sum_j (\bar{X}_{.j} - \bar{X}_{..})^2 ,$$

with

$$\Delta = \tau_{00} + \sigma^2/n ,$$

and

$$\mathrm{Var}(\hat{\beta}_w) = \sigma^2 / \sum_j \sum_i (X_{ij} - \bar{X}_{.j})^2 .$$

In this specific case, the estimator of β provided in Column 4 of Table 5.9,

$$\hat{\gamma}_{10} = \hat{\beta} = \frac{W_1 \hat{\beta}_b + W_2 \hat{\beta}_w}{W_1 + W_2} \qquad [5.38]$$

simplifies in that

$$W_1 = [\hat{\mathrm{V}}\mathrm{ar}(\hat{\beta}_b)]^{-1} = \sum (\bar{X}_{.j} - \bar{X}_{..})^2 / \hat{\Delta}$$

and

$$W_2 = [\hat{\mathrm{V}}\mathrm{ar}(\hat{\beta}_w)]^{-1} = \sum \sum (X_{ij} - \bar{X}_{.j})^2 / \hat{\sigma}^2 .$$

In this specific case, $\hat{\gamma}_{10}$ is a weighted average of $\hat{\beta}_b$ and $\hat{\beta}_w$ where the weights are the precisions of each estimator. Because both $\hat{\beta}_b$ and $\hat{\beta}_w$ contain information about β, the hierarchical estimator optimally combines the information to yield a single estimator with greater precision than either of the two component estimators. Formally,

$$[\mathrm{Var}(\hat{\beta}_{\mathrm{hierarchical}})]^{-1} = W_1 + W_2 , \qquad [5.39]$$

that is, the precision of the hierarchical estimate is the sum of the precisions of $\hat{\beta}_b$ and $\hat{\beta}_w$. It is of interest that W_1 is approximately proportional to J and W_2 to Jn.

In unbalanced designs, the formulas become more complicated. The same principal still applies, however. Assuming $\beta_w = \beta_b$, the hierarchical estimator with grand-mean centering will be most efficient.

When $\beta_b \neq \beta_w$, as appears true in this application, the hierarchical estimator under grand-mean centering is an inappropriate estimator of the person-level effect. It too is an uninterpretable blend: neither β_w nor β_b nor β_t . Thus, when an unbiased estimate of β_w is desired, group-mean centering will produce it. Two alternative hierarchical models that allow joint estimation of β_w and β_b are presented below.

Disentangling Person-Level and Compositional Effects

Compositional or contextual effects are of enduring interest in organizational sociology (see Erbring & Young, 1979; Firebaugh, 1978). Such effects are said to occur when the aggregate of a person-level characteristic, $\overline{X}_{.j}$, is related to the outcome, Y_{ij}, even after controlling for the effect of the individual characteristic, X_{ij} . In an OLS Level-1 regression analysis, these effects are represented through the inclusion of both $(X_{ij} - \overline{X}_{.j})$ and $\overline{X}_{.j}$ as predictors:

$$Y_{ij} = \beta_0 + \beta_1(X_{ij} - \overline{X}_{.j}) + \beta_2\overline{X}_{.j} + r_{ij} . \qquad [5.40]$$

The compositional effect is the extent to which the magnitude of the organization-level relationship, β_b, differs from the person-level effect, β_w . Formally, the compositional effect is

$$\beta_c = \beta_2 - \beta_1 = \beta_b - \beta_w . \qquad [5.41]$$

We note that a nonzero estimate for β_2 does not necessarily imply a compositional effect. If β_1 and β_2 are equal, no compositional effect is present.

Compositional effects are open to widely varying interpretations. Such effects may occur because of normative effects associated with an organization (Erbring & Young, 1979) or because $\overline{X}_{.j}$ acts as a proxy for other important organizational variables omitted from the model. They may also signal a statistical artifact where $\overline{X}_{.j}$ carries part of the effect of a poorly measured X_{ij} (Hauser, 1970). Whatever their source, past empirical research indicates that compositional effects occur with considerable regularity (see Willms's [1986] review).

Within a hierarchical modeling framework, these effects can be estimated in two different ways. In both cases, the person-level X_{ij} is included

TABLE 5.10 Illustration of Person-Level and Compositional (or Contextual) Effects

Statistical Model

Group-Mean Centering	*Grand-Mean Centering*
$Y_{ij} = \beta_{0j} + \beta_{1j}(X_{ij} - \overline{X}_{.j}) + r_{ij}$	$Y_{ij} = \beta_{0j} + \beta_{1j}(X_{ij} - \overline{X}_{..}) + r_{ij}$
$\beta_{0j} = \gamma_{00} + \gamma_{01}\overline{X}_{.j} + u_{0j}$	$\beta_{0j} = \gamma_{00} + \gamma_{01}\overline{X}_{.j} + u_{0j}$
$\beta_{1j} = \gamma_{10}$	$\beta_{1j} = \gamma_{10}$
$\gamma_{01} = \beta_b$	$\gamma_{01} = \beta_c$
$\gamma_{10} = \beta_w$	$\gamma_{10} = \beta_w$
$\beta_c = \gamma_{01} - \gamma_{10}$	$\beta_b = \gamma_{01} + \gamma_{10}$

Estimates Using High School and Beyond Data

	Coefficient	*se*		*Coefficient*	*se*
$\hat{\gamma}_{00}$	12.648	0.149	$\hat{\gamma}_{00}$	12.661	0.149
$\hat{\gamma}_{01} = \hat{\beta}_b$	5.866	0.362	$\hat{\gamma}_{01} = \hat{\beta}_c$	3.675	0.378
$\hat{\gamma}_{10} = \hat{\beta}_w$	2.191	0.109	$\hat{\gamma}_{10} = \hat{\beta}_w$	2.191	0.109
$\hat{\beta}_c$	3.675	0.378*	$\hat{\beta}_b$	5.866	0.362*

* Not directly estimated but can be determined from the sampling variance-covariance matrix for the γ coefficients.

in the Level-1 model and its aggregate, $\overline{X}_{.j}$, is included in the Level-2 model for the intercept. The difference between the two approaches, as displayed in columns 1 and 2 of Table 5.10, is in the choice of centering for X_{ij}. When group-mean centering is chosen as in column 1, the relationship between X_{ij} and Y_{ij} is directly decomposed into its within- and between-group components. Specifically, γ_{01} is β_b and γ_{10} is β_w. The compositional effect can be derived by simple subtraction. Alternatively, if X_{ij} is centered around the grand mean, as in column 2, the compositional effect is estimated directly and β_b is derived by simple addition.

In terms of the High School and Beyond data, the student-level effect was 2.191 (the same as in column 3 of Table 5.9), the school-level effect was 5.866 and the difference between these two, the compositional effect, was 3.675. Identical estimates result from the two alternative formulations. Clearly, the social-class composition of the school has a substantial effect on math achievement, even larger than the individual student-level effect.

We should note that similar point estimates for β_b, β_w, and β_c can be obtained through use of a Level-1 OLS regression based on Equation 5.40. In general, the OLS estimates are unbiased but not as efficient as the hierarchical linear model estimators (see Chapter 3). Also, the OLS standard errors for $\hat{\beta}_c$ and $\hat{\beta}_b$ are negatively biased because Equation 5.40 fails to represent explicitly the random variation among schools captured in the u_{0j}.

Estimating the Effects of Individual Organizations

Conceptualization of Organization Specific Effects

An important practical use of multilevel data is to monitor the performance of individual organizations—firms, schools, or classrooms, for example. One might use such data to hold organizational leaders accountable, to rank units for purposes of evaluation, or to identify for further study organizations that are unusually effective or ineffective.

Recently, governments in many countries and several states within the United States have developed educational accountability systems based on quantitative indicators of student progress. Considerable controversy surrounds these efforts, both substantive and methodological. Because empirical Bayes estimates of Level-1 coefficients are increasingly being employed in these systems, some discussion of the issues embedded in this use seems warranted.

Commonly Used Estimates of School Performance

The most common estimator of school performance uses the predicted mean outcome for each school based on the background and prior ability of students in that school. Schools that score higher than predicted are viewed as effective. Typically, the effectiveness score or performance indicator is just the actual mean achievement minus the predicted mean score for each school. Specifically, in the case of one background variable, the performance indicator or school effect is

$$\bar{Y}_{\cdot j} - \bar{Y}_{\cdot\cdot} - \beta(\bar{X}_{\cdot j} - \bar{X}_{\cdot\cdot}) \quad [5.42]$$

where

$\bar{Y}_{\cdot j}$ is the mean outcome for school j;

$\bar{Y}_{\cdot\cdot}$ is the grand mean outcome across all schools;

$\bar{X}_{\cdot j}$ is the school mean on the background variable X_{ij};

$\bar{X}_{\cdot\cdot}$ is the grand mean of X; and

β is a coefficient of adjustment.

A focus of the methodological controversy has been the choice of method for estimating β. Aitkin and Longford (1986) summarize common alternatives. One of their key conclusions is that estimates of β based on OLS regression (ignoring students' membership in schools) can be quite misleading. An alternative method is to use an ANCOVA model in which school membership is included as a series of dummy variables. However, this approach quickly becomes impractical as the number of schools increases. Both OLS regression (ignoring group membership) and the ANCOVA can produce unstable estimates of school effects when sample sizes per school are small.

Use of Empirical Bayes Estimators as Indicators of School Performance

The empirical Bayes residuals estimated under a hierarchical linear model provide an alternative indicator for judging individual school performance. These empirical Bayes estimates (a) take into account group membership even when the number of groups is large, and (b) produce relatively stable estimates even when sample sizes per school are modest.

The random-intercepts model discussed earlier is a common choice for those applications. At the student level,

$$Y_{ij} = \beta_{0j} + \sum_q \beta_{qj}(X_{qij} - \bar{X}_{q\cdot\cdot}) + r_{ij}. \quad [5.43]$$

At the school level,

$$\beta_{0j} = \gamma_{00} + u_{0j} \quad [5.44a]$$

and

$$\beta_{qj} = \gamma_{q0} \quad \text{for } q = 1, \ldots, Q, \quad [5.44b]$$

where the γ_{00} is the overall intercept. Notice that all Level-1 regression coefficients except the intercept are constrained to be constant across schools, and the unique individual-school effect is just u_{0j}.

In the combined form, the model is

$$Y_{ij} = \gamma_{00} + \sum_q \gamma_{q0}(X_{qij} - \bar{X}_{q\cdot\cdot}) + u_{0j} + r_{ij}. \quad [5.45]$$

This model hypothesizes that all students within school j have an effect, u_{0j}, added to their expected score as a result of attending that school. It is essentially the same as Model 5 of Aitkin and Longford (1986) and can be viewed as an ANCOVA where the Xs are covariates and the set of J schools constitute independent groups in a one-way random-effects ANCOVA. A key difference from a traditional random-effects ANCOVA, however, is that our goal here is literally to estimate the effects for each Level-2 unit and not just their variance.

Estimation. An OLS estimator of the effect for each school J is

$$\hat{u}_{0j} = \bar{Y}_{\cdot j} - \hat{\gamma}_{00} - \sum_{q} \hat{\gamma}_{qs}(\bar{X}_{q \cdot j} - \bar{X}_{q \cdot \cdot}) . \qquad [5.46]$$

Note that $\hat{u}_{0j}$ in Equation 5.46 is just the school mean residual for the ANCOVA. Schools with the small samples, n_j, will tend to yield unstable estimates for $\hat{u}_{0j}$. As a result, these schools are more likely to appear extreme purely as a result of chance. Thus, to select out the largest or smallest values of $\hat{u}_{0j}$ as indicators of the most or least effective organizations is likely to capitalize on extreme chance occurrences.

As noted in Chapter 4 and further detailed in Chapter 10, the estimator for u_{0j} in the hierarchical analysis, u^*_{0j}, is an empirical Bayes or shrinkage estimator. The u^*_{0j} shrinks the OLS school-effect estimate proportional to the unreliability of $\hat{u}_{0j}$. The more reliable the OLS estimate from a school is, the less shrinkage occurs. Hence values that are extreme because they are unstable will be pulled toward zero.

Specifically, the estimated school effect under a hierarchical analysis is

$$u^*_{0j} = \lambda_j \hat{u}_{0j} , \qquad [5.47]$$

where

$$\lambda_j = \tau_{00} / [\tau_{00} + \sigma^2 / n_j]$$

is a measure of the reliability of $\hat{u}_{0j}$ as an estimate of u_{0j}. Both theoretical and empirical evidence, reviewed by Efron and Morris (1975) and Morris (1983), indicate that u^*_{0j} will be a more accurate estimator of the school effect u_{0j} than will $\hat{u}_{0j}$. Raudenbush (1988) reviews educational applications of this estimator.

Threats to Valid Inference Regarding Performance Indicators

Despite the technical advantages of empirical Bayes estimators, major validity issues remain in using such statistics as performance indicators. We consider some of these below.

Bias. Studies of school performance indicators may profitably be viewed as quasi-experiments in which each school is a treatment group. The problem of valid causal inference in such settings has been extensively studied (Cook & Campbell, 1979). When random assignment of subjects to treatments is impossible, an attempt must be made to identify and control for individual background differences that are related to group membership and also to the outcome. This poses two problems: First, one can never be confident that all of the relevant background variables have been identified and controlled. Second, reasonable people can disagree about proper models for computing adjustment coefficients, and this choice of adjustments can have a substantial impact on inferences about the individual school effects. One general principle does emerge, however, in considering adjustments: The more dramatically different the groups are on background characteristics, the more sensitive inferences are likely to be to different methods of adjustment and the less credible the resulting inferences.

This principle can be illustrated by a deliberately exaggerated and hypothetical example. Consider Figure 5.1. Student achievement (vertical axis) is plotted against student SES (horizontal axis). Associated with each school is a regression line describing the relationship between social class and achievement. The length of each line represents the range of social class within each school. Notice that there are two types of schools: The students in Group 1 schools are of low SES, and in Group 2 schools they are considerably higher. Within Groups 1 and 2, schools vary only slightly in their effectiveness, as indicated by the small distances between the parallel regression lines. Notice also that there is a compositional effect, D. That is, Group 1 and Group 2 schools differ by more than one would predict given the regression of student achievement on individual SES, and this appears related to the average SES of the schools.

Now we shall consider two alternative models for estimating the individual school effects. The first is a fixed-effects ANCOVA controlling for student social class but ignoring the compositional effect. Formally, using the model implied by Equation 5.42,

$$Y_{ij} = \beta_{0j} + \beta_1(X_{ij} - \overline{X}_{..}) + r_{ij} \qquad [5.48]$$

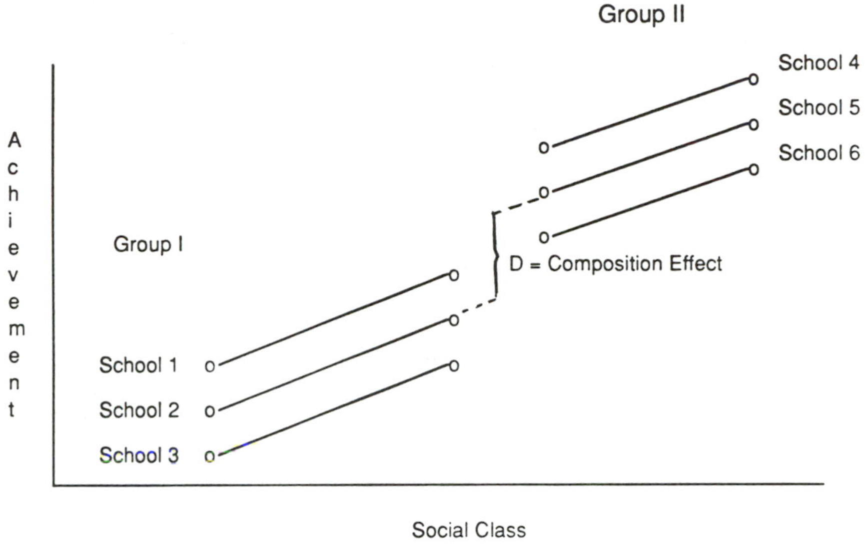

Figure 5.1. A Hypothetical Example of the Relationship Between Achievement and Student Social Class in Two Groups of Schools: Low Social-Class Schools (Group 1) and High Social-Class Schools (Group 2)

where β_1 is the adjustment coefficient associated with student SES and β_{0j} represents the fixed school effect in this case. Because the achievement-SES relationship is homogeneous across the six schools, the difference in effects between any two schools is the distance between their regression lines. For example, the difference between School 2 and School 5 is very large. Notice that under this model every Group 2 school will appear substantially more effective than any Group 1 school.

The second model explicitly controls for school SES when estimating the school effects. This involves extending Equation 5.48 to include mean school SES, $\overline{X}_{.j}$, as a second covariate. For example,

$$Y_{ij} = \beta_{0j} + \beta_1(X_{ij} - \overline{X}_{.j}) + \beta_2(\overline{X}_{.j} - \overline{X}_{..}) + r_{ij} \qquad [5.49]$$

In practice, Equation 5.49 implies comparing "like with like." Now Group 1 schools are compared to each other, and Group 2 schools are compared to each other. From Figure 5.1, we see that Schools 2 and 5 are now viewed as equally effective: Each is about average compared with schools in its group (schools having similar social composition).

This strategy may seem fairer than the first, but is it? Suppose that the Group 2 schools have more effective staff and that staff quality, not student composition, causes the elevated test scores. The results in Figure 5.1 could occur, for example, if the school district assigned its best principals and teachers to the more affluent schools. If so, the second strategy would give no credit to these leaders for their effective practices.

The key concern is that without having formulated an explicit model of school quality, we can never be sure that we have disentangled the effect of school composition from other school factors with which composition is often correlated.

Heterogeneity of Regression. Problematic as this may seem, the example above is far simpler than reality is likely to be. Our example assumes that the SES-achievement regression lines are identical in all schools. In many cases, the regressions may be heterogeneous, as indicated in Figure 5.2. Now, regardless of the method of adjustment, the estimate of a school's effectiveness will depend upon the social class of the child in question. For example, School 1 appears very effective relative to School 2 for low-SES students (i.e., effect 1 in Figure 5.2). However, for high-SES students, the differences between two schools are negligible (i.e., effect 2).

Shrinkage as a Self-Fulfilling Prophecy. As discussed in Chapter 3, the shrinkage estimator, u^*_{0j}, has a smaller expected mean square error than does the least squares estimator, $\hat{u}_{0j}$, and protects us against capitalizing on chance. However, shrinkage estimators are conditionally biased. From Equation 5.46, we can see that the expected value of $\hat{u}_{0j}$ given the true value of u_{0j} is

$$E(\hat{u}_{0j} \mid u_{0j}) = u_{0j} = \mu_{Y_j} - \sum_q \gamma_{qs}(\bar{X}_{q \cdot j} - \bar{X}_{q \cdot \cdot}) , \qquad [5.50]$$

where μ_{Y_j} is the unadjusted mean outcome in group j. Notice that u_{0j} is the deviation of group j's unadjusted mean, μ_{Y_j}, from a value predicted on the basis of student-background variables. The conditional expectation of the empirical Bayes estimator, u^*_{0j}, is

$$E(u^*_{0j} \mid u_{0j}) = \lambda_j u_{0j} , \qquad [5.51]$$

so the bias is

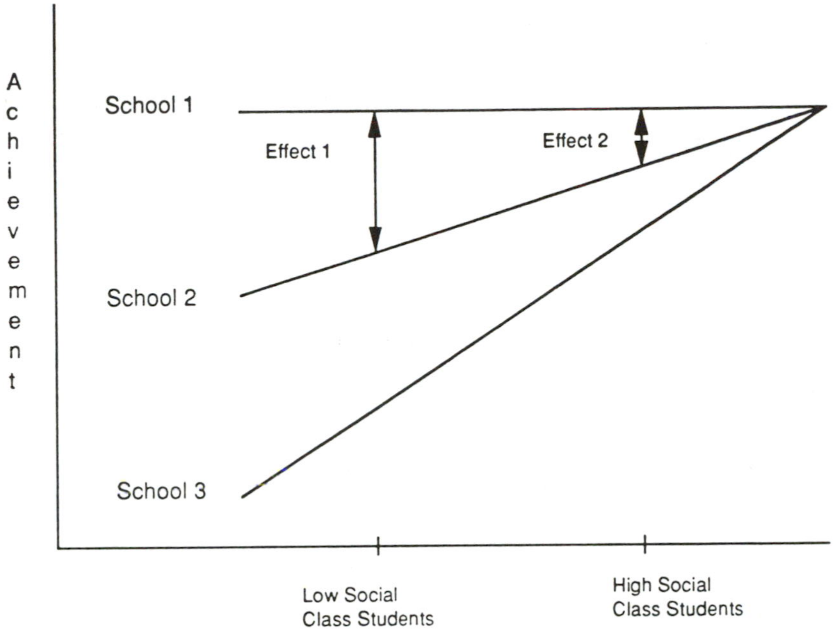

Figure 5.2. Identifying School Effects When the Relationship Between Achievement and Student Background Is Heterogeneous

$$\text{Bias}(u^*_{0j} \mid u_{0j}) = -(1 - \lambda_j)[\mu_{Y_j} - \sum_q \gamma_{qs}(\overline{X}_{q\cdot j} - \overline{X}_{q\cdot\cdot})]\,. \qquad [5.52]$$

This formula indicates that to the extent $\hat{u}_{0j}$ is unreliable, the estimate u^*_{0j} will be biased *toward* the value predicted on the basis of student background0. For example, unusually effective schools that have children of disadvantaged backgrounds will have their high mean effect estimates biased downward toward the value typically displayed by other, similarly disadvantaged schools. This procedure then operates as a kind of statistical self-fulfilling prophecy in which, to the extent the data are unreliable, schools effects are made to conform more to expectations than they do in actuality.

6 Applications in the Study of Individual Change

Background Issues in Research on Individual Change

Finding adequate measures of individual change and valid techniques for research on change are problems that have long perplexed behavioral scientists. Many concerns catalogued by Harris (1963) still continue to trouble quantitative studies of growth. These methodological problems have led to a bewildering array of well-intentioned but misdirected suggestions about design and analysis. Recent efforts (Rogosa, Brand, & Zimowski, 1982; Rogosa & Willett, 1985), however, have gone a long way toward dispelling these misconceptions. Willett (1988) provides an excellent review of both past problems and recent developments.

In brief, research on change has been plagued by inadequacies in conceptualization, measurement, and design. The conceptual concern is that a model is needed to guide inquiry into the phenomenon under study. Yet research on individual change rarely identifies an explicit model of individual growth. Regarding measurement, studies of change typically use instruments that were developed to discriminate among individuals at a fixed point in time. The adequacy of such measures for distinguishing differences in rates of change among individuals is rarely considered. In addition, the practice of scaling instruments to have a constant variance over time is fatal to studying change and the determinants of change (Rogosa et al., 1982). Finally, and perhaps most importantly, is the problem of design. Most studies of change collect data at only two time points. Such designs are often inadequate for studying individual growth (Bryk & Raudenbush, 1987; Bryk & Weisberg, 1977; Rogosa et al., 1982).

The development of hierarchical linear models, however, now offers a powerful set of techniques for research on individual change. When applied with valid measurements from a multiple-time-point design, they afford an integrated approach for studying the structure and predictors of individual growth.

Formulating Models

Many individual change phenomena can be represented through a two-level hierarchical model. At Level 1, each person's development is represented by an individual growth trajectory that depends on a unique set of parameters. These individual growth parameters become the outcome variables in a Level-2 model, where they may depend on some person-level characteristics. Formally, we view the multiple observations on each individual as nested within the person. This treatment of multiple observations as nested allows the investigator to proceed without difficulty when the number and spacing of time points vary across cases.

We introduce a new notation in this chapter for representing the two-level hierarchical model. The Level-1 coefficients are now denoted by π and the Level-2 coefficients by β. The Level-1 and Level-2 predictors are a_{ti} and X_{pq}, and the random effects are now e_{ti} and r_{pi}, respectively. This new notation facilitates our presentation in Chapter 8 where we bring together the study of individual growth and organizational effects in a three-level model.

Repeated-Observations Model (Level 1)

We assume that Y_{ti}, the observed status at time t for individual i, is a function of a systematic growth trajectory or growth curve plus random error. It is especially convenient when systematic growth over time can be represented as a polynomial of degree P. Then, the Level-1 model is

$$Y_{ti} = \pi_{0i} + \pi_{1i}a_{ti} + \pi_{2i}a_{ti}^2 + \ldots + \pi_{Pi}a_{ti}^P + e_{ti} \qquad [6.1]$$

for $i = 1, \ldots, n$ subjects, where a_{ti} is the age at time t for person i and π_{pi} is the growth trajectory parameter p for subject i associated with the polynomial of degree P (i.e., $p = 0, \ldots, P$). Each person is observed on T_i occasions. Note that the number and spacing of measurement occasions may vary across persons.

It is most common to assume a simple error structure for e_{ti}, namely that each e_{ti} is independently and normally distributed with a mean of zero and constant variance, σ^2. The error structure, however, can take on a variety of forms. The variance may be person specific, for example, $\text{Var}(e_{ti}) = \sigma_i^2$. Autocorrelation might exist among the e_{ti} for each person (Louis & Spiro, 1984; Ware, 1985). Or, e_{ti} may depend on measured characteristics such as age (Goldstein, 1986). These more complex models for e_{ti} seem most useful when there are many time points per subject. For short time series, the assumption of independent errors with constant variance is most practical and unlikely to significantly distort the analysis in most cases. We assume this in each of the applications discussed below.

Person-Level Model (Level 2)

An important feature of Equation 6.1 is the assumption that the growth parameters vary across individuals. We formulate a Level-2 model to represent this variation. Specifically, for each of the $P + 1$ individual growth parameters,

$$\pi_{pi} = \beta_{p0} + \sum_{q=1}^{Q_p} \beta_{pq} X_{qi} + r_{pi}, \qquad [6.2]$$

where

X_{qi} is either a measured characteristic of the individual's background (e.g., sex or social class) or of an experimental treatment (e.g., type of curriculum employed or amount of instruction);

β_{pq} represents the effect of X_q on the pth growth parameter; and

r_{pi} is a random effect with a mean of zero. The set of $P + 1$ random effects for person i are assumed multivariate normally distributed with full covariance matrix, $\mathbf{T}$, dimensioned $(P + 1) \times (P + 1)$.

We assume this multivariate normality for all applications discussed in this chapter.

Comparison with Conventional Multivariate Repeated Measures (MRM) Methods

The statistical techniques discussed in this chapter have appeared in the growth-curve literature under a variety of terms, including the random-effects model (Laird & Ware, 1982) and the general mixed-linear model (Goldstein, 1986), as well as the hierarchical linear model (Strenio et al., 1983). Ware (1985) provides a thorough comparison of these new techniques with more conventional MRM methods.

In brief, five key points should be made about use of the hierarchical linear model in studying individual growth. First, the model explicitly represents the individual growth at Level 1. In contrast, in an MRM model individual variation in growth is not directly modeled but rather appears in the interaction of repeated occasions by subjects. Conceptually, the hierarchical model is more in the spirit of the growth-curve analysis, as articulated in a series of papers by Rogosa and Willett and their associates (see Willett, 1988, for a review).

Second, the hierarchical model is generally more flexible in terms of its data requirements because the repeated observations are viewed as nested within the person rather than as the same fixed set for all persons as in MRM. In an hierarchical model, both the number of observations per person and the spacing among the observations may vary. The time or age variable may also be continuous rather than a fixed set of points. Although missing observations can now be handled in MRM through an application of the EM algorithm (Jennrich & Schlucter, 1986), this poses no special problem in a hierarchical analysis. Other Level-1 predictors besides age or time also can be incorporated (see Chapter 8). Their effects can be specified as fixed, nonrandomly varying, or random.

Third, the hierarchical model permits flexible specification of the covariance structure among the repeated observations and provides methods for direct hypothesis testing about possible determinants of this structure. This is accomplished through specification of both the structural features of the individual growth model in Equation 6.1 and the Level-1 and Level-2 random effects. For further discussion see Goldstein (1987) and Bryk and Raudenbush (1987).

Fourth, when the restrictive data requirements and assumptions of MRM apply, a hierarchical analysis produces the same point estimates for the fixed effects as in an MRM analysis. The *t*-ratios computed in the hierarchical analysis are also identical to those obtained using a priori contrasts in MRM. In sum, the results of a hierarchical analysis can be formally related to the MRM model when the MRM conditions apply.

Fifth, the formulation of growth models via the hierarchical approach leads naturally to the study of organizational effects on growth, a topic considered in detail in Chapter 8.

Application of a Linear Growth Model

In many situations, particularly when the number of observations per individual are few (e.g., three or four occasions), it is convenient to employ a linear individual growth model for Equation 6.1. When the time period is relatively short, this model can provide a good approximation for more complex processes that cannot be fully modeled because of the sparse number of observations.

Under a linear model at Level 1, Equation 6.1 simplifies to

$$Y_{ti} = \pi_{0i} + \pi_{1i} a_{ti} + e_{ti}, \qquad [6.3]$$

where we assume that the errors e_{ti} are independent and normally distributed with common variance σ^2.

Here, π_{1i} is the growth rate for person i over the data-collection period and represents the expected change during a fixed unit of time. The intercept parameter, π_{0i}, is the true ability of person i at $a_{ti} = 0$. Thus, the specific meaning of π_{0i} depends on the scaling of the age metric.

Both the intercept and growth-rate parameters are allowed to vary at Level 2 as a function of measured person characteristics. Thus, Equation 6.2 becomes

$$\pi_{0i} = \beta_{00} + \sum_{q=1}^{Q_0} \beta_{0q} X_{0qi} + r_{0i} \qquad [6.4]$$

$$\pi_{1i} = \beta_{10} + \sum_{q=1}^{Q_1} \beta_{1q} X_{1qi} + r_{1i}.$$

Note there are two Level-2 random effects, r_{0i} and r_{1i}, with variances τ_{00} and τ_{11}, respectively, and with covariance τ_{01}.

In this section, we illustrate how the linear individual growth model can be applied to (a) estimate a mean growth curve and the extent of individual variation around it; (b) assess the reliability of measures for studying both status and change; (c) estimate the correlation between initial status and rate of change; and (d) model relations of person-level predictors to both status and change.

Example: The Effect of Instruction on Cognitive Growth

The data consist of test results on a measure of natural science knowledge from 143 children enrolled in the Head Start program. They were collected as part of a large effort to develop measures of children's growth (rather than just status) during the preschool and early elementary years. The measures were generated through an item-response-theory scaling of a set of test items (Lord, 1980). As is customary in such applications, the natural science measure is represented in "a logit metric." The latter references a person's ability to the log of the odds of a correct response to items of selected difficulty.

The original design called for each child to be tested on four occasions approximately equally spaced throughout the year. In practice, the testing dates varied across children and not every child was assessed at each time point. The age variable, a_{ti}, was defined as the amount of time in months that had elapsed from the first data-collection point. Under this specification, π_{0i} in Equation 6.3 represents the true ability level of person i at the onset of data collection, or what we call the *initial status.* In addition to the test data, information was collected on students' home language (Spanish or English) and amount of direct instruction (hours per academic year).

A Random-Coefficient Regression Model

Equation 6.3 specifies the Level-1 model. At Level 2, we begin with the simplest person-level model:

$$\pi_{0i} = \beta_{00} + r_{0i} \qquad [6.5]$$

$$\pi_{1i} = \beta_{10} + r_{1i}.$$

We note that Equation 6.5 is an unconditional model in that no Level-2 predictors for either π_{0i} or π_{1i} have been introduced. As in the organizational research application discussed in the previous chapter, a hierarchical analysis typically begins with the fitting of an unconditional model. This model provides useful empirical evidence for determining a proper specification of the individual growth equation and baseline statistics for evaluating subsequent Level-2 models. Table 6.1 presents the results for this analysis.

TABLE 6.1 Linear Model of Growth in Natural Science Knowledge (unconditional model)

Fixed Effect	*Coefficient*	*se*	*t ratio*	
Mean initial status, β_{00}	−0.135	0.005	−27.00	
Mean growth rate, β_{10}	0.182	0.025	7.27	
Random Effect	*Variance Component*	*df*	χ^2	*p value*
Initial status, r_{0i}	1.689	139	356.90	< 0.001
Growth rate, r_{1i}	0.041	139	724.91	< 0.001
Level-1 error, e_{ti}	0.419			
Reliability of OLS Regression Coefficient Estimate				
Initial status, π_{0i}	0.854			
Growth rate, π_{1i}	0.799			

Mean Growth Trajectory. The estimated mean intercept, $\hat{\beta}_{00}$, and mean growth rate, $\hat{\beta}_{10}$, for the natural science data were −0.135 and 0.182, respectively. This means that the average natural science score at the first testing was −0.135 logits and children were gaining an average 0.182 logits per month during the study.

As discussed in Chapter 3, hypothesis tests for fixed effects, now denoted β, use the ratio of the estimated effects to their standard error. Both the mean intercept and growth rate have large t statistics indicating that both parameters are necessary for describing the mean growth trajectory.

Individual Variation in Growth Trajectories. Next, we consider the nature of the deviations of the individual growth trajectories from the mean curve. The estimates for the variances of individual growth parameters π_{0i} and π_{1i} were 1.689 and 0.041, respectively. As discussed in Chapter 3, the simplest test of homogeneity, that there is no true variation in individual growth parameters, involves use of a χ^2 statistic. Application of Equation 3.71 resulted in a test statistic for the intercept term of 356.90 (df = 139, $p < .001$). This leads us to reject the null hypotheses and conclude that children vary significantly in their knowledge of natural science at entry into Head Start. The corresponding χ^2 test statistic for the hypothesis that there are no individual differences among children's growth rates (i.e., H_0: $\tau_{11} = 0$) was 724.91 (df = 139, $p < .001$), which leads us to conclude that there is also significant variation in their learning rates.

The variance estimate $\hat{\tau}_{11} = .041$ implies an estimated standard deviation of 0.202. Thus, a child whose growth is one standard deviation above average is expected to grow at the rate of .182 + .202 = .384 logits per month.

Reliability of Initial Status and Change. Estimation of the unconditional model also allows us to investigate the psychometric characteristics of the estimated individual growth parameters. If most of the variability in the OLS estimate, $\hat{\pi}_{pi}$, of a person's growth parameters, π_{pi}, were due to model error, we would be unlikely to find any systematic relations between these estimates and person-level variables. Without knowledge of the reliability of the estimated growth parameters, we might falsely conclude that there are no relations, when in fact the data may simply be incapable of detecting such relations.

Recall from Equation 3.25 that the total variability in the OLS estimated Level-1 coefficients consists of error variance and parameter variance. In the notation of this chapter,

$$\begin{aligned} \mathrm{Var}(\hat{\pi}_{p\,i}) &= \mathrm{Var}(\hat{\pi}_{p\,i} \mid \pi_{p\,i}) + \mathrm{Var}(\pi_{p\,i}) \\ &= v_{p\,p\,i} + \tau_{p\,p}\,. \end{aligned} \qquad [6.6]$$

Following classical measurement theory, the ratio of the "true" parameter variance, $\mathrm{Var}(\pi_{pi})$, to the "total" observed variance, $\mathrm{Var}(\hat{\pi}_{pi})$, is the reliability of the OLS estimate, $\hat{\pi}_{pi}$, as a measure of the "true" growth parameters, π_{pi} . Analogous to Equation 3.52, for any person i,

$$\text{reliability of } (\hat{\pi}_{p\,i}) = \mathrm{Var}(\pi_{p\,i})/\mathrm{Var}(\hat{\pi}_{p\,i}) = \tau_{p\,p}/(v_{p\,p\,i} + \tau_{p\,p})\,, \qquad [6.7]$$

for the $p = 0, \ldots, P$ growth parameter estimates.[1] Averaging across the n persons (as in Equation 3.53) provides a summary index of the reliability of each growth parameter estimate for this population of persons. For the natural science data, the estimated reliabilities for initial status and growth rates were .854 and .799, respectively (see Table 6.1). These results indicate that there is a substantial signal in these data in terms of individual differences in both initial status and growth rates. Modeling each parameter as a function of person-level variables is certainly warranted.

Correlation of Change with Initial Status. The correlation between individual change and initial status is an important characteristic of interest in much research on change. It is impossible, however, to obtain a consistent estimate of this relationship in a simple pretest-posttest design.

Researchers have typically found spurious negative correlations between initial status and rate of growth in pre-post studies, correlations that occur because the measurement errors in the pretest and the observed change score are negatively correlated (Bereiter, 1963; Blomqvist, 1977).

With multiwave data, however, a consistent estimate of the correlation of true initial status and true change can be obtained. Under a linear individual growth model, this correlation is just the correlation between π_{0i} and π_{1i}. Analogous to Equation 2.3,

$$\hat{\rho}(\pi_{0i}, \pi_{1i}) = \hat{\tau}_{01}/(\hat{\tau}_{00} + \hat{\tau}_{11})^{1/2}. \quad [6.8]$$

For the natural science data, the estimated correlation between true change and true initial status was −.278. This means that students who had limited natural science knowledge at entry into Head Start tended to gain at a somewhat faster rate. We can infer this is a true negative relationship and not a spurious result of the measurement process. Note that the correlation between initial status and rate of growth will vary depending on the specific time point selected for initial status. As noted earlier, the meaning of π_{0i} depends on the scaling of the age or time variable, a_{ti}.

An Intercept- and Slopes-as-Outcomes Model

The Level-1 model remains as in Equation 6.3. We now introduce two predictors into the Level-2 model: LANGUAGE (a dummy variable indicating home language: 1 = non-English, 0 = English); and HOURS (a continuous measure of the number of hours of direct classroom instruction received by the child in that program year). The person-level model is now

$$\pi_{0i} = \beta_{00} + \beta_{01}(\text{LANGUAGE})_i + \beta_{02}(\text{HOURS})_i + r_{0i}, \quad [6.9]$$

and

$$\pi_{1i} = \beta_{10} + \beta_{11}(\text{LANGUAGE})_i + \beta_{12}(\text{HOURS})_i + r_{1i}. \quad [6.10]$$

Table 6.2 presents the estimated fixed-effects results for this analysis.

Neither home language nor hours of instruction was strongly related to entry ability. The t ratios were less than 2.0 in both cases. The estimated effects were plausible, however. On average, Spanish speakers started behind English-speaking children by .463 logits, that is, $\hat{\beta}_{01} = -.463$. It is commonly encountered in Head Start that children from non-English-speaking families tend to score lower initially but are also likely to show rapid progress.

TABLE 6.2 Linear Model of Growth in Natural Science Knowledge (Effects of Home Language and Hours of Instruction)

Fixed Effect	*Coefficient*	*se*	*t ratio*
Model for initial status, π_{0i}			
BASE, β_{00}	0.895	0.267	3.35
LANGUAGE, β_{01}	−0.463	0.304	−1.52
HOURS, β_{02}	1.523×10^{-3}	0.853×10^{-3}	1.79
Model for growth rate, π_{1i}			
BASE, β_{10}	0.029	0.039	0.74
LANGUAGE, β_{11}	0.187	0.045	4.20
HOURS, β_{12}	4.735×10^{-4}	1.252×10^{-4}	3.78

The positive relation between total hours of instruction and initial status was also reasonable because the first testing occasion, t_1, occurred between 6 and 14 weeks into the program year. Because a substantial amount of instruction had already been given, the observed effect was not surprising.

Both home language and hours of instruction related significantly to individual growth rates. The test scores for children whose home language was Spanish increased, on average, at a rate .187 logits per month faster than the scores of their English-speaking companions (i.e., $\hat{\beta}_{11} = .187$). Similarly, each additional hour of instruction per year was associated with a .000474 logit increment to the growth rate (i.e., $\hat{\beta}_{12} = .000474$). To understand the latter result, consider the expected growth rates for two children who had the same home language but received varying amounts of instruction. Specifically, suppose the first child received 40 hours per month of instruction and the second 80 hours. (These numbers approximate the minimum and maximum hours of instruction in the Head Start sample.) The model predicts that over a 9-month period, the extra 40 hours per month of instruction received by the second child will yield an increment to that child's growth rate of $9 \times 40 \times .0004735$, or .170 logits per month. That is, the child in the 80-hour-per-month program will be expected to grow at a rate of .170 logits per month faster than his counterpart in the 40-hour-per-month program.

Table 6.3 displays the estimated variances for the random effects in this model and compares these results with those from the unconditional model (Equation 6.5). As in Equation 4.17, the proportion of variance explained is the difference between the total parameter variance (estimated from the unconditional model) and the residual parameter variance (based on the fitted model) relative to the total parameter variance. In the Head Start

TABLE 6.3 Variance Explained in Initial Status and Growth Rate as a Result of Home Language and Hours of Instruction

Model	*Initial Status* $Var(\pi_{0i})$	*Growth Rate* $Var(\pi_{1i})$
Unconditional[a]	1.689	0.041
Conditional on LANGUAGE and HOURS[b]	0.761	0.010
Proportion of variance explained	54.9	75.0

a. From Table 6.1.
b. These are residual variances based on the model estimated in Table 6.2.

application, home language and hours of instruction account for 54.9% of the parameter variance in the initial status and 75.0% of the parameter variance in growth rates on the natural science test.

Application of a Quadratic Growth Model

We illustrate in this section the use of a quadratic growth model and demonstrate how various hypothesis testing procedures can be used during the process of developing a model. The model at Level 1 is now of the form

$$Y_{ti} = \pi_{0i} + \pi_{1i}(a_{ti} - L) + \pi_{2i}(a_{ti} - L)^2 + e_{ti}. \qquad [6.11]$$

Note that we have introduced a specific or a priori centering constant, L, for the Level-1 predictors that are powers of a_{ti} . Each of the growth parameters in Equation 6.11 has a substantive meaning. The intercept, π_{0i}, represents the status of person i at time L. The linear component, π_{1i} is the instantaneous growth rate for person i at time L, and π_{2i} captures the curvature or acceleration in each growth trajectory. Although acceleration is a characteristic of the entire trajectory, the status and instantaneous rate parameters depend on the particular choice of value for L.

At Level 2, we have a separate equation for each Level-1 coefficient, π_{pi}, where $p = 0, 1, 2$. That is,

$$\pi_{pi} = \beta_{p0} + \sum_{q=1}^{Q_p} \beta_{pq} X_{qi} + r_{pi}. \qquad [6.12]$$

The variances and covariances for the Level-2 random effects, r_{pi}, now form a 3×3 matrix:

$$\mathbf{T} = \begin{bmatrix} \tau_{00} & \text{Symmetric} & \\ \tau_{10} & \tau_{11} & \\ \tau_{20} & \tau_{21} & \tau_{22} \end{bmatrix} = \begin{bmatrix} \text{Var}(\pi_{0i}) & & \text{Symmetric} \\ \text{Cov}(\pi_{1i}, \pi_{0i}) & \text{Var}(\pi_{1i}) & \\ \text{Cov}(\pi_{2i}, \pi_{0i}) & \text{Cov}(\pi_{2i}, \pi_{1i}) & \text{Var}(\pi_{2i}) \end{bmatrix}.$$

Example: The Effects of Maternal Speech on Children's Vocabulary

We reanalyze data from a recent study of children's vocabulary development during the second year of life (Huttenlocher et al., 1991). The Huttenlocher et al. study hypothesized that maternal use of language in the home affects a child's early vocabulary acquisition. Sex differences in vocabulary growth were also expected.

The data actually consist of results from two closely related studies. In the first study, 11 children were observed in the home on six or seven occasions at 2-month intervals during the period from 14 to 26 months of age. (For some cases, the 14-month data point is missing.) A measure of the child's vocabulary size at each measurement occasion, Y_{ti}, was derived from these observations. In the second study, another 11 children were observed at 16, 20, and 24 months. In both studies, the amount of maternal speech was also recorded when the child was 16 months.

One of the strengths of a hierarchical analysis of individual change is that diverse repeated measure data patterns such as the above can be combined into a single analysis. Because of slight differences in research procedures employed in two studies, however, the investigators worried about combining the data. Yet to treat the two studies separately ran the risk of failing to detect substantively important relations because of possible low power in each of the individual studies. The analysis described here illustrates how to combine data from two studies while still permitting a rigorous test of study effects and study-person interaction effects.

A Random-Coefficient Regression Model

A visual examination of the individual child vocabulary growth trajectories, displayed in Figure 6.1, clearly indicated a nonlinear growth pattern. In fact, all 22 trajectories displayed upward curvature, indicating that the rate of new word acquisition was increasing over time. These observations suggested fitting a quadratic individual growth model as in Equation 6.11.

The centering parameter, L, was deliberately set at 12 months, because this is about the time that most children begin to express their first words. Thus, π_{0i} represents the child's vocabulary size at 12 months, which should be close to 0; and π_{1i} is the instantaneous growth rate at 12 months, which

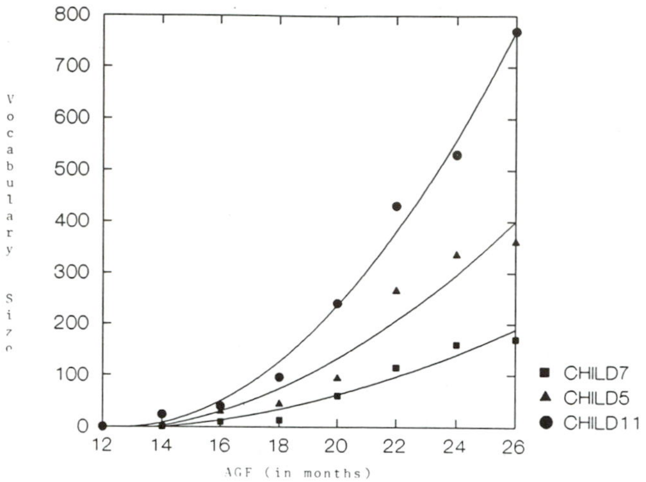

Figure 6.1. A Sample of Individual Vocabulary Growth Trajectories
SOURCE: Huttenlocher, Haight, Bryk, & Seltzer, 1991.
NOTE: □, O, Δ represent the actual observations. The smooth curves result from fitting a separate quadratic polynomial to each child's vocabulary data.

also should be close to zero because prior research has demonstrated that initial vocabulary acquisition occurs very slowly.

As is customary, the researchers began with an unconditional Level-2 model. That is,

$$\pi_{0i} = \beta_{00} + r_{0i} \quad [6.13a]$$

$$\pi_{1i} = \beta_{10} + r_{1i} \quad [6.13b]$$

$$\pi_{2i} = \beta_{20} + r_{2i}. \quad [6.13c]$$

Table 6.4 presents the results. Both the mean vocabulary size at 12 months and the mean growth rate were very close to zero. (Note that the estimated coefficients for both of these parameters were considerably smaller than their respective standard errors.) The mean acceleration was positive ($\hat{\beta}_{20}$ = 2.305) and highly significant. This indicates that, on average, children were acquiring new words at an increasing rate over time.

In general, the growth rate at any particular age is the first derivative of the growth model evaluated at that age. For quadratic growth,

TABLE 6.4 Model 1: Full Quadratic Model of Vocabulary Growth

Fixed Effect	*Coefficient*	*se*	*t ratio*	
Mean vocabulary size at 12 months, β_{00}	−3.879	5.427	−0.715	
Mean growth rate at 12 months, β_{10}	−0.327	2.295	−0.143	
Mean acceleration, β_{20}	2.035	0.200	10.172	
Random Effect	*Variance Component*	*df*	χ^2	*p value*[a]
12-month status, r_{0i}	62.307	10	0.790	> 0.500
Growth rate, r_{1i}	46.949	10	6.211	> 0.500
Acceleration, r_{2i}	0.510	10	17.434	0.065
Level-1 error, e_{ti}	676.882			

Deviance = 1,277.03 with 7 df

a. These results are based on only the 11 cases for whom sufficient data exist to compute separate OLS estimates for each individual child. The χ^2 statistics and p values are rough approximations given the small number of persons.

$$\text{growth rate at age } t = \pi_{1i} + 2\pi_{2i}(a_{ti} - L)\,. \qquad [6.14]$$

At 14 months of age, for example, the average growth rate was 7.81 new words per month [−.327 + 2(2.035)(14 − 12)]. By 16 months, the average growth rate had grown to 15.91 new words per month.

The standard deviation of the individual observations around any individual growth trajectory was 26.02 words^2 (i.e., $\hat{\sigma} = 676.88^{1/2}$). The χ^2 statistics associated with π_{0i} and π_{1i} suggest that the observed variability in both vocabulary size and instantaneous growth rates at 12 months reflects mostly error variability in the OLS estimates. In reality, there probably are significant differences among children in these parameters, but we have relatively little information in this study to detect these effects, because no direct observations were made before 14 months. We also note that reliability statistics were not reported in this application because half of the cases had only three observations. As a result, the OLS estimates fit these data perfectly and the reliability statistics would be quite misleading.

These results suggest that some simplification of the Level-1 model is in order. The estimates for the mean initial status and growth rate at 12 months were not significantly different from zero (and are in fact small in absolute terms). The homogeneity hypothesis was also sustained for both of these random parameters. Further evidence for a model simplification is provided by the estimated correlations among the random effects (see

TABLE 6.5 Correlations Among Random Coefficients in the Full Quadratic Model

	π_{0i}	π_{1i}	π_{2i}
12 month status, π_{0i}	1.000		
Growth rate at 12 months, π_{1i}	−0.982	1.000	
Acceleration, π_{2i}	−0.895	0.842	1.000

Table 6.5). The intercept coefficient, π_{0i}, is nearly colinear with both the growth rate, π_{1i}, and acceleration, π_{2i} . At a minimum this suggests that a "no-intercept" model be fitted. That is, the Level-1 model reduces to

$$Y_{ti} = \pi_{1i}(a_{ti} - L) + \pi_{2i}(a_{ti} - L)^2 + e_{ti} . \qquad [6.15]$$

The results for this model are presented in Table 6.6.

The basic findings of the first model are sustained in the reduced model. The average growth rate at 12 months is still close to zero and the average acceleration is virtually unchanged. The standard deviation around the individual growth trajectories has risen only slightly ($\hat{\sigma} = \text{Var}(e_{ti})^{1/2} = 26.63$), which indicates that a no-intercept Level-1 model fits the data about as well as the initial model. The χ^2 statistics associated with the random growth rate and acceleration parameters indicate that there is substantial individual variation in both of these parameters.

The correlation between these two random coefficients remains very high at .904. The latter suggests that the χ^2 tests for parameter homogeniety might be misleading, because these are independent univariate tests that do not take into account the relations among the random effects.

As a check, a likelihood-ratio test was computed (see Chapter 3). Specifically, the deviance statistic from the second model (1,285.02 with 4 df) was compared with the corresponding statistic from a model where the instantaneous growth rate, π_{1i}, was specified as a fixed effect. As a result the variance in the growth rates and the covariance between growth rate and acceleration were constrained to 0. That is, the Level-1 model remained as in Equation 6.15, but at Level 2

$$\pi_{1i} = \beta_{10} \qquad [6.16]$$

$$\pi_{2i} = \beta_{20} + r_{2i} .$$

TABLE 6.6 Model 2: Quadratic Model of Vocabulary Growth (No Intercept)

Fixed Effect	*Coefficient*	*se*	*t ratio*	
Mean growth rate at 12 months, β_{10}	−1.294	1.557	−0.831	
Mean acceleration, β_{20}	2.087	0.205	10.201	
Random Effect	*Variance Component*	*df*	χ^2	*p value*
Growth rate, r_{1i}	21.908	21	37.532	0.015
Acceleration, r_{2i}	0.663	21	89.359	0.000
Level-1 error, e_{it}	709.231			

Deviance = 1,285.02 with 4 df

The deviance statistic for the alternative model was 1,292.03 with 2 df. The difference between these two deviance statistics is 7.01, which is distributed as approximately χ^2 with 2 df. The test result is highly significant ($p < .001$) and implies that the model reduction is not warranted. This result confirms the univariate homogenity test. A random growth rate component should remain in the model.

We can, however, make one further simplification by constraining the average growth rate coefficient to 0. That is, the Level-1 model remains as is in Equation 6.15, but the Level-2 model is reduced to

$$\pi_{1i} = r_{1i} \qquad [6.17]$$

$$\pi_{2i} = \beta_{20} + r_{2i}.$$

The results for this "best" specification are presented in Table 6.7.

An Intercept- and Slopes-as-Outcomes Model of the Effects of Maternal Speech, Sex, and Study Group

Having identified an appropriate Level-1 model, the researchers proceeded to test the formal hypotheses of the study. Specifically, they posed the following person-level model:

$$\pi_{1i} = r_{1i} \qquad [6.18a]$$

TABLE 6.7 Model 3: Quadratic Model of Vocabulary Growth (No Intercept Term and No Fixed Effect for the Linear Rate)

Fixed Effect	*Coefficient*	*se*	*t ratio*	
Mean acceleration, β_{20}	2.098	0.206	10.172	
Random Effect	*Variance Component*	*df*	χ^2	*p value*
Growth rate, r_{1i}	20.158	22	40.947	0.006
Acceleration, r_{2i}	0.685	21	88.528	0.000
Level-1 error, e_{ti}	708.085			
Deviance = 1,286.57 with 4 df				

$$\pi_{2i} = \beta_{20} + \beta_{21}(\text{STUDY})_i + \beta_{22}(\text{SEX})_i + \beta_{23}(\text{MOMSPEECH})_i \quad [6.18b]$$

$$+ \beta_{24}(\text{STUDY} \times \text{SEX})_i + \beta_{25}(\text{STUDY} \times \text{MOMSPEECH})_i + r_{2i}\,.$$

Equation 6.18a specifies a pure random-effects model for π_{1i}. No intercept term appears in this Level-2 equation because, as in the previous model, the mean rate was constrained to 0. Variation in the individual acceleration parameters was modeled as a function of STUDY (−1 = study 1 and 1 = study 2), child's SEX (−1 = male, 1 = female), MOMSPEECH (count of words spoken, in natural log metric, and centered around the grand mean), and interaction terms of STUDY with SEX and MOMSPEECH. (Note, the −1/1 coding scheme for STUDY and SEX was adopted in order to test these interaction effects.) The results for this model appear in Table 6.8.

There was a significant difference in the average acceleration rates between the two studies of .866 words/month^2 [i.e., effect of study 1 – effect of study 2 = (−1)(−.433) − (1)(−.433)]. This difference resulted from the somewhat different procedures employed in the two studies to estimate total vocabulary size at each age. As hypothesized, the average acceleration was significantly higher for girls than boys by .624 words/month^2. Similarly, the amount of mother's speech was positively related to vocabulary acquisition ($\hat{\beta}_{23} = 0.793$, t ratio = 2.370). There was no evidence that the child-sex and mother-speech effects vary across the two studies; that is, both the interaction terms were small and insignificant (t ratios < 1.0 for both $\hat{\beta}_{24}$ and $\hat{\beta}_{25}$). Thus, we have some confidence in interpreting the results from the pooling of data across the two studies. The residual vari-

TABLE 6.8 Final Quadratic Growth Model

Fixed Effect	*Coefficient*	*se*	*t ratio*	
Model for acceleration, π_{2i}				
Base, β_{20}	2.031	0.157	12.887	
Study effect, β_{21}	−0.433	0.157	−2.747	
Sex effect, β_{22}	0.312	0.165	1.891	
Momspeech effect, β_{23}	0.793	0.334	2.370	
Study × sex, β_{24}	0.144	0.165	0.876	
Study × speech, β_{25}	−0.158	0.334	−0.473	
Random Effect	*Variance Component*	*df*	χ^2	*p value*
Growth rate, r_{1i}	18.778	22	39.547	0.010
Acceleration, r_{2i}	0.282	16	39.864	0.001
Level-1 error, e_{ti}	707.156			
Deviance = 1,284.3 with 4 df[a]				

a. The deviance statistics in Tables 6.6 through 6.8 cannot be compared because the fixed effects vary across these three models (see Chapter 3).

ance in the acceleration parameters, π_{2i}, was reduced to .282 from the total parameter variance of .685 estimated in the unconditional model (Table 6.7). Almost 59% of the total variability in individual acceleration, [(.685 − .282)/.685)], was associated with study-group, child-sex, and maternal-speech effects.

In general, the hierarchical analysis provided strong evidence of effects for maternal speech and child's sex on early vocabulary acquisition. The residual variability in vocabulary acceleration after controlling only for study group (i.e., a reduced version of Equation 6.18b where only the STUDY variable was included) was .551. When the nonsignificant interaction terms were deleted from Equation 6.18b and the final model reestimated, the residual variability in π_{2i} was .257. Comparing these results indicates that an estimated 53.4% of the remaining variability in acceleration parameters after controlling for study group was associated with child's sex and maternal speech.

Some Other Growth Models

The procedures illustrated in the previous two sections generalize directly to more complex growth models. In principle, a polynomial of any degree can be fitted and tested as long as the time series is sufficiently long. For at least some Level-2 units (e.g., children in the above application), the number of observations, T_i, must exceed the number of random parameters, $P + 1$, specified in the individual growth model (Equation 6.1). So long as this is true, however, other units that fail to meet this criterion can be still be included in the analysis. (See Chapter 10 for technical details of estimation when some units have insufficient data for separate OLS estimation.)

Alternative age metrics can also be easily accomodated by transforming either the outcome or the age variable first, and then proceeding as above. For example, $(Y_{ti})^{1/2}$ could have been used as the outcome variable in the vocabulary study and a linear growth model posed for this square-root metric. In general, we suggest visual examination of the individual time series and mean trajectories to identify possible models that might be fitted to the data. We note that the mean growth curve and the individual growth curves can have different forms. For example, in fitting a quadratic model to the data, we might find that some individual trajectories with positive curvatures cancel out others with negative curvatures. In this case, a line might be a fine description for the mean curve but an inadequate representation for individual growth. It is for this reason that we examined in the random-coefficient regression model both the mean growth parameters and the amount of individual variation around them.

Piecewise Linear Growth Models

When an exploratory examination of the data suggests nonlinearity, one option to consider is breaking up the curvilinear growth trajectories into separate linear components. This approach is particular attractive where, for substantive reasons, we wish to compare growth rates during two different periods. Possible research questions include "Is growth more variable in period 1 than period 2?" and "Are the correlates of growth different in the two periods?"

For example, Frank and Seltzer (1990) analyzed data on the acquisition of reading ability for students in the Chicago public schools in Grades 1 through 6. Each student was scheduled to be tested at the end of each academic year, but for a variety of logistical reasons some children missed one or more testing occasions. Exploratory analysis of growth trajectories for a sample of individual students and selected subgroups by gender, race, and school membership indicated that the acquisition of reading ability in Grades 1 through 3 followed a different pattern than in Grades 4 and beyond. Growth rates appeared faster and more variable in the early grades

TABLE 6.9 Some Possible Coding Schemes for a Two-Piece Linear Model (Reading Achievement Example)

(a) Two-Rate model

	Grades 1	2	3	4	5	6	Interpretation of πs:
a_{1t}	0	1	2	2	2	2	π_1 growth rate period 1
a_{2t}	0	0	0	1	2	3	π_2 growth rate period 2
							π_0 status Grade 1
a_{1t}	−2	−1	0	0	0	0	π_1 growth rate period 1
a_{2t}	0	0	0	1	2	3	π_2 growth rate period 2
							π_0 status Grade 3

(b) Increment (Decrement) Model

	Grades 1	2	3	4	5	6	Interpretation of πs:
a_{1t}	0	1	2	3	4	5	π_1 base growth rate
a_{2t}	0	0	0	1	2	3	π_2 increment (decrement) to growth in period 2
							π_0 status Grade 1
a_{1t}	−2	−1	0	1	2	3	π_1 base growth rate
a_{2t}	0	0	0	1	2	3	π_2 increment (decrement) to growth in period 2
							π_0 status Grade 3

than later. These results suggested the possibility of a two-piece linear growth model: one individual growth rate for period 1, and a second, different growth rate for period 2. Specifically, the Level-1 model was of the form

$$Y_{ti} = \pi_{0i} + \pi_{1i}a_{1ti} + \pi_{2i}a_{2ti} + e_{ti} \qquad [6.19]$$

where a_{1ti} and a_{2ti} are coded variables, as defined in Table 6.9a, to represent the piecewise regression.

Although the coding schemes of Table 6.9 may seem a bit odd at first glance, their operation can be easily seen through a simple substitution of values for a_{1t} and a_{2t} into Equation 6.19 to generate predicted outcomes. For example, using the first coding scheme in Table 6.9a, the predicted status at each grade level would be π_0, $\pi_0 + \pi_1$, $\pi_0 + 2\pi_1$, $\pi_0 + 2\pi_1 + \pi_2$, $\pi_0 + 2\pi_1 + 2\pi_2$, and $\pi_0 + 2\pi_1 + 3\pi_2$, respectively. Thus, the growth rate is

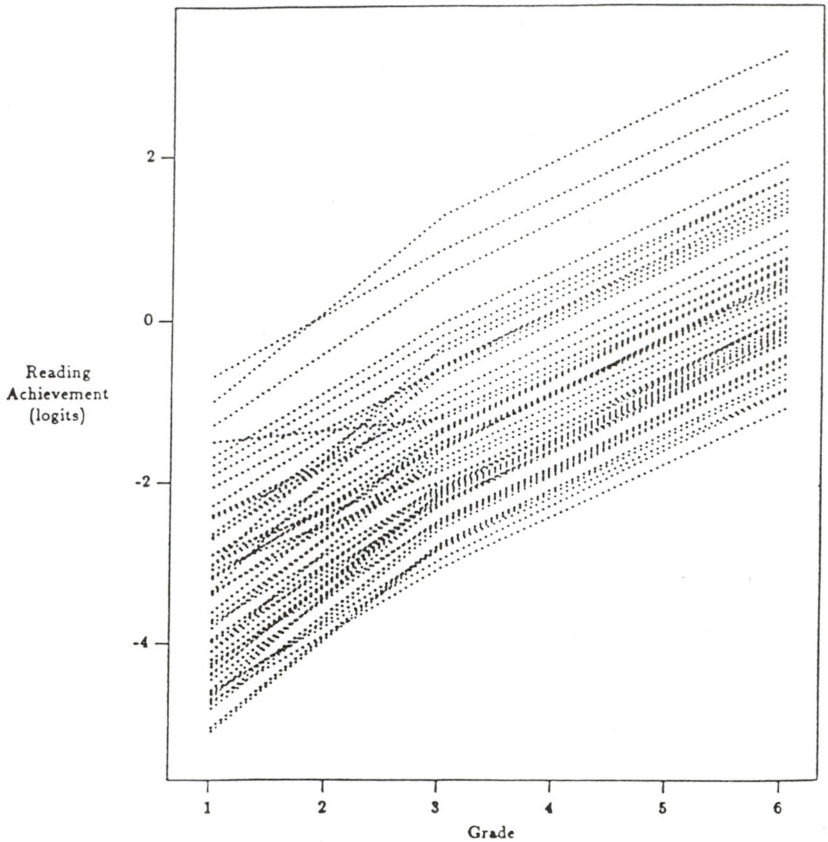

Figure 6.2. A Sample of Reading Achievement Trajectories (empirical Bayes estimates, Chicago public schools data)

π_1 per grade during Grades 2 and 3, and π_2 per grade during Grades 4, 5, and 6.

Figure 6.2 presents a sample of 50 fitted growth trajectories reported by Frank and Seltzer (1990), based on Equation 6.19 and an unconditional Level-2 model with π_{0i}, π_{1i}, and π_{2i} random. The trajectories displayed are empirical Bayes or shrunken estimates based on the formula

$$\pi_i^* = \Lambda_i \hat{\pi}_i + (\mathbf{I} - \Lambda_i)\beta^* \quad [6.20]$$

where

$\hat{\pi}_i$ is a 3 by 1 vector of OLS estimates $(\hat{\pi}_{0i}, \hat{\pi}_{1i}, \hat{\pi}_{2i})'$ for each individual's growth parameter based only on that person's data;

β^* is a 3 by 1 vector containing estimates of the three parameters describing the mean growth trajectory; and

Λ_i is a 3 by 3 multivariate reliability matrix for subject i (as introduced in Chapter 3).

We note that the two-piece linear growth model in Equation 6.19 could have been parameterized as base rate for the entire period (Grades 1 through 6) and increment (or decrement) to the base rate in either period 1 or 2. This would have been accomplished by using an alternative coding scheme for a_{1t} and a_{2t} as detailed in Table 6.9b.

Time-Varying Covariates

In some applications we may have other Level-1 predictors, besides age or time, that explain variation in Y_{ti} . We term these *time-varying covariates.* For example, suppose in the reading achievement research that we had a measure of student absenteeism in each grade. Presumably, if a child is absent a good deal during a particular academic year, then the achievement for that child at year end might be somewhat below the value predicted by that individual's growth trajectory. This temporal variation can be captured by adding a measure of student's absenteeism at each grade to the Level-1 model of Equation 6.19. Specifically, if we define a_{3ti} as the student's absenteeism in a particular period, the Level-1 model would be

$$Y_{ti} = \pi_{0i} + \pi_{1i}a_{1ti} + \pi_{2i}a_{2ti} + \pi_{3i}a_{3ti} + e_{ti}. \qquad [6.21]$$

Because student absenteeism was intended as a covariate, it would normally be specified at Level 2 as fixed (i.e., $\pi_{3i} = \gamma_{30}$). However, it also could be specified as nonrandomly varying, allowing, for example, for different effects in Grades 1 through 3 versus Grades 4 and above. It could even be specified as random. We illustrate use of a time-varying covariate in Chapter 8 in a three-level analysis of student learning and summer-drop-off effects.

Using an Hierarchical Model to Predict Future Status

Our primary purpose in this chapter has been to demonstrate how studies of change can be constructively pursued by means of hierarchical linear models. We have illustrated the formulation and interpretation of some commonly employed Level-1 models and the testing of growth hypotheses.

Another advantage of hierarchical models, as noted in Chapters 1 and 3, is that the empirical Bayes estimates of the Level-1 coefficients, such as the growth parameters in Equation 6.20, have smaller mean squared error than do the OLS estimates that use only the separate time trend data from each individual. This feature can prove advantageous when the individual estimates are employed (e.g., to predict future status). We now illustrate this feature with a subset of the vocabulary data analyzed earlier.

For purposes of this comparision we used the study data through 22 months as a basis for predicting vocabulary size at 24 months. We then compared these predicted values with the actual observed values. Specifically, we posed a Level-1 model as in Equation 6.15 and an unconditional Level-2 model as in Equation 6.17. We compared the predictions at 24 months based on the empirical Bayes estimates of π_{pi} (see Equation 6.20) with those based on OLS estimation of a no-intercept quadratic regression for each child. The results are presented in Table 6.10. The first column presents the measured vocabulary size for the 22 children at 24 months. The second and third columns are the OLS and empirical Bayes predictions. The corresponding prediction errors appear in columns 4 and 5.

Notice that, as expected, the standard deviation of the prediction errors based on the empirical Bayes estimates is smaller than for OLS (66.51 versus 75.30). This is mainly achieved because empirical Bayes provides somewhat better predictions for the extreme cases, such as 4, 7, 10, 18, and especially 21. The empirical Bayes advantage in this particular application is modest because the OLS estimates are fairly reliable, given the careful measurement procedures employed in this study. For the model employed in this prediction application, the hierarchical analysis estimated the reliability of the linear rate component at .51 and the quadratic term at .88. This can also be seen in Figure 6.1, where the individual OLS quadratic trajectories provide a close fit to the data.

In general, the empirical Bayes advantage over OLS would be greater in applications where the time trend data have more random noise. Even so, the conventional caution still applies. Polynomial growth models can

TABLE 6.10 Comparison of Hierarchical Model Predictions with Ordinary Least Squares at 24 Months

Case	*Actual Vocabulary Size*	*OLS Prediction*	*Empirical Bayes Prediction*	*OLS Error*	*Empirical Bayes Error*
1	139.00	126.649	127.898	12.351	11.102
2	449.00	505.802	512.202	–56.802	–63.202
3	142.00	111.458	111.028	30.542	30.972
4	579.00	723.594	702.335	–144.594	–123.335
5	317.00	326.472	311.864	–9.472	5.136
6	78.00	56.648	55.519	21.352	22.481
7	577.00	703.864	690.083	–126.864	–113.083
8	491.00	489.922	492.341	1.078	–1.341
9	595.00	634.180	656.442	–39.180	–61.442
10	604.00	727.508	715.186	–123.508	–111.186
11	137.00	145.040	138.352	–8.040	–1.352
12	350.00	366.000	346.939	–16.000	3.061
13	149.00	126.007	134.250	22.993	14.750
14	56.00	6.007	28.904	49.993	27.096
15	188.00	186.000	239.329	2.000	–51.329
16	172.00	228.007	240.512	–56.007	–68.512
17	240.00	174.007	190.903	65.993	49.097
18	292.00	153.007	167.123	138.993	124.877
19	99.00	111.007	127.636	–12.007	–28.636
20	142.00	174.000	176.779	–32.000	–34.779
21	265.00	120.000	163.448	145.000	101.552
22	329.00	432.007	432.892	–103.007	–103.892
Root mean square error of prediction				75.30	66.51

provide reliable predictions only for time points that are relatively near to the time points represented in the data. In our example, prediction to age 24 months seemed reasonable. Predictors much beyond 24 months, however, might not be trustworthy.

Notes

1. The notion that each person has a unique set of reliabilities may seem strange in the light of classical measurement theory, which defines reliability as a characteristic of a measurement instrument applied to a population. The classical definition assumes, however, that a standard instrument has been applied to all persons sampled. In more modern applications, such as tailored testing, each person may receive a somewhat different set of test items.

Analogous to the current situation, we can define and estimate the reliability of the measurement process as it applies to each person.

2. Note, there is some evidence in the data of heterogeneity of Level-1 errors as a function of Y_{ti}. Not surprisingly, the Level-1 residual variability is smaller when vocabulary size is small. Because the heterogeneity does not materially effect the key results reported here, we have chosen to ignore it in this illustration.

7 Applications in Meta-Analysis and Other Cases Where Level-1 Variances Are Known

- Introduction
- Formulating Models for Meta-Analysis
- Example: The Effect of Teacher Expectancy on Pupil IQ
- Other Level-1 Variance-Known Problems
- The Multivariate *V*-Known Model

Introduction

There has been a recent surge of interest in quantitative methods for summarizing results from a series of related studies. In this form of inquiry, called *meta-analysis* (Glass, 1976), individual studies conducting tests of the same hypothesis become cases in a "study of the studies."

A key question in meta-analysis is the consistency of study results. If each implementation of a new experimental treatment produces the same effect, it is sensible to summarize the entire stream of studies by a single common-effect size estimate. However, if the study results are inconsistent, so that the magnitude of the treatment effect varies from study to study, the meta-analyst's task becomes more complicated. Hunter and Schmidt (1990) advocate estimating both the mean and the standard deviation of the true-effect sizes. Hedges (1982; see also Hedges & Olkin, 1985) provides methods for testing a series of models formulated to account for the variation in the true-effect sizes. This approach encourages investigators to formulate and test explanations for *why* study results vary. What characteristics of treatment implementation, subject background, study context, or study methodology might predict differences in study results?

The central difficulty in assessing consistency of study results and in accounting for inconsistency is that even when every study produces a common "true" effect, the estimates of that effect will vary from study to study as a result of sampling error. For example, in a true experiment, the estimated treatment effect is influenced both by the treatment's effectiveness and by random differences between the experimental and control group. Therefore, variations will appear in a set of estimated effects from a series of studies, even if the studies are identically designed and implemented, and even if the studies draw random samples from the same population. The task facing the meta-analyst is to distinguish between components of variation in the estimated effects, where one component arises from sampling error, and a second component represents inconsistency in the effect-size parameters.

If inconsistency is discovered, one may formulate a model to account for it. The question of components of variation again arises: Of the residual variation in the estimated study effects, how much reflects sampling error, and how much represents true inconsistency that the model fails to explain?

The hierarchical model provides a useful framework for addressing the problem of components of variation in meta-analysis. This model enables the meta-analyst (a) to estimate the average effect size across a set of studies; (b) to estimate the variance of the effect-size parameters (as distinguished from the variance of the estimates); (c) to pose and test a series of linear models to explain variation in the effect-size parameters; (d) to estimate the residual variance of the effect-size parameters for each linear model; and (e) to use information from all studies to derive empirical Bayes estimates of each study's effect.

This last goal is important when research interest focuses on the true effect sizes for particular studies. We illustrate such a case later (see "Unconditional Analysis").

The Hierarchical Structure of Meta-Analytic Data

It is natural to apply hierarchical linear models to meta-analytic data because such data are hierarchically structured: subjects are "nested" within studies. Models are needed that take into account variation at the subject and the study level. Indeed, each study's investigator seeks to learn about sources of variation among subjects. It is the task of the meta-analyst to sort out variation across studies.

Applications discussed previously in this book may themselves be viewed as meta-analyses. In Chapter 5, for example, we conceived of each school as characterized by a relationship between student background and student mathematics achievement. The Level-2 model enabled us to compare differences in this relationship across schools. In a sense, each school yielded a study of the relationship between social background and achievement. The Level-2 model enabled us to combine results from these "studies," to assess consistency in that relationship, and to account for inconsistency. Similarly, the growth examples presented in Chapter 6 may be viewed as meta-analytic. Each child's data provides a "study" of the relationship between time and an outcome. By combining data across children we are able to study variation in that relationship.

Two features, however, distinguish meta-analysis from the kinds of application described in previous chapters. First, in meta-analysis, the raw data from each study are rarely available. Instead, only summary statistics published in research reports are accessible to the meta-analyst. Second, different studies typically use different outcome measures, even though these are viewed as measures of the same construct. For example, in the series of studies of teacher expectancy on pupil IQ reported below, investigators used different IQ tests, each measured on a different scale.

To cope with these problems, meta-analysts have employed a variety of standardized measures of effect, the most common being standardized mean differences and correlation coefficients. Using standardized measures of effect translates each study's results to a common scale so that they may be compared.

Extensions to Other Level-1 "Variance-Known" Problems

If these standardized effect measures are based on moderately large samples, say 30 or more cases per study, the sampling distribution of the statistics will be approximately normally distributed with a sampling variance that can be assumed known (see below). Thus, from a statistical point of view, meta-analysis presents the analyst with a series of independent effect estimates, each normally distributed with known variance at Level 1.

Interestingly, a variety of other research problems, in addition to meta-analysis, have this same structure. A single statistic (say a standard deviation, proportion, or correlation) is available from each of many contexts and the goal is to compare these statistics. Often a transformation of the statistic justifies the assumptions of normality and known variance. We label such cases *Level-1 variance-known* (or *V-known*) applications. Meta-analysis thus represents a particular and important instance of this type.

Organization of this Chapter

We first consider applications of the hierarchical linear model to meta-analyses in which a single standardized effect is available for each of a series of studies. The next section presents the formulation of the model, and the one following illustrates its application in research on the effect of teacher expectancy on pupil IQ. The following section generalizes the meta-analytic methods to the broader class of "Level-1 variance-known" problems, and last section considers the case of multiple-outcome variables at Level 1.

Formulating Models for Meta-Analysis

Standardized Mean Differences

As mentioned, a meta-analyst rarely has access to the raw data from each study. Instead, data on subjects from each study are summarized by a statistic. This statistic characterizes the magnitude of an effect or the strength of association between variables. We denote this statistic d_j as the "effect-size estimate" for study j.

In many applications, d_j is the standardized mean difference between an experimental group and a control:

$$d_j = (\bar{Y}_{Ej} - \bar{Y}_{Cj})/S_j\,, \qquad [7.1]$$

where

$\bar{Y}_{Ej}$ is the mean outcome for the experimental group;
$\bar{Y}_{Cj}$ is the mean outcome for the control group; and
S_j is the pooled, within-group standard deviation.

Each d_j estimates the population mean difference between the experimental and control groups in standard deviation units. For example, d_j = .50 indicates that experimental subjects in study j were estimated to score half a standard deviation higher, on average, than controls.

The statistic d_j may be viewed as estimating the corresponding population parameter, δ_j, where

$$\delta_j = (\mu_{Ej} - \mu_{Cj})/\sigma_j\,. \qquad [7.2]$$

Of course, the accuracy of d_j as an estimate of δ_j depends on the experimental- and control-group sample sizes, n_{Ej} and n_{Cj}, respectively. Hedges (1981) showed that for a fixed value of δ_j, the statistic d_j is approximately unbiased and normally distributed with variance V_j, that is,

$$d_j \mid \delta_j \sim \mathrm{N}(\delta_j,\ V_j) \qquad [7.3]$$

with

$$V_j = (n_{Ej} + n_{Cj})/(n_{Ej}n_{Cj}) + \delta_j^2/[2(n_{Ej} + n_{Cj})]\,. \qquad [7.4]$$

Actually, d_j is not exactly unbiased. Hedges (1981) also presents a correction for bias that is especially helpful when n_{Ej} or n_{Cj} is very small. It is common to substitute d_j for δ_j in Equation 7.4 and then to assume V_j is "known."[1]

Level-1 (Within-Studies) Model

The Level-1 model is simply

$$d_j = \delta_j + e_j \qquad [7.5]$$

for studies $j = 1, \ldots, J$, where e_j is the sampling error associated with d_j as an estimate of δ_j and for which we assume $e_j \sim \mathrm{N}(0, V_j)$.

We note that Equation 7.5 generalizes to meta-analyses using effect-size measures other than standardized mean differences. That is, d_j is any standardized effect measure from study j; δ_j is the corresponding parameter; and V_j is the sampling variance of d_j as an estimate of δ_j. For example, suppose a correlation, r_j, is reported for a series of studies. The standardized effect measure, d_j, is

$$d_j = \frac{1}{2}\log[(1 + r_j)/(1 - r_j)]\,, \qquad [7.6]$$

and the corresponding parameter is

$$\delta_j = \frac{1}{2}\log[(1 + \rho_j)/(1 - \rho_j)]\,. \qquad [7.7]$$

The sampling variance of d_j is

$$V_j = 1/(n_j - 3)\,, \qquad [7.8]$$

where

r_j is the sample correlation between two variables observed in study j;
ρ_j is the corresponding population correlation; and
n_j is the sample size is study j.

In this case d_j is "Fisher's r to Z" transformation. Note that V_j is independent of the unknown ρ_j, which is an advantage.

Level-2 (Between-Studies) Model

In the Level-2 model, the true unknown-effect size, δ_j, depends on study characteristics and a Level-2 random error:

$$\delta_j = \gamma_0 + \gamma_1 W_{1j} + \gamma_2 W_{2j} + \ldots + \gamma_S W_{Sj} + u_j \qquad [7.9]$$

$$= \gamma_0 + \sum_s \gamma_s W_{sj} + u_j ,$$

where

$W_{1j}, \ldots, W_{Sj}$ are study characteristics predicting these effect sizes;
$\gamma_0, \ldots, \gamma_S$ are regression coefficients; and
u_j is a Level-2 random error for which we assume $u_j \sim \mathrm{N}(0, \tau)$.

Combined Model

Substituting Equation 7.9 into Equation 7.5 yields the single model for the observed d_j :

$$d_j = \gamma_0 + \sum_s \gamma_s W_{sj} + u_j + e_j , \qquad [7.10]$$

from which it is clear that d_j is normally distributed,

$$d_j \sim \mathrm{N}(\gamma_0 + \sum_s \gamma_s W_{sj} ,\ \tau + V_j) ,$$

and for simplicity we denote

$$\mathrm{Var}(d_j) = \tau + V_j = \Delta_j \,. \qquad [7.11]$$

Estimation

Estimation follows the basic procedure outlined in Chapter 3, except that it simplifies because each V_j is assumed known. Now there is only one variance component to estimate, τ. Given a maximum likelihood estimate of τ, the Level-2 coefficients (the γs) are estimated by means of weighted least squares where the weights are the precisions, Δ_j^{-1}, as previously seen in Equation 3.17.

The empirical Bayes estimator, δ_j^*, of each study's effect, δ_j, is

$$\delta_j^* = \lambda_j d_j + (1 - \lambda_j)(\hat{\gamma}_0 + \sum_s \hat{\gamma}_s W_{sj}) \,, \qquad [7.12]$$

where $\lambda_j = \tau/(\tau + V_j)$. See Chapter 10 for details on the estimation algorithm.

Example: The Effect of Teacher Expectancy on Pupil IQ

The hypothesis that teachers' expectations influence pupils' intellectual development as measured by IQ (intelligence quotient) scores has been the source of sustained and acrimonious controversy for over 20 years. (See, for example, Wineburg's [1987] review and Rosenthal's [1987] response). Raudenbush (1984b) was able to find 19 reports of experiments testing this hypothesis. In these studies, the experimental group consisted of children for whom teachers were encouraged to have "high" expectations. The controls were children for whom no particular expectations were encouraged. The studies, their sample sizes, and the reported standardized mean differences are presented in Table 7.1.

The reported effect sizes seem to vary a great deal, from −0.32 to 1.18. However, some of the most extreme results (e.g., Study 4) are based on studies with small samples and large standard errors (i.e., $V_j^{1/2}$). Because the estimated effects in Table 7.1 vary, in part because of sampling errors in each d_j, the total variation among the d_js is probably substantially greater than the variability among the unknown-effect parameters, the δ_js.

We perform two analyses below. The goal of the first analysis is to assess the variability in the true-effect parameters. The goal of the second is to account for that variation. Specifically, in the first analysis we estimate

TABLE 7.1 Experimental Studies of Teacher Expectancy Effects on Pupil IQ

Study	*Weeks of Prior Contact*	*Effect Size Estimate, dj*	*Standard Error of dj*	*Empirical Bayes Estimates, δ_j^* Unconditional Model*	*Conditional Model*
1. Rosenthal et al (1974)	2	0.03	0.125	0.05	0.09
2. Conn et al (1968)	3	0.12	0.147	0.10	−0.06
3. Jose & Cody (1971)	3	−0.14	0.167	−0.00	−0.06
4. Pellegrini & Hicks (1972)	0	1.18	0.373	0.22	0.41
5. Pellegrini & Hicks (1972)	0	0.26	0.369	0.11	0.41
6. Evans & Rosenthal (1969)	3	−0.06	0.103	−0.01	−0.06
7. Fielder et al (1971)	3	−0.02	0.103	0.02	−0.06
8. Claiborn (1969)	3	−0.32	0.220	−0.03	−0.06
9. Kester & Letchworth (1972)	0	0.27	0.164	0.16	0.41
10. Maxwell (1970)	1	0.80	0.251	0.25	0.25
11. Carter (1970)	0	0.54	0.302	0.16	0.41
12. Flowers (1966)	0	0.18	0.223	0.11	0.41
13. Keshock (1970)	1	−0.02	0.289	0.06	0.25
14. Henrickson (1970)	2	0.23	0.290	0.11	0.09
15. Fine (1972)	3	−0.18	0.159	−0.03	−0.06
16. Greiger (1970)	3	−0.06	0.167	0.03	−0.06
17. Rosenthal & Jacobson (1968)	1	0.30	0.139	0.19	0.25
18. Fleming & Anttonen (1971)	2	0.07	0.094	0.07	0.09
19. Ginsburg (1970)	3	−0.07	0.174	0.02	−0.06

the mean and variance of the true effects and the empirical Bayes estimates of each study's effect size. In the second analysis, we formulate a model to predict the effect sizes, to estimate the residual variance in the true effects, and to compute new empirical Bayes estimates for each study.

Unconditional Analysis

Using Equation 7.5, the Level-1 model is

$$d_j = \delta_j + e_j \qquad [7.13]$$

where d_j (as reported in column 3 of Table 7.1) is the estimated standardized mean difference in study j between experimental children (those assigned to a "high expectancy" condition) and control children, and δ_j is the corresponding parameter value. Hence, each d_j estimates δ_j with a known sampling variance, V_j (given by Equation 7.4 with d_j substituted for δ_j).

TABLE 7.2 Unconditional Model for the Meta-Analysis of Teacher Expectancy Effects

Fixed Effect	*Coefficient*	*se*	*t ratio*	
Grand mean, γ_0	0.083	0.052	1.62	
Random Effect	*Variance Component*	*df*	χ^2	*p value*
True effect sizes, δ_j	0.019	18	35.85	.009

In an unconditional analysis, no predictors are involved in the Level-2 model. We view the true-effect sizes, δ_j, as simply varying around a grand mean, γ_0, plus a Level-2 error, u_j . Thus, at Level 2,

$$\delta_j = \gamma_0 + u_j\,. \qquad [7.14]$$

Substituting Equation 7.14 into Equation 7.13 yields the combined model

$$d_j = \gamma_0 + u_j + e_j\,, \qquad [7.15]$$

implying $d_j \sim \mathrm{N}(\gamma_0, \Delta_j)$ with $\Delta_j = \tau + V_j$.

Results. Table 7.2 presents estimates of the grand mean, γ_0, and Level-2 variance, τ. The estimated grand-mean effect size is small, $\hat{\gamma}_0 = .083$, implying that on average experimental students scored about .083 standard deviation units above the controls. However, the estimated variance of the effect parameters is $\hat{\tau} = .019$. This corresponds to a standard deviation of .138, which implies that important variability exists in the true-effect sizes. For example, an effect one standard deviation above the average would be $\delta_j = .22$, which is of nontrivial magnitude.

One might wonder whether the estimate $\hat{\tau} = .019$ is a chance result. Using the procedure introduced in Chapter 3, we test this null hypothesis, H_0: $\tau = 0$, with the statistic

$$H = \sum V_j^{-1}(d_j - \bar{d}.)^2\,, \qquad [7.16]$$

where $\bar{d}. = \Sigma V_j^{-1} d_j / \Sigma V_j^{-1}$. This statistic has a χ^2 distribution with $J - 1$ degrees of freedom, and is the "*H* statistic" discussed by Hedges (1982) and Rosenthal and Rubin (1982). Here $H = 35.85$, df = 18, $p < .01$, implying that studies do vary significantly in their effects.

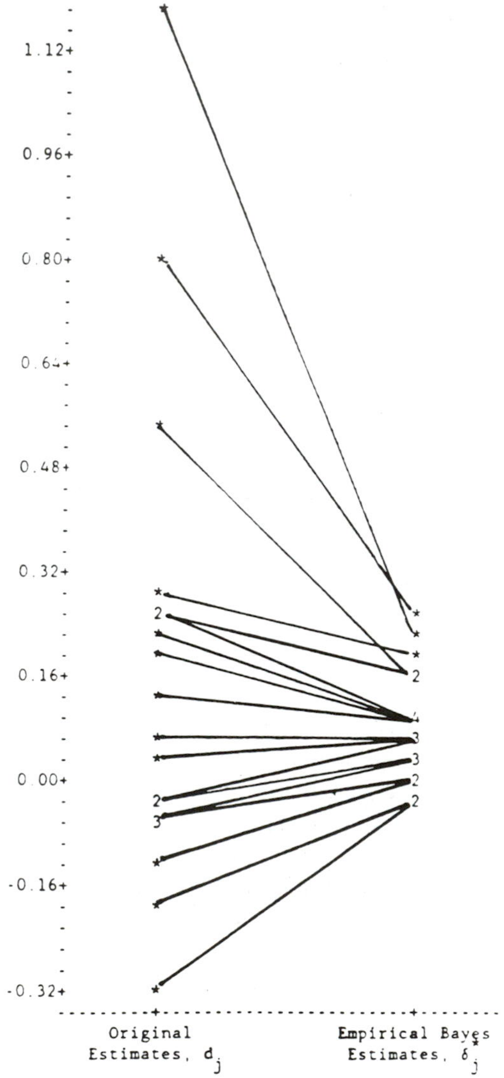

Figure 7.1. Comparison Between Original Standardized Mean Difference Estimates, d_j, and Empirical Bayes Estimates, δ_j^*, Based on the Unconditional Model

Table 7.1 (column 5) lists the empirical Bayes estimates, $d_j^* = \lambda_j d_j + (1 - \lambda_j)\,\hat{\gamma}_0$, for each study. A comparison between these estimates and the original estimates, d_j, is displayed in Figure 7.1. Lines connect the two estimates from each study. Notice that the empirical Bayes estimates are substantially more concentrated about $\hat{\gamma}_0 = .083$ than are the d_j values. Some values of d_j, especially those with small samples and those far from .083, have experienced substantial shrinkage. For example, in Study 4 the d_4 of 1.18 is "shrunk" to 0.22.

Conditional Analysis

The "expectancy" treatment depended upon deception for its effectiveness. In some cases experimenters presented teachers with a list of pupils who allegedly displayed potential for dramatic intellectual growth. In fact these "high expectancy" pupils had been assigned at random to the experimental condition. In other cases, researchers presented teachers with inflated IQs for pupils assigned at random to the high expectancy condition. In either case, if the deception failed and teachers refused to believe the experimenter's information, no treatment effect could have been observed, simply because no treatment had been implemented. Such an implementation failure does not refute expectancy theory, which can only be tested if the experimenters had successfully modified the teachers' expectations for their students.

Raudenbush (1984) hypothesized that the variability in teacher expectancy effects might be related to how well the teachers knew their pupils at the time they encountered the deceptive information, as indicated by the number of weeks of pupil-teacher contact prior to the experiment. This hypothesis was based on past research suggesting that when teachers know their pupils well, they are likely to ignore new information that is discrepant from their established views.

The effect sizes from the 19 studies are plotted against weeks of pupil-teacher contact prior to experiment in Figure 7.2. This graphical display is consistent with Raudenbush's (1984) hypothesis. Estimation of a conditional model provides an explicit test of this hypothesis.

The Level-1 model remains unchanged (Equation 7.5). At Level 2, we now use the information about prior contact between teachers and children to predict the effect sizes. The model is

$$\delta_j = \gamma_0 + \gamma_1(\text{WEEKS})_j + u_j\,, \qquad [7.17]$$

where

γ_0 is the expected effect size for a study with no prior teacher-pupil contact;

γ_1 is the expected difference in effect size between two studies differing by one week in prior contact;

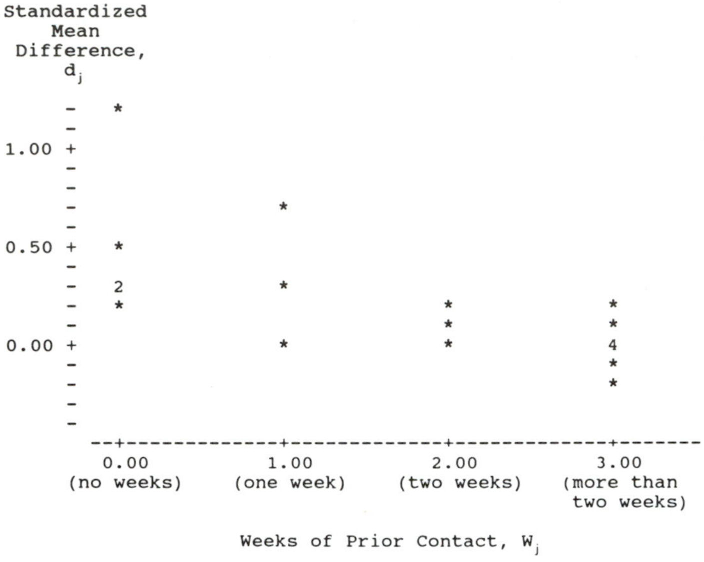

Figure 7.2. Plot of Observed Standardized Mean Difference, d_j (vertical axis), as a Function of Weeks of Prior Teacher-Pupil Contact, W_j (horizontal axis)

TABLE 7.3 Conditional Model for the Meta-Analysis of Teacher Expectancy Effects

Fixed Effect	*Coefficient*	*se*	*t ratio*	
INTERCEPT, γ_0	0.407	0.087	4.67	
WEEKS, γ_1	−0.157	0.036	−4.38	
Random Effect	*Variance Component*	*df*	χ^2	*p value*
True effect size, δ_j	0.000	17	16.57	> 0.500

$(\text{WEEKS})_j$ is 0, 1, 2, or 3, respectively, if prior teacher-pupil contact had occurred for 0, 1, 2, or more than 2 weeks prior to the experiment; and

u_j is the residual effect size in study j unexplained by amount of prior content where $u_j \sim N(0, \tau)$.

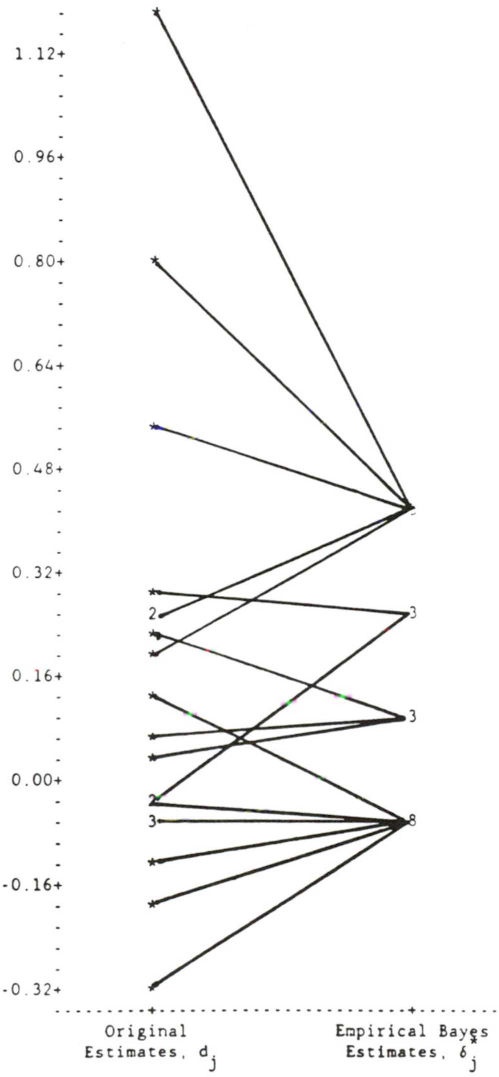

Figure 7.3. Comparison Between Original Standardized Mean Difference Estimates, d_j, and Empirical Bayes Estimates, δ_j^*, Based on a Conditional Model

We note that τ is now the residual or conditional variance of the effect sizes, that is, the variance of the true-effect-size residuals, $\delta_j - \gamma_0 - \gamma_1(\text{WEEKS})_j$.

Substituting Equation 7.17 into Equation 7.5 yields

$$d_j = \gamma_0 + \gamma_1(\text{WEEKS})_j + u_j + e_j\,, \tag{7.18}$$

implying $d_j \sim \text{N}[\gamma_0 + \gamma_1(\text{WEEKS})_j, \Delta_j]$, where $\Delta_j = \tau + V_j$ is the conditional variance in d_j after controlling for weeks of prior contact.

Results. Table 7.3 displays the estimates of γ_0, γ_1, and τ. The results indicate that treatment effects are smaller in those studies where teachers and students had prior contact. The largest predicted effects occur in studies with no prior teacher-pupil contact, $\hat{\gamma}_0 = .407$, $t = 4.67$. With each week of contact, the expected effect size diminishes by .157 (i.e., $\hat{\gamma}_1 = -.157$, $t = -4.38$). In studies with more than 2 weeks of prior contact, expected effects are near zero. Clearly, much of the variability in teacher-expectancy effects is accounted for by knowledge of the amount of prior contact. In fact, the maximum likelihood point estimate for the residual variation in δ_j after controlling for W_j was virtually zero.

The empirical Bayes estimates of δ_j^* under the model specified by Equation 7.18 are

$$\delta_j^* = \lambda_j d_j + (1 - \lambda_j)[\hat{\gamma}_0 + \hat{\gamma}_1(\text{WEEKS})_j]\,. \tag{7.19}$$

However, if $\hat{\tau} = 0$, then $\lambda_j = \tau/(\tau + V_j) = 0$ for all j, so that, in this case,

$$\delta_j^* = \hat{\gamma}_0 + \hat{\gamma}_1(\text{WEEKS})_j\,.$$

Figure 7.3 displays the shrinkage for each d_j toward δ_j^* under this model. (The empirical Bayes estimates of δ_j^* yielded by Equation 7.19 are located in Table 7.1, column 6.) This is another instance of *conditional* shrinkage (as introduced in Chapter 3 and previously illustrated in Chapter 4). In contrast with Figure 7.1, where each d_j was shrunk in the direction of the estimated grand mean of .083, now each d_j is shrunk toward a value that is conditional on the amount of prior contact. Because $(\text{WEEKS})_j$ can take on four values, the shrinkage is toward four points.

Other Level-1 Variance-Known Problems

The essential statistical features of meta-analysis applications that distinguish them from the others discussed in this book are two: Only summary data are available at Level 1; and the sampling variance, V_j, of the Level-1

TABLE 7.4 Some Univariate *V*-Known Cases

	Level-1 Parameter, δ_j	*Sample Estimator, d_j*	*Approximate Variance, V_j*
Standardized mean difference[a]	$(\mu_E - \mu_C)/\sigma$	$(\bar{Y}_E - \bar{Y}_C)/S$	$(n_E + n_C)/(n_E n_C) + d^2/[2(n_E + n_C)]$
Correlation	$\frac{1}{2}\log[(1+\rho)/(1-\rho)]$	$\frac{1}{2}\log[(1+r)/(1-r)]$	$1/(n-3)$
Logit[b]	$\log[p/(1-p)]$	$\log[\hat{p}/(1-\hat{p})]$	$n^{-1}\hat{p}^{-1}(1-\hat{p})^{-1}$
Log(sd)[c]	$\log(\sigma)$	$\log(S) + [1/(2f)]$	$1/(2f)$

a. Typically, σ is the pooled, within-treatment standard deviation, μ_E, μ_C are the experimental and control population means, and $\bar{Y}_E$ and $\bar{Y}_C$ the corresponding sample estimates.
b. We denote p as the proportion of subjects in the population with a given characteristic; $\hat{p}$ is the sample proportion.
c. We denote σ as a standard deviation, S as the sample estimate, and f as the degrees of freedom associated with S. Thus $f = n - 1$ when σ is a standard deviation, but $f = n - p$ when σ is the residual standard deviation estimated in a regression model with p parameters.

parameter estimate, d_j, can be assumed known. A variety of non-meta-analysis research problems have a similar structure. We refer to this class of problems, which includes meta-analysis as a specific case, as Level-1 *V*-known problems.

In a *V*-known analysis some statistic or set of statistics is computed separately for each study, organization, or other Level-2 unit. In addition to standardized mean differences, these statistics might be correlations, proportions, or standard deviations. Often a transformation of these statistics will improve the tenability of the normality and *V*-known assumptions. For example, the sample correlation, r, has a sampling distribution that is approximately normal, but this approximation is poor, especially when the parameter value is near −1.0 or 1.0. Fisher's transformation (Equation 7.6) has a sampling distribution that is much more nearly normal for nonzero values of ρ. Also, the sampling variance of r depends on the unknown value of ρ, whereas the sampling variance of Fisher's transformed r does not.

Table 7.4 lists some parameters that might be studied in a *V*-known analysis (column 1). For each parameter, its sample estimator (column 2) and approximate sampling variance (column 3) are provided. The hierarchical linear model of Equations 7.5 and 7.9 can be applied to any of these statistics.

Example: Correlates of Diversity

Most studies of school effects focus on *mean* differences. However, Raudenbush and Bryk (1987) sought to study school differences in the *disper-*

sion of mathematics achievement using a sample of data from the High School and Beyond survey, similar to that employed in Chapter 4. Of special interest was the question of whether school differences in organization, policy, and practice affect dispersion in achievement. Do large schools produce greater inequality than smaller schools? If students within a school differ widely in course taking, do wide differences in achievement result?

Choice of the Outcome. Such questions suggest using the standard deviation in mathematics achievement, computed separately for each school, as the outcome to be explained by differences in school-level predictors. To be credible, an analysis must also take into account that schools differ in their student composition. Therefore, the investigators first computed a *residual* standard deviation (i.e., the standard deviation for each school) after controlling for SES, minority status, sex, and a measure of prior academic background (see Raudenbush & Bryk [1987] for details).

The sampling distribution of a standard deviation (or a residual standard deviation) is approximately normal when samples are large, but positively skewed otherwise. Moreover, the sample variance of the sample standard deviation, S_j, is approximately $\sigma_j^2/(2n)$, which depends on the unknown population standard deviation, σ_j. A logarithmic transformation of S_j helps on both counts. The sampling distribution of $\log(S_j)$ is more nearly normal than that of S_j, and its sampling variance does not depend upon σ_j. Specifically, the investigators used the following:

$$\delta_j = \log(\sigma_j) \qquad [7.20]$$

$$d_j = \log(S_j) + 1/(2f_j)$$

$$V_j = 1/(2f_j)$$

where

S_j is the estimated residual standard deviation in school j;

σ_j is the population residual standard deviation for school j;

δ_j is the natural logarithm of σ_j;

f_j is the degrees of freedom associated with S_j;

d_j is an estimate of δ_j where $1/(2f_j)$ is a small-sample correction for a negative bias; and

V_j is the sampling variance of d_j.

As in the meta-analysis case, the Level-1 model (Equation 7.5) simply describes the sampling distribution of the estimate, d_j, where now d_j, δ_j, and V_j are defined as above.

At the school level, the dispersions, δ_j, were presumed to vary as a function of certain school characteristics. Specifically, smaller schools and schools where students were similar in math course taking were expected to have smaller variation in math achievement. Other school-level predictors included the heterogeneity of each school's student membership in terms of SES and academic background and public versus Catholic sector:

$$\delta_j = \gamma_0 + \gamma_1(\text{SD SES})_j + \gamma_2(\text{SD BACKGROUND})_j + \gamma_3(\text{SECTOR})_j \quad [7.21]$$
$$+ \gamma_4(\text{SIZE})_j + \gamma_5(\text{SD MATH COURSES})_j + u_j\,,$$

where

SD SES is the standard deviation of the socioeconomic status of students in the school;

SD BACKGROUND is the standard deviation of a measure of academic background of students in the school;

SECTOR is an indicator variable (0 = Public, 1 = Catholic);

SIZE is the number of pupils enrolled in the school;

SD MATH COURSES is the standard deviation of the number of math courses taken by students in the school; and

u_j is a residual for which we assume $u_j \sim N(0, \tau)$.

The results in Table 7.5 indicate that schools that were heterogeneous in student SES (i.e., large positive values on SD SES) tended to display greater diversity in math achievement ($\hat{\gamma}_1 = .231$, $t = 4.64$). Similarly, heterogeneity in students' academic background also predicted diversity in math achievement ($\hat{\gamma}_2 = .525$, $t = 5.78$). Catholic schools tended to have less dispersion in math achievement than did public schools ($\hat{\gamma}_3 = -.048$, $t = -2.05$). Larger schools were more diverse in math achievement than were smaller schools ($\hat{\gamma}_4 = 4.15 \times 10^{-5}$, $t = 2.47$). And schools characterized by substantial dispersion in math course taking were also more diverse in math achievement ($\hat{\gamma}_5 = .139$, $t = 4.06$).

The investigators noted that an earlier analysis, without SIZE and SD MATH COURSES included as predictors, had shown a substantial SECTOR effect with Catholic schools displaying much less variation in math achievement than public schools. In their final analysis (see Table 7.5),

TABLE 7.5 Effects of School Characteristics on Mathematics Dispersion

Fixed Effect	*Coefficient*	*se*	*t ratio*	
INTERCEPT, γ_0	1.324	0.1007	—	
SD SES, γ_1	0.231	0.0498	4.64	
SD BACKGROUND, γ_2	0.525	0.0909	5.78	
SECTOR, γ_3	−0.048	0.0235	−2.05	
SIZE, γ_4	4.15×10^{-5}	1.68×10^{-5}	2.47	
SD MATH, γ_5	0.139	0.0342	4.06	
Random Effect	*Variance Component*	*df*	χ^2	*p value*
True school dispersion, δ_j	0.0019	154	179.81	0.075

the estimate of the effect of SECTOR is much smaller. The investigators concluded that the smaller variation in achievement within Catholic schools was largely explainable by the small average size of those schools and by their more restrictive course-taking requirements.

It is useful at this point to test the hypothesis that all of the variability among δ_j has been accounted for in the model (i.e., H_0: $\tau = 0$). If this hypothesis were true, the only unexplained variation in the estimates, d_j, would have resulted from "estimation error" (i.e., imprecise estimation of the true dispersion, δ_j, by its sample estimate, d_j). The test statistic (see Equation 3.82) under such a null hypothesis is distributed as a χ^2 variate with $J - S - 1$ degrees of freedom. In this case, the statistic was 179.81 with $160 - 6 = 154$ df and $p = .075$. These results suggest that little if any variability in δ_j remains to be explained. Our model has, in fact, accounted for over 85% of the total variability in δ_j . (This variance-explained statistic is computed by comparing the τ estimates from the unconditional and conditional models using the procedures previously illustrated, as in Equation 5.6.)

The Multivariate *V*-Known Model

Level-1 Model

The multivariate model is a straightforward extension of the univariate case. Within each unit, Q parameters $\delta_{1j}, \delta_{2j}, \ldots, \delta_{Qj}$ are estimated by means of statistics $d_{1j}, d_{2j}, \ldots, d_{Qj}$. Conditional on the true parameters, the statistics are assumed to have a multivariate normal sampling distribution with variances V_{qqj} and covariances $V_{qq'j}$ for each pair of statistics q and q'. These variances and covariances are assumed known. The Level-1 model is then

$$d_{qj} = \delta_{qj} + e_{qj} \qquad [7.22]$$

for each of the $q = 1, \ldots, Q$ separate statistics.

Level-2 Model

The true parameter, δ_{qj}, varies as a function of predictor variables measured at Level 2, plus error:

$$\delta_{qj} = \gamma_{q0} + \sum_{s=1}^{S_q} \gamma_{qs} W_{sj} + u_{qj}, \qquad [7.23]$$

where

W_{sj} is a predictor variable;
γ_{qs} is the corresponding regression coefficient; and
u_{qj} is the unique effect for each unit j.

These effects are assumed multivariate normally distributed, each with a mean of 0, variance τ_{qq}, and with covariances of $\tau_{qq'}$ between u_{qj} and $u_{q'j}$. We note that a different set of Level-2 predictors can be specified for each δ_{qj}.

Like the univariate *V*-known model, the multivariate model can be applied to a variety of parameters. Table 7.6 presents some of these possibilities. Again, transformations can improve the tenability of the assumptions of multivariate normality for d_{qj} and of the assumption of known variances and covariances.

For an application of the multivariate *V*-known model, see Becker (1988), who utilized it in a meta-analysis of five mental practice studies. Each study produced two effect-size estimates. The analysis enabled her to take into account the Level-2 variation between studies in their effect sizes and to estimate the correlations between effect sizes computed from the same study.

TABLE 7.6 Some Multivariate *V*-Known Cases[a]

Level-1 Parameters, δ_q	*Sample Estimators,* d_q	*Variances,* V_{qq}	*Covariances,* $V_{qq'}$
Standardized mean difference[b, c]			
$(\mu_{Eq} - \mu_{Cq})/\sigma_q$	$(\bar{Y}_{Eq} - \bar{Y}_{Cq})/S_q$	$\sigma^2(d_q)$	$\frac{\rho_{qq'}(n_E + n_C)}{n_E n_C} + \frac{\rho_{qq'}^2 d_q d_{q'}}{2(n_E + n_C)}$
Multinomial proportion[d]			
$\log[p_q/(1 - p_q)]$	$\log[\hat{p}_q/(1 - \hat{p}_q)]$	$n^{-1}\hat{p}_q^{-1}(1 - \hat{p}_q)^{-1}$	$-n^{-1}(1 - \hat{p}_q)^{-1}(1 - \hat{p}_{q'})^{-1}$
Standard deviation[e]			
$\log(\sigma_q)$	$\log(S_q) + [1/(2f)]$	$1/(2f)$	$\rho_{qq'}^2/(2f)$

a. Each sample is said to produce Q statistics $q = 1, \ldots, Q$, where d_q and $d_{q'}$ are estimates of any pair of parameters δ_q and $\delta_{q'}$ respectively.
b. Here $\sigma^2(d_q) = (n_E + n_C)/(n_E n_C) + d_q^2/[2(n_E + n_C)]$.
c. Here $\rho_{qq'}$ is the correlation between the variates Y_q and $Y_{q'}$ used in estimates effect sizes d_q and $d_{q'}$ (Hedges & Olkin, 1985).
d. We assume that objects have fallen into category q with probability p_q where $\Sigma p_q = 1$.
e. Here $\rho_{qq'}$ is the correlation between variates Y_q and $Y_{q'}$ used in estimating σ_q and $\sigma_{q'}$.

Note

1. Hedges and Olkin (1983) present a transformation of d_j that eliminates the dependence of the sampling variance on δ_j. This transformation is especially useful when n_{Ej} or n_{Cj} is small.

8 Three-Level Models

- Formulating and Testing Three-Level Models
- Studying Individual Change Within Organizations
- A Measurement Model at Level 1
- Estimating Random Coefficients in Three-Level Models

We have demonstrated in the last three chapters how two-level models can be used to represent a wide range of psychological, sociological, and educational phenomena. We have also shown how these models address chronic methodological problems of multiple units of analysis, slopes-as-outcomes, assessing change, studying correlates of growth, and synthesizing research. Clearly, two-level models provide powerful new tools for behavioral and social scientists. Further, as we noted in Chapter 1, hierarchical data may involve any number of levels, not just two, and the basic modeling features and procedures for estimation and inference extend directly. This chapter introduces the three-level model and provides several illustrations from recent research.

Formulating and Testing Three-Level Models

In the interests of clarity, we introduce the three-level model in the context of a specific problem: a single cross-section of data with a three-level structure consisting of students (Level 1) nested within classrooms (Level 2) nested within schools (Level 3). Other common examples of three-level cross-sections involve individuals within households within geographic areas or workers within firms within different industries. Longitudinal applications involving three-level models are considered in the next section, and the following section considers an application to the study of latent variables.

A Fully Unconditional Model

The simplest three-level model is fully unconditional: that is, no predictor variables are specified at any level. Such a model represents how variation in an outcome measure is allocated across the three different levels (child, classroom, and school).

Child-Level Model. We model academic achievement for each child as a function of a classroom mean plus a random error:

$$Y_{ijk} = \pi_{0jk} + e_{ijk}, \qquad [8.1]$$

where

Y_{ijk} is the achievement of child i in classroom j and school k;
π_{0jk} is the mean achievement of classroom j in school k; and
e_{ijk} is a random "child effect," that is, the deviation of child ijk's score from the classroom mean. These effects are assumed normally distributed with a mean of 0 and variance σ^2.

The indices i, j, and k denote children, classrooms, and schools where there are

$i = 1, 2, \ldots, n_{jk}$ children within classroom j in school k;
$j = 1, 2, \ldots, J_k$ classrooms within school k; and
$k = 1, 2, \ldots, K$ schools.

Classroom-Level Model. We view each classroom mean, π_{0jk}, as an outcome varying randomly around some school mean:

$$\pi_{0jk} = \beta_{00k} + r_{0jk}, \qquad [8.2]$$

where

β_{00k} is the mean achievement in school k;
r_{0jk} is a random "classroom effect," that is, the deviation of classroom jk's mean from the school mean. These effects are assumed normally distributed with a

mean of 0 and variance τ_π. Within each of the K schools, the variability among classrooms is assumed the same.

School-Level Model. The Level-3 model represents the variability among schools. We view the school means, β_{00k}, as varying randomly around a grand mean:

$$\beta_{00k} = \gamma_{000} + u_{00k}, \quad [8.3]$$

where

γ_{000} is the grand mean;

u_{00k} is a random "school effect," that is, the deviation of school k's mean from the grand mean. These effects are assumed normally distributed with a mean of 0 and variance τ_β.

Variance Partitioning and Reliabilities

This simple three-level model partitions the total variability in the outcome Y_{ijk} into its three components: (Level 1) among children within classrooms, σ^2; (Level 2) among classrooms within schools, τ_π; and (Level 3) among schools, τ_β. It also allows us to estimate the proportion of variation that is within classrooms, among classrooms within schools, and among schools. That is,

$\sigma^2/(\sigma^2 + \tau_\pi + \tau_\beta)$ is the proportion of variance within classrooms; [8.4]

$\tau_\pi/(\sigma^2 + \tau_\pi + \tau_\beta)$ is the proportion of variance among classrooms within schools; and [8.5]

$\tau_\beta/(\sigma^2 + \tau_\pi + \tau_\beta)$ is the proportion of variance among schools. [8.6]

As in the two-level model, we can also examine the reliability of the least squares estimated coefficients. Now, however, reliabilities are estimated at two levels: classrooms, $\hat{\pi}_{0jk}$, and schools, $\hat{\beta}_{00k}$. For each classroom jk at Level 2,

$$\text{reliability}\,(\hat{\pi}_{0jk}) = \tau_\pi / [\tau_\pi + \sigma^2/n_{jk}] \quad [8.7]$$

is the reliability of a classroom sample mean for use in discrimination among classrooms within the same school. For any school k at Level 3,

$$\text{reliability } (\hat{\beta}_{00k}) = \frac{\tau_\beta}{\tau_\beta + \left\{\sum [\tau_\pi + \sigma^2/n_{jk}]^{-1}\right\}^{-1}} \quad [8.8]$$

is the reliability of the school's sample mean as an estimate of its true mean.

The averages of these reliabilities across classrooms (Equation 8.7) and schools (Equation 8.8) may be viewed as summary measures of the reliability of the class and school means, respectively.

Conditional Models

The fully unconditional model, Equations 8.1 to 8.3, allows estimation of variability associated with the three levels—students, classes, and schools. Presumably, part of the variability at each level can be explained or accounted for by measured variables at each level. That is, child background characteristics, classroom characteristics, and school characteristics could be utilized as predictors. Further, some of the relationships at the class and school levels may vary randomly among these units. For example, suppose that within classrooms child's sex was related to academic achievement. The magnitude of this sex difference might depend perhaps on certain teacher characteristics (e.g., teacher expectations or methods of classroom organization). In such a situation, the regression coefficient representing the sex effect might vary depending on characteristics of teachers and classrooms.

Similarly, regression coefficients can vary randomly at the school level. School intercepts would typically be random; regression slopes could also differ across schools. For example, the effect of student social class on achievement might vary from school to school. These possibilities encourage us to formulate a general structural model at each level.

General Level-1 Model. Within each classroom, we model student achievement as a function of student-level predictors plus a random student-level error:

$$Y_{ijk} = \pi_{0jk} + \pi_{1jk}a_{1ijk} + \pi_{2jk}a_{2ijk} + \ldots + \pi_{Pjk}a_{Pijk} + e_{ijk}, \quad [8.9]$$

where

Y_{ijk} is the achievement of child i in classroom j and school k;

π_{0jk} is the intercept for classroom j in school k;

a_{pijk} are $p = 1, \ldots, P$ child characteristics that predict achievement;

π_{pjk} are the corresponding Level-1 coefficients that indicate the direction and strength of association between each child characteristic, a_p, and the outcome in classroom jk; and

e_{ijk} is a Level-1 random effect that represents the deviation of child ijk's score from the predicted score based on the student-level model. These residual child effects are assumed normally distributed with a mean of 0 and variance σ^2.

General Level-2 Model. Each of the regression coefficients in the child-level model (including the intercept) can be viewed as either fixed, nonrandomly varying, or random. In addition, each Level-1 coefficient may be predicted or modeled by some classroom-level characteristics. These possibilities lead to the following general formulation of the model for variation among classrooms within schools. For each classroom effect, π_{pjk},

$$\pi_{pjk} = \beta_{p0k} + \sum_{q=1}^{Q_p} \beta_{pqk} X_{qjk} + r_{pjk}, \qquad [8.10]$$

where

β_{p0k} is the intercept for school k in modeling the classroom effect π_{pjk};

X_{qjk} is a classroom characteristic used as a predictor of the classroom effect π_{pjk} (note that each π_p may have a unique set of these Level-2 predictors X_{qjk}, $q = 1, \ldots, Q_p$);

β_{pqk} is the corresponding coefficient that represents the direction and strength of association between classroom characteristic X_{qjk} and π_{pjk}; and

r_{pjk} is a Level-2 random effect that represents the deviation of classroom jk's Level-1 coefficient, π_{pjk}, from its predicted value based on the classroom-level model.

Note that there are $P + 1$ equations in the Level-2 model: one for each of the Level-1 coefficients. The random effects in these equations are assumed to be correlated. Formally, we assume that the set of r_{pjk} are multivariate normally distributed each with a mean of 0, some variance τ_{pp}, and some covariance between elements r_{pjk} and $r_{p'jk}$ of $\tau_{pp'}$. We collect these variances and covariances in a matrix labeled $\mathbf{T}_\pi$ whose dimensionality depends on the number of Level-1 coefficients specified as random. For example, if a classroom effect, π_{pjk}, is specified as fixed, no Level-2 predictors would be included in Equation 8.10 for that effect and the corresponding r_{pjk} would be set to zero. If π_{pjk} is specified as nonrandomly varying, X variables would appear, but r_{pjk} would still be zero.

General Level-3 Model. A similar modeling process is replicated at the school level. Each Level-3 "outcome" (i.e., each β_{pq} coefficient) may be predicted by some school-level characteristic. That is,

$$\beta_{pqk} = \gamma_{pq0} + \sum_{s=1}^{S_{pq}} \gamma_{pqs} W_{sk} + u_{pqk}, \qquad [8.11]$$

where

γ_{pq0} is the intercept term in the school-level model for β_{pqk};

W_{sk} is a school characteristic used as a predictor for the school effect, β_{pqk} (note that each β_{pq} may have a unique set of the Level-3 predictors, W_{sk}, $s = 1, \ldots, S_{pq}$);

γ_{pqs} is the corresponding Level-3 coefficient that represents the direction and strength of association between school characteristic W_{sk} and β_{pqk}; and

u_{pqk} is a Level-3 random effect that represents the deviation of school k's coefficient, β_{pqk}, from its predicted value based on the school-level model.

Note that for each school there are $\Sigma_{p=0}^{P}(Q_p + 1)$ equations in the Level-3 model. The residuals from these equations are assumed multivariate normally distributed. Each is assumed to have a mean of zero, some variance, and covariance among all pairs of elements. Here too, the variances and covariances are collected in a matrix, $\mathbf{T}_\beta$. The dimensionality of $\mathbf{T}_\beta$ depends on the number of Level-2 coefficients that are specified as random. As was true for the π coefficients in the Level-2 model, each of the β coefficients (including the intercept) can be viewed as either fixed, nonrandomly varying, or random in the Level-3 model. If β_{pq} is specified as either fixed or nonrandomly varying, the corresponding u_{pqk} is assumed zero.

Many Alternative Modeling Possibilities

Between the fully unconditional model of Equations 8.1 to 8.3 and the full three-level model of Equations 8.9 through 8.11, many alternative formulations are possible. If we introduce predictors into the Level-1 model, specify all corresponding π parameters as random at Levels 2 and 3, and pose unconditional models at both levels, we would have a random-coefficient model with two sources of variation in the π coefficients: classrooms and schools.

Alternatively, perhaps only the intercept in the child-level model might be random with the child-level predictors having fixed effects at both Levels 2 and 3. If the child-level predictors were grand-mean centered (i.e., $a_{pijk} - \bar{a}_{p\cdots}$), then π_{0jk} would be the mean outcome in classroom jk adjusted for mean differences among classrooms on the child-level predictors. A variety of classroom and school variables may be introduced in the Level-2 and Level-3 models, respectively, to explain variability in these adjusted classroom means.

A different application might not have any predictors in the Level-1 model. That is, the Level-1 model might simply represent the variation of individuals around their classroom means. Variations in these classroom means may be fully modeled at Levels 2 and 3. In addition, some of the predictors introduced at Level 2 might be specified as random or nonrandomly varying to be subsequently modeled at Level 3. This application is illustrated later.

There are far more possibilities than we are able to illustrate or even fully describe here. In most general terms, the analyst using a three-level model may choose to (a) introduce predictors at each level (i.e., specify a structural model at each level); (b) specify whether the structural effects in each model (i.e., intercepts and slopes) are considered fixed, nonrandomly varying, or random at that level; and (c) specify alternative models for the variance-covariance components other that those assumed in Equations 8.9 to 8.11.

On the latter point, many options are possible for σ^2, $\mathbf{T}_\pi$, and $\mathbf{T}_\beta$ depending upon both the substantive hypotheses under study and the availability of sufficient data for estimating model parameters implied by these hypotheses. For example, the covariances among the classroom-level effects might have a different structure in each of the K schools—that is, a set of $\mathbf{T}_{\pi k}$, $k = 1, \ldots, K$, might be estimated. Alternatively, the Level-1 variation could be heteroscedastic among classrooms or schools—for example, a set of $k = 1, \ldots, K$ variances, σ_k^2, might be estimated. In general, the more complex the model specified, the greater the amount of data needed for estimation and inference.

Hypothesis Testing in the Three-Level Model

Testing hypotheses in three-level models is directly analogous to the procedures introduced in Chapter 3 for two-level models. In brief, we can pose and test hypotheses about fixed effects, random coefficients, and variance-covariance components at any of the three levels. For each of these types of hypotheses, both single and multiparameter tests are available.

Univariate tests for the fixed effects help the analyst decide which specific coefficients are needed. Multiparameter tests for the fixed effects enable both *omnibus tests* and a priori comparisons among fixed effects. Suppose, for example, that schools are classified according to sector (public, Catholic, or other private) and that two dummy variables are used to represent this. An omnibus test would be that the effects of both dummy variables were null. If this hypothesis were retained, school sector could be dropped from the model. Alternatively, single degree-of-freedom comparisons might be considered, such as the difference between private schools and public schools or between Catholic schools and other private schools.

Single parameter tests for variance components may be posed at either Level 2 or Level 3. That is, any diagonal element of either $\mathbf{T}_\pi$ or $\mathbf{T}_\beta$ could be hypothesized as zero. Multiparameter tests for variance components can be used to examine hypotheses about more than one variance component, including elements at both Levels 2 and 3. For example, suppose that a model were fitted in which the effects of sex and social class were allowed to vary randomly at Level 2 (among classes in the schools). Perhaps the investigator wonders whether a simpler model—in which both of these effects were presumed constant among classes in the same school—would be adequate. To test this hypothesis, the investigator reestimates the model, now fixing the effects of sex and social class. A comparison of the deviance statistics from the restricted model (with fixed slopes for sex and social class within schools) and the more general alternative (i.e., the random slopes model) is a likelihood-ratio test, as previously discussed in Chapter 3.

Example: Research on Teaching

This illustration is based on data from 57 high school math teachers working in 14 schools in the United States (Raudenbush, Rowan, & Cheong, 1991).[1] These teachers were assigned to teach four math classes, on average, per day. The teachers' objectives tended to vary across classes. Raudenbush et al. focused on the extent to which each teacher emphasized higher order thinking (HOT). For each class, each teacher was asked to respond to a four-item scale indicating the degree of emphasis on construction of proofs, the formulation of mathematical arguments, and the articulation of reasoning underlying mathematical algorithms. The HOT index was constructed as the mean of these four items. Here the Level-1 units are classes, the Level-2 units are teachers, and the Level-3 units are schools.

We consider the fully unconditional model given by Equations 8.1, 8.2, and 8.3, where

TABLE 8.1 Three-Level Analysis of HOT Data (Fully Unconditional Model)

Fixed Effect		*Coefficient*	*se*	*t ratio*
Average classroom mean, γ_{000}		−0.252	0.262	−0.959
Random Effect	*Variance Component*	*df*	χ^2	*p value*
Classes (Level 1), e_{ijk}	5.85			
Teachers (Level 2), r_{0jk}	3.11	56	195.2	0.000
Schools (Level 3), u_{00k}	0.01	13	11.7	> 0.500
Variance Decomposition (percentage by level)				
Level 1	65.2			
Level 2	34.7			
Level 3	0.1			

Y_{ijk} is the HOT score for class i of teacher j in school k;

π_{0jk} is teacher jk's mean on HOT;

β_{00k} is school k's mean on HOT; and

γ_{000} is the grand mean.

Results. In a fully unconditional model, there is only one fixed effect, γ_{000}, which in this case is the average classroom mean. For the HOT data, $\hat{\gamma}_{000} = -0.252$, $t = -0.959$ (see Table 8.1). The average HOT classroom mean was not significantly different from zero, an expected result because the scale was standardized to a mean of zero.

In terms of the variance partitioning, $\sigma^2 = \text{Var}(e_{ijk})$ is the variance within teachers over classes, $\tau_\pi = \text{Var}(r_{0jk})$ is the variance between teachers within schools, and $\tau_\beta = \text{Var}(u_{00k})$ is the variance between schools. Substituting the estimates for each of these variance components into Equations 8.4, 8.5, and 8.6 yields estimates of the percentage of variance in Y_{ijk} at each level (see third panel of Table 8.1). The largest percentage (65.2%) lies between classes within teachers (i.e., at Level 1); a substantial, though smaller, percentage (34.7%) lies between teachers within schools (i.e., at Level 2); and only a trivial portion (0.1%) lies between schools (i.e., at Level 3). The variation between teachers is statistically significant, $\chi^2 = 195.2$ with 56 df ($p < .001$), but the variance between schools is not, $\chi^2 = 11.7$ with 13 df ($p > .500$).

These results imply that teachers tend to tailor their objectives differently for different math classes. Raudenbush et al. (1991) therefore formulated a Level-1 model to predict HOT:

$$Y_{ijk} = \pi_{0jk} + \pi_{1jk}(\text{TRACK})_{ijk} + e_{ijk} \quad [8.12]$$

where $(\text{TRACK})_{ijk}$ measures the track or level of each class and was coded −1 for vocational and general classes, 0 for academic classes, and 1 for academic honors classes. (This contrast seemed to adequately capture the variation among the four tracks.) The coefficients π_{0jk} and π_{1jk} were allowed to vary randomly over teachers and schools but were not predicted by teacher- or school-level variables. Thus, the Level-2 model was

$$\pi_{0jk} = \beta_{0jk} + r_{0jk} \quad [8.13a]$$

$$\pi_{1jk} = \beta_{1jk} + r_{1jk}. \quad [8.13b]$$

Note, there were two random effects at Level 2 and, as a result, $\mathbf{T}_\pi$ was a 2 by 2 matrix. At Level 3,

$$\beta_{0jk} = \gamma_{000} + u_{00k} \quad [8.14a]$$

$$\beta_{1jk} = \gamma_{100} + u_{10k} \quad [8.14b]$$

where there were also two random effects and $\mathbf{T}_\beta$ was a 2 by 2 matrix. The results (not reproduced here) indicated that HOT was strongly related to track. That is, $\hat{\gamma}_{100}$ was a large, significant positive effect. This means that teachers were more likely to emphasize higher order thinking in high track classes. The magnitude of this track effect, π_{1jk}, however, varied across teachers. That is, $\hat{\tau}_{\pi 11} = \text{Var}(r_{1jk})$ was significantly greater than zero. In contrast, there was no evidence that the track effect varied among schools. That is, the hypothesis that $\tau_{\beta 11} = \text{Var}(u_{10k}) = 0$ was sustained.

The next step in the analysis was to introduce additional class-level predictors (for example, grade level, type of math taught) in the Level-1 model and additional teacher-level predictors (amount of education, preparation in math, and professional experience) in the Level-2 model. The teacher-level predictors were hypothesized to explain both variation in teacher means on HOT, π_{0jk}, and variation among teachers in their tendency to emphasize HOT in high-track classes, π_{1jk}.

Because the number of schools was small and because there was little evidence of school-to-school variation, no Level-3 predictors were specified. In fact, the apparent absence of any school-level variation in either β_{0jk} or β_{1jk} provides an argument for considering a simpler, two-level analysis of classes at Level 1 and teachers at Level 2, ignoring schools.

Studying Individual Change Within Organizations

A fundamental phenomenon of interest in educational research is the growth of the individual learner within the organizational context of classrooms and schools. To study the growth of children who are nested within schools, we combine the approaches developed in Chapter 5 for modeling individuals nested within organizations, and that of Chapter 6 for modeling individual change over time. Individual growth trajectories comprise the Level-1 model; the variation in growth parameters among children within a school is captured in the Level-2 model; and the variation among schools is represented in the Level-3 model.

Bryk and Raudenbush (1988) illustrated this approach with a small subsample of the longitudinal data from the Sustaining Effects Study (Carter, 1984). The data are from 618 students in 86 schools, each measured at five occasions between the spring of first grade and the spring of third grade.

Unconditional Model

Level-1 Model. We begin with an individual growth model of the academic achievement at time t of student i in school j:

$$Y_{tij} = \pi_{0ij} + \pi_{1ij}(\text{TIME POINT})_{tij} + \pi_{2ij}(\text{SUMMER DROP})_{tij} + e_{tij} \qquad [8.15]$$

where

Y_{tij} is the outcome at time t for child i in school j;

$(\text{TIME POINT})_{tij}$ is 0 at spring of Grade 1, 1 at fall of Grade 2, 2 at spring of Grade 2, 3 at fall of Grade 3, and 4 at spring of Grade 3;

$(\text{SUMMER DROP})_{tij}$ takes on a value of 1 in the fall (time points 1 and 3) and 0 at the spring time points;

π_{0ij} is the initial status of child ij, that is, the expected outcome for that child in the spring of first grade (when TIME POINT = 0 and SUMMER DROP = 0);

π_{1ij} is the learning rate for child ij during the academic year; and

π_{2ij} is the summer effect on mathematics learning for child ij.

According to the model, the expected learning rate for child ij during the academic year is π_{1ij}. The coefficient π_{2ij} captures the summer drop-off in student learning. As a result, $\pi_{1ij} + \pi_{2ij}$ is the expected learning rate during the summer.

The results of a preliminary analysis suggested considerable random variation in π_0 and π_1 at both Levels 2 and 3. The student-level reliability for π_{2ij}, however, was less than .02, and the null hypothesis that $\tau_{\pi 22} = 0$ was retained. In contrast, the school-level reliability was about .20, and the corresponding null hypothesis that $\tau_{\beta 22} = 0$ was rejected. These results suggested that we retain π_{2ij} in the Level-1 model, treat it as fixed at Level 2, and then as random at Level 3. This means that all children within any school j would have the same summer-drop-off effect, but this effect would vary among schools. Formally, SUMMER DROP is a time-varying covariate in the Level-1 model.

Specifically, at Level 2,

$$\pi_{0ij} = \beta_{00j} + r_{0ij} \quad [8.16a]$$

$$\pi_{1ij} = \beta_{10j} + r_{1ij} \quad [8.16b]$$

$$\pi_{2ij} = \beta_{20j}; \quad [8.16c]$$

and, at Level 3,

$$\beta_{00j} = \gamma_{000} + u_{00j} \quad [8.17a]$$

$$\beta_{10j} = \gamma_{100} + u_{10j} \quad [8.17b]$$

$$\beta_{20j} = \gamma_{200} + u_{20j}. \quad [8.17c]$$

Note that β_{00j} represents the mean initial status within school j while γ_{000} is the overall mean initial status; β_{10j} is the mean growth rate within school j while γ_{100} is the overall mean growth rate; and β_{20j} is the SUMMER DROP effect in school j while γ_{200} is the overall mean SUMMER DROP effect.

Results. The results presented in Table 8.2 indicate, as expected, a strong positive overall growth trajectory averaged across all children and schools. The estimated initial status, $\hat{\gamma}_{000}$, was 403.267 points. The average learning rate per academic year was estimated at 28.511 (i.e., $\hat{\gamma}_{100}$) with a mean summer drop-off of 27.782 (i.e., $\hat{\gamma}_{200} = -27.782$). As a result, the average summer learning was approximately zero (i.e., $\hat{\gamma}_{100} + \hat{\gamma}_{200}$).

Of more substantive interest in this application was the decomposition of the variance in π_{0jk} and π_{1jk} into their within- and between-schools

TABLE 8.2 Three-Level Analysis of Sustaining Effects Study Data (Unconditional Model at Levels 2 and 3)

Fixed Effect	*Coefficient*	*se*	*t ratio*
Average initial status, γ_{000}	403.267	2.279	176.932
Average learning rate, γ_{100}	28.511	0.619	46.048
Average summer drop, γ_{200}	−27.782	1.229	−22.602

Random Effect	*Variance Component*	*df*	χ^2	*p value*
Level 1				
Temporal variation, e_{tij}	613.100			
Level 2 (students within schools)				
Individual initial status, r_{0ij}	1,033.054	532	2,148.8	.000
Individual learning rate, r_{1ij}	3.976	532	694.2	.000
Level 3 (between schools)				
School mean status, u_{00j}	173.041	85	154.5	.000
School mean learning, u_{10j}	19.082	85	235.8	.000
School summer drop-off, u_{20j}	44.603	85	121.6	.000

Level-1 Coefficient	*Percentage of Variance Between Schools*
Initial status, π_{0ij}	14.3
Learning rate, π_{1ij}	82.7

Variance-Covariance Components and Correlations Among the Level-2 and Level-3 Random Effects[a]

Level 2
$$\begin{pmatrix} 1033.054 & 0.742 \\ 47.530 & 3.976 \end{pmatrix} = \mathbf{T}_\pi = \begin{pmatrix} \tau_{\pi 11} & \\ \tau_{\pi 12} & \tau_{\pi 22} \end{pmatrix}$$

Level 3
$$\begin{pmatrix} 173.041 & 0.069 & -0.766 \\ 3.940 & 19.082 & -0.595 \\ -67.321 & -17.360 & 44.603 \end{pmatrix} = \mathbf{T}_\beta = \begin{pmatrix} \tau_{\beta 11} & & \\ \tau_{\beta 12} & \tau_{\beta 22} & \\ \tau_{\beta 13} & \tau_{\beta 23} & \tau_{\beta 33} \end{pmatrix}$$

a. The lower triangles contain the covariances; the upper triangles contain the correlations.

components. The estimates for these variance components appear in the second panel of Table 8.2. The χ^2 statistics accompanying these variance components indicate significant variation among children within schools for initial status and learning rates (i.e., π_{0ij} and π_{1ij}) and significant variation between schools for mean status, mean learning rates, and summer-drop-off effects (i.e., β_{00j}, β_{10j}, and β_{20j}).

Based on these variance components estimates, we can also compute the percentage of variation that lies between schools for both initial status and learning rates. Formally,

$$\begin{array}{c}\%\ \text{variance} \\ \text{between schools} \\ \text{on } \pi_{pjk}\end{array} = \frac{\tau_{\beta pp}}{\tau_{\beta pp} + \tau_{\pi pp}} \qquad [8.18]$$

for $p = 0, \ldots, P$. In this case, $p = 0, 1$. Substituting the corresponding estimates for the variance components into Equation 8.18 yields the results presented in the third panel of Table 8.2. We find that about 14% of the variance in initial status lies between schools. This result is consistent with results typically encountered in cross-sectional studies of school effects where 10% to 30% of the achievement variability is between schools. The results for learning rates, however, are startling: Almost 83% of the variance is between schools.

Also illuminating are the correlations between initial status and rate of growth (last panel of Table 8.2). Within schools (i.e., at Level 2), the estimated correlation is .742. However, between schools (i.e., at Level 3), the estimated correlation is .069. These results suggest that children with relatively high initial status within a school will tend to grow at faster rates than their schoolmates with low initial status. However, mean differences among schools on initial status are not very predictive of school effects on learning.

In general, unconditional Level-2 and Level-3 models should be fit prior to consideration of any explanatory models at either level. The unconditional model provides important statistics for studying individual growth, including the partitioning of variability in the individual growth parameters into Level-2 and Level-3 components; the correlations among the growth parameters; and the reliability of effects at each level (as in Equations 8.7 and 8.8).

In this particular application, the variance component decomposition highlighted two important features of the data: the high percentage of variation in learning rates lying between schools, and the different initial status and learning rate correlations between and within schools. The reliability estimates also help us to discern whether certain random effects in the Level-2 and Level-3 models might be constrained to zero.

Conditional Model

We now consider an explanatory model that allows estimation of the separate effects of child poverty and school poverty concentration on individual mathematics learning. The Level-1 model remains as in Equation

8.15. The Level-2 model represents the variability in each of the growth parameters, π_{pij} among students within schools. The effects of CHILD POVERTY are represented here. Specifically, we formulated the following Level-2 model:

$$\pi_{0ij} = \beta_{00j} + \beta_{01j}(\text{CHILD POVERTY})_{ij} + r_{0ij}, \qquad [8.19a]$$

$$\pi_{1ij} = \beta_{10j} + \beta_{11j}(\text{CHILD POVERTY})_{ij} + r_{1ij}, \qquad [8.19b]$$

$$\pi_{2ij} = \beta_{20j}. \qquad [8.19c]$$

We hypothesize in Equations 8.19a and 8.19b that CHILD POVERTY (a dummy variable indicating whether the child comes from a poor family) is related to initial status and learning rate. Equation 8.19c specifies that the summer-drop-off effect is the same for all students within school j. Because CHILD POVERTY is a dummy variable, the corresponding regression coefficients can be interpreted as poverty-gap effects. That is, β_{01j} is the poverty gap on initial status (i.e., the extent to which a poor child starts school behind his or her more advantaged counterparts within school j), and β_{11j} is the poverty gap on learning rates in school j (i.e., the difference between the two groups in subsequent rates of learning).

The Level-3 model represents the variability among schools in the five β coefficients. We hypothesize in this illustration that school poverty predicts school mean initial status and learning rate and that the effect of child poverty on initial status is constant across all schools, but that the poverty gap on learning rates varies across schools as a function of school poverty. We also hypothesize, for reasons discussed below, that school poverty is related to the size of the summer-drop-off effect. Thus, we pose the following Level-3 model:

$$\beta_{00j} = \begin{array}{l}\text{mean status in}\\ \text{school } j \text{ for an}\\ \text{“advantaged” child}\end{array} = \gamma_{000} + \gamma_{001}(\text{SCHOOL POVERTY})_j + u_{00j} \qquad [8.20a]$$

$$\beta_{01j} = \begin{array}{l}\text{poverty gap on}\\ \text{initial status}\\ \text{constant across}\\ \text{all schools}\end{array} = \gamma_{010} \quad (\text{note } \beta_{01j} \text{ is a fixed effect}) \qquad [8.20b]$$

$$\beta_{10j} = \begin{array}{l}\text{learning rate}\\ \text{for an advantaged}\\ \text{child in school } j\end{array} = \gamma_{100} + \gamma_{101}(\text{SCHOOL POVERTY})_j + u_{10j} \qquad [8.20c]$$

$$\beta_{11j} = \begin{array}{l}\text{child poverty} \\ \text{gap on the} \\ \text{learning rate} \\ \text{in school } j\end{array} = \gamma_{110} + \gamma_{111}(\text{SCHOOL POVERTY})_j \quad \text{(note } \beta_{11j} \text{ is a nonrandomly varying effect)} \qquad [8.20d]$$

$$\beta_{20j} = \begin{array}{l}\text{summer drop–off} \\ \text{in school } j\end{array} = \gamma_{200} + \gamma_{201}(\text{SCHOOL POVERTY})_j + u_{20j}. \qquad [8.20e]$$

Note that there are three random effects per school: u_{00j}, u_{10j}, and u_{20j}. The estimated fixed effects for this model are presented in Table 8.3.

The γ_{000} coefficient represents in this application the predicted initial status for an "advantaged child" (CHILD POVERTY = 0) in an "affluent school" (SCHOOL POVERTY = % poor = 0). For such a student, the predicted math achievement is 414.614. For each 10% increment in SCHOOL POVERTY, the expected initial status is reduced by 4.666 points (i.e., 10 $\times\ \hat{\gamma}_{001}$). At the initial data-collection point, the child poverty gap, $\hat{\gamma}_{010}$, is 10.372 points. This means that children from poor families (CHILD POVERTY = 1) start out 10.372 points behind their more advantaged schoolmates.

The predicted academic-year learning rate for an advantaged child in an affluent school, $\hat{\gamma}_{100}$, is 29.115. On average, such children gain about 29 points per academic year. Further, the learning rate for advantaged children does not depend on school poverty concentration ($\hat{\gamma}_{101} = -.019$, $t = -.527$). For a poor child in an affluent school, the academic year learning rate is 4.526 points lower than for the advantaged child (i.e., $\hat{\gamma}_{110}$). The average gain for such children from one year of instruction is $\hat{\gamma}_{100} + \hat{\gamma}_{110} =$ 29.115 − 4.526 = 24.589 points. SCHOOL POVERTY may have a small positive effect on academic year learning for the poor child. After adjusting for CHILD POVERTY, a 10% increase in school poverty concentration predicts an *increment* to learning of .80 points (i.e., 10 $\times\ \hat{\gamma}_{111}$). Presumably, the SCHOOL POVERTY measure is acting in this analysis as a proxy for the amount of compensatory education resources available in the school, which depends directly on the poverty level of the school.

This pattern of effects for SCHOOL POVERTY also appears in modeling the summer drop-off. For the advantaged child in an affluent school, the expected summer learning gain is approximately zero (i.e., $\hat{\gamma}_{100} + \hat{\gamma}_{200} =$ 29.115 − 30.818). In schools with higher levels of poverty concentration, however, the summer drop-off is less. For example, in a school with all poor children (SCHOOL POVERTY = 100), the expected summer effect would be $\hat{\gamma}_{200} + 100 \times \hat{\gamma}_{201} = -30.818 + (.139)100 = -16.92$. In such contexts, the summer decline is reduced by more than one third as compared

TABLE 8.3 Effects of Child and School Poverty on Student Learning (a Three-Level Analysis of Sustaining Effects Study Data)

Fixed Effect	*Coefficient*	*se*	*t ratio*
Model for initial status, π_{0ij}			
Model for mean status of advantaged child, β_{00j}			
INTERCEPT, γ_{000}	414.614	2.633	157.482
SCHOOL POVERTY, γ_{001}	−0.466	0.104	−4.478
Model for child poverty gap on initial status, β_{01j}			
INTERCEPT, γ_{010}	−10.372	4.924	−2.106
Model for learning rates, π_{1ij}			
Model for learning rates of an advantaged child, β_{10j}			
INTERCEPT, γ_{100}	29.115	0.946	30.786
SCHOOL POVERTY, γ_{101}	−0.019	0.036	−0.527
Model for child poverty gap on learning rate, β_{11j}			
INTERCEPT, γ_{110}	−4.526	2.046	−2.122
SCHOOL POVERTY, γ_{111}	0.080	0.049	1.650
Model for summer drop-off, π_{2ij}			
Model for school effect, β_{20j}			
INTERCEPT, γ_{200}	−30.818	1.701	−18.122
SCHOOL POVERTY, γ_{201}	0.139	0.060	2.306

to the expected decline of −30.818 in an affluent school. Although we do not have data on the specific summer programs available in schools, we know that in general, compensatory funds were used for this purpose. Thus, these results suggest possible compensatory education effects on student learning during the summer.

Table 8.4 presents estimated variances and related χ^2 statistics from the three-level decomposition. These results suggest that residual parameter variance still remains to be explained in both the student-level (π) and school-level (β) coefficients.

A Measurement Model at Level 1

Studies of organizational climate are often based on individuals' perceptions. For example, Pallas (1988) reported on U.S. high school teachers' perceptions about the degree of principal leadership, staff cooperation, staff control, and other characteristics of school climate. Typically, climate measures are constructed from several survey items. In the Pallas study, for example, 14 items were combined to create a principal leadership measure as reported by each teacher. These individual measures are

TABLE 8.4 Variance Decomposition from a Three-Level Analysis of the Effects of Child and School Poverty on Student Learning

Random Effect	*Variance Component*	*df*	χ^2	*p value*
Level-1 variance				
Temporal variation, e_{tij}	613.76			
Level-2 (student within schools)				
Individual initial status, r_{0ij}	1,015.95	446	2,132.4	0.000
Individual learning rate, r_{1ij}	3.46	530	688.8	0.000
Level-3 (between schools)				
School mean status, u_{00j}	50.63	84	103.39	0.057
School mean learning rate, u_{10j}	19.19	84	238.53	0.000
School summer drop-off, u_{20j}	33.73	84	111.40	0.024

Deviance = 29,930.3
Number of estimated variance and covariance components = 19

then aggregated to the organizational level to create an overall measure of the climate. The problem is that the climate measures at the person or organizational level may have different meanings and different measurement properties. Correlations will be attenuated by measurement error to different degrees at each level, potentially rendering the research uninterpretable.

The three-level model can be formulated to address this problem. We illustrate this in a case with five climate measures: principal leadership, staff cooperation, teacher control, teacher efficacy, and teacher satisfaction.

Example: Research on School Climate

Raudenbush, Rowan, and Kang (1991) analyzed data from questionnaires administered to 1,867 teachers nested within 110 schools. The data consisted of 35 Likert-scaled items measuring five latent constructs: principal leadership, staff cooperation, teacher control, teacher efficacy, and teacher satisfaction. The analyses sought to examine the psychometric properties of the measures and to investigate structural relations between school characteristics and the latent constructs.

We reproduce the results of their unconditional analysis below. Level 1 of the model represents variation among the item scores within each teacher. Level 2 represents variation among teachers within schools, and Level 3 represents variation across schools.

Level-1 Model. For simplicity, we assume that each item measuring a given construct will be equally weighted. Further, items at Level 1 were rescaled to have approximately equal error variances. The Level-1 model is

$$Y_{ijk} = \sum_p \pi_{pjk} a_{pijk} + e_{ijk}, \tag{8.21}$$

where

a_{pijk} takes on a value of 1 if item i measures construct p and 0 otherwise, for constructs $p = 1, \ldots, 5$;

π_{pjk} is the latent true score for person j in school k on construct p; and

e_{ijk} is an error assumed to be normally distributed with a mean of 0 and a variance σ^2.

The assumption that e_{ijk} is normal will have little effect in cases where the item is, for example, a Likert scale with a reasonably symmetric distribution.

Level-2 Model. The Level-2 model describes the distribution of the true scores, π_p, across teachers within schools:

$$\pi_{pjk} = \beta_{pk0} + r_{pjk}, \tag{8.22}$$

where β_{pk0} is the true score mean on construct p for school k, and r_{pjk} is a person-specific effect. For each person, the five random effects $r_{1jk}, \ldots, r_{5jk}$ are assumed multivariate normal with means of 0 and a 5 by 5 covariance matrix $\mathbf{T}_\pi$.

Level-3 Model. At Level 3, the school means scores vary around their respective grand means:

$$\beta_{pk0} = \gamma_{pk0} + u_{pk0}. \tag{8.23}$$

For each school, the random effects $u_{1k}, \ldots, u_{5k}$ are assumed multivariate normal with means of 0 and a 5 by 5 covariance matrix, $\mathbf{T}_\beta$.

Results. The results appear in Table 8.5. The fixed effects are the five grand means. The table also presents maximum likelihood estimates of the two covariance matrices, $\mathbf{T}_\pi$ and $\mathbf{T}_\beta$, and the Level-1 variance σ^2. (Note that variance-covariances appear in the lower triangle and the corresponding correlations are located in the upper triangle of the two matrices.)

TABLE 8.5 Psychometric Analysis

Fixed Effect	*Coefficient*	*se*	*t ratio*
Mean principal leadership, γ_{100}	3.76	5.36	0.70
Mean staff cooperation, γ_{200}	9.63	4.42	2.18
Mean teacher control, γ_{300}	14.24	3.66	3.89
Mean teacher efficacy, γ_{400}	9.65	3.04	3.17
Mean teacher satisfaction, γ_{500}	10.79	4.05	2.66

Variance-Covariance Components for Random Effects at Level 1, 2 and 3 and Correlations Among the Level-2 and Level-3 Random Effects.

Level 1, $\hat{\sigma}^2 = 9979$

$$\text{Level 2, } \hat{\mathbf{T}}_\pi = \begin{pmatrix} 6052 & .615 & .579 & .578 & .561 \\ 3436 & 5156 & .382 & .527 & .531 \\ 2324 & 1413 & 2660 & .561 & .468 \\ 2964 & 2498 & 1909 & 4351 & .980 \\ 4241 & 3709 & 2347 & 6285 & 9447 \end{pmatrix}$$

$$\text{Level 3, } \hat{\mathbf{T}}_\beta = \begin{pmatrix} 2957 & .746 & .560 & .633 & .690 \\ 1584 & 1694 & .605 & .709 & .734 \\ 1000 & 862 & 1198 & .648 & .579 \\ 694 & 621 & 478 & 453 & .898 \\ 1077 & 915 & 607 & 579 & 916 \end{pmatrix}$$

NOTE: The lower triangles contain the covariances; the upper triangles contain the correlations.

Perhaps the most interesting feature of the results is the insight they provide about the correlations among the latent constructs. For example, we see that the estimated correlation between the teacher efficacy and teacher satisfaction (constructs 4 and 5) at the teacher level is .98. The implication is that these two constructs are virtually indistinguishable at the teacher level. This inference, however, contrasts markedly with what might have been concluded by examining the correlations among the observed scores. These comparisons are provided in Table 8.6. Note that the correlation among the observed score is .56. The explanation for the difference is that only two items are used to measure each of these constructs. As a result, the observed score correlation is actually remarkably high given the paucity of items used in each case. Not surprisingly, the hierarchical estimates of the correlations among the true constructs are larger than the observed correlations at both the teacher and school levels.

The results also show that the correlation structure is not the same at the two levels. Essentially, the three-level analysis corrects the correlations for measurement error, which yields different corrections at each level because the measurement error structure at each level is quite different.

TABLE 8.6 Correlations at Each Level

	Teacher Level		*School Level*	
	Ordinary[a]	*Hierarchical*	*Ordinary*[b]	*Hierarchical*
Principal leadership with:				
Staff cooperation	.57	.62	.68	.75
Teacher control	.48	.58	.55	.56
Teacher efficacy	.38	.58	.46	.63
Teacher satisfaction	.44	.56	.56	.69
Staff cooperation with:				
Teacher control	.35	.38	.52	.61
Teacher efficacy	.35	.53	.53	.71
Teacher satisfaction	.41	.53	.61	.73
Teacher control with:				
Teacher efficacy	.35	.56	.51	.65
Teacher satisfaction	.34	.47	.51	.58
Teacher efficacy with:				
Teacher satisfaction	.56	.98	.74	.90

a. Based on teacher-level observations, ignoring school membership.
b. Based on school means.

At the teacher level, the reliability depends upon the number of items in the scale and the interitem agreement. At the school level, although affected somewhat by these factors, the reliability depends more heavily upon the number of teachers sampled per school and the level of teacher agreement within schools.

Raudenbush, Rowan, and Kang (1991) extended this analysis by employing characteristics of teachers (e.g., education and social background) and of schools (e.g., sector, size, social composition) to explain variation in the latent-climate variables. In essence, their analyses involved a multivariate two-level model (i.e., multiple latent-climate constructs defined on teachers within schools). This explanatory model enabled the investigators to assess the relative strength of school- and teacher-level predictors for each of the five different latent-climate constructs.

Estimating Random Coefficients in Three-Level Models

This chapter has focused on the use of three-level models for estimating multi-level fixed effects and variance-covariance components. The three-level model can also provide empirical Bayes estimates of the random coefficients at both Level 2 and Level 3. We return to the simple model introduced earlier (see "A Fully Unconditional Model") of academic achievement of students nested within classrooms that are in turn nested within schools. For this unconditional three-level model, the hierarchical analysis provides the following composite estimates (empirical Bayes) for each classroom (Level-2) and school (Level-3) mean:

$$\pi^*_{0jk} = \hat{\lambda}_{\pi_{jk}} \bar{Y}_{\cdot jk} + (1 - \hat{\lambda}_{\pi_{jk}}) \beta^*_{00k} \qquad [8.24]$$

$$\beta^*_{00k} = \hat{\lambda}_{\beta_k} \hat{\beta}_{00k} + (1 - \hat{\lambda}_{\beta_k}) \hat{\gamma}_{000} \qquad [8.25]$$

where $\lambda_{\pi_{jk}}$ and λ_{β_k} are the reliabilities of the class- and school-level means defined in Equation 8.7 and 8.8; $\hat{\gamma}_{000}$ is the estimate of the grand mean; and $\hat{\beta}_{00k}$ is the weighted least squares estimator of β_{00k}:

$$\hat{\beta}_{00k} = \frac{\sum_j [\hat{\tau}_\pi + \hat{\sigma}^2/n_{jk}]^{-1} \bar{Y}_{\cdot jk}}{\sum_j [\hat{\tau}_\pi + \hat{\sigma}^2/n_{jk}]^{-1}} . \qquad [8.26]$$

Note that β^*_{00k} shrinks the classical weighted least squares estimator $\hat{\beta}_{00k}$ toward the grand mean, $\hat{\gamma}_{000}$, by an amount proportional to $1 - \hat{\lambda}_{\beta_k}$, the unreliability of $\hat{\beta}_{00k}$. Similarly, π^*_{0jk} shrinks the sample mean $\bar{Y}_{\cdot jk}$ toward β^*_{00k} by an amount proportional to $1 - \hat{\lambda}_{\pi_{jk}}$, the unreliability of $\bar{Y}_{\cdot jk}$ computed within school k. Estimation formulas for the Level-2 and Level-3 random coefficients in more general models are supplied in Chapter 10.

Note

1. We wish to thank the Center for Research on the Context of Secondary School Teaching at Stanford University (funded by the Office of Educational Research and Improvement, U.S. Department of Education, Cooperative Agreement No. OERI-G0089C235) for use of this data.

9 Assessing the Adequacy of Hierarchical Models

Introduction

A good data analysis begins with a careful examination of the univariate frequency distribution of each variable that may be employed in a subsequent multivariate analysis. Examination of the shape and scale of each variable provides a check on the quality of the data, identifies outlying observations, and may suggest a need for a variable transformation. The next step in model building involves exploration of the bivariate relationships. Plots of two continuous variables can identify possible nonlinear relationships and identify discrepant cases that could arise from some erroneous observations. Prior to fitting a hierarchical model, such analyses are needed at each level.

In addition, cross-level exploratory analyses are needed. For example, prior to a school effects study, it is useful to examine the OLS regressions for each school. This enables the analyst to look for *outlier* schools, that is, schools with implausible regression intercepts or slopes. One may then investigate the possible causes of these odd results, which could arise because of small samples, unusual characteristics of the school in question, or even coding errors. Implausible results arising from units with small sample size are not a problem because the estimation methods detailed in Chapter 3 are robust in this regard. Distorted regressions from bad data, however, are more serious because discrepant schools may exert undue influence on estimation.

Thinking About Model Assumptions

Inferences based on standard linear models depend for their validity on the tenability of assumptions about both the structural and random parts of the model. In terms of the structural part, OLS requires a properly specified model where the outcome is a linear function of the regression coefficients. Misspecification occurs when some component included in the error term is associated with one or more of the predictors in the model.

In hierarchical linear models, specification assumptions apply at each level. Moreover, misspecification at one level can affect results at other levels. Further, because Level-2 equations may have correlated errors, the misspecification of one equation can bias the estimates in another. For example, in Chapter 4 we modeled each school's intercept and slope as a bivariate outcome in the Level-2 model. It is important to know how misspecification of the model for the intercept might affect estimates of the Level-2 coefficients in the slope model.

In terms of the random part of the model, OLS regression assumes independent errors with equal variances. Standard hypothesis tests also require that the errors be normally distributed. In a hierarchical analysis, similar assumptions are made at both Level 1 and Level 2. Although a violation of these assumptions will not bias the Level-2 coefficient estimates, it can adversely influence their estimated standard errors and inferential statistics. Similarly, estimation of random Level-1 coefficients and variance-covariance components can be distorted.

Skillful data analysts pay close attention to the assumptions required by their models. They investigate the tenability of assumptions in light of the available data; they consider how sensitive their conclusions are likely to be to violations of these assumptions; and they seek ameliorative strategies when significant violations are discovered. In this regard, a caveat is in order. Hierarchical linear models are relatively new and there are few in-depth studies of the consequences of violating model assumptions. Thus, we rely heavily in this chapter on principles drawn from general linear model theory and on our best judgments based on accumulated data analytic experiences to date. Our remarks focus on the estimated fixed effects, their standard errors, and inferential statistics because these are of primary interest in most applications and because most is known about their properties. Some implications for inference regarding the random coefficients and variance-covariance components are also sketched.

Organization of the Chapter

Chapters 5 through 7 sought to illustrate the logic of hierarchical modeling through a range of applications of two-level models. In this chapter, we focus on key decisions involved in formulating such models, the assumptions on which we rely, and empirical procedures that can assist us in the model-building process. Although a hierarchical linear model involves an interrrelated set of specifications and assumptions at both Level 1 and Level 2, for purposes of clarity of presentation we proceed by first discussing the Level-1 model and then the Level-2 model. This discussion actually follows the general flow of the model-building process. The analyst settles on a tentative Level-1 model, then considers the Level-2 model, which may eventuate in some changes at Level 1. We assume throughout most of this chapter that the conditions for large sample theory of maximum likelihood estimation hold. The final section, however, discusses the properties of estimates when the samples sizes at Level 1 and 2 are modest.

The illustrations presented in this chapter use data on high school mathematics achievement similar to those discussed in Chapter 4. We consider a Level-1 model

$$Y_{ij} = \beta_{0j} + \beta_{1j}(\text{SES})_{ij} + r_{ij} \qquad [9.1]$$

where Y_{ij} is the mathematics achievement of student i in school j, which depends on the student's social class. At Level 2,

$$\beta_{0j} = \gamma_{00} + \gamma_{01}(\text{MEAN SES})_j + \gamma_{02}(\text{SECTOR})_j + u_{0j}$$

and

$$\beta_{1j} = \gamma_{10} + \gamma_{11}(\text{MEAN SES})_j + \gamma_{12}(\text{SECTOR})_j + u_{1j}. \qquad [9.2]$$

Key Assumptions of a Two-Level Hierarchical Linear Model

Equations 9.1 and 9.2 are a specific case from the general two-level model, where at Level 1,

$$Y_{ij} = \beta_{0j} + \sum_{q=1}^{Q} \beta_{qj} X_{qij} + r_{ij} \quad [9.3]$$

and at Level 2, for each β_{qj},

$$\beta_{qj} = \gamma_{q0} + \sum_{s=1}^{S_q} \gamma_{qs} W_{sj} + u_{qj}. \quad [9.4]$$

Formally, we assumed the following:

1. Each r_{ij} is independent and normally distributed with a mean of 0 and variance σ^2 for every Level-1 unit i within each Level-2 unit j [i.e., $r_{ij} \sim N(0, \sigma^2)$].
2. The Level-1 predictors, X_{qij}, are independent of r_{ij} [i.e., $\mathrm{Cov}(X_{qij}, r_{ij}) = 0$ for all q].
3. The vector of $Q + 1$ random errors at Level 2 are multivariate normal, each with a mean of 0, some variance, τ_{qq}, and covariance among the random elements, q and q', of $\tau_{qq'}$. The random-error vectors are independent among the J Level-2 units [i.e., $\mathbf{u}_j = (u_{0j}, \ldots, u_{Qj})' \sim N(0, \mathbf{T})$].
4. The set of Level-2 predictors (i.e., all the unique elements in W_{sj} across the $Q + 1$ equations) are independent of every u_{qj}. [i.e., for every W_{sj} and u_{qj}, $\mathrm{Cov}(W_{sj}, u_{qj}) = 0$].
5. The errors at Level 1 and Level 2 are also independent [i.e., $\mathrm{Cov}(r_{ij}, u_{qj}) = 0$ for all q].

Assumptions 2, 4, and 5 focus on the relationship between the variables included in the structural portion of the model—the Xs and Ws—and those factors relegated to the error terms, r_{ij} and u_{qj}. They pertain to the adequacy of model specification. Their tenability affects the bias of γ_{qs}, that is, whether $E(\hat{\gamma}_{qs}) = \gamma_{qs}$. Assumptions 1 and 3 focus only on the random portion of the model (i.e., r_{ij} and u_{qj}). Their tenability affects the accuracy of the estimates of $\mathrm{se}(\hat{\gamma}_{qs})$, the accuracy of β^*_{qj}, $\hat{\sigma}^2$, and $\hat{\mathbf{T}}$.

In terms of the simple two-level model of Equations 9.1 and 9.2, we are assuming the following:

1. Conditional on a student's social class, the within-school errors are normal and independent with a mean of zero in each school and equal variances across schools (assumption 1).
2. Whatever student-level predictors of math achievement are excluded from the model and thereby relegated to the error term, r_{ij}, are independent of student social class (assumption 2).
3. The residual school effects, u_{0j} and u_{1j}, are assumed bivariate normal with variances τ_{00} and τ_{11}, respectively, and covariance τ_{01} (assumption 3).

4. The effects of whatever school predictors are excluded from the model for the intercept and SES slope are independent of MEAN SES and SECTOR (assumption 4).
5. The error at Level 1, r_{ij}, is independent of the residual school effects u_{0j} and u_{1j}.

We now proceed to consider each of these assumptions in the process of building the Level-1 and Level-2 models.

Building the Level-1 Model

The early phases of model building involve an interplay of theoretical and empirical considerations. The substantive theory under study should suggest a relatively small number of predictors for possible consideration in the Level-1 model. There are two questions here: (a) Should a candidate X_q be included in the model? If yes, (b) how should its coefficient be specified: random, fixed, or nonrandomly varying?

Initially, the Level-2 predictors are held aside and the analysis focuses on comparing some alternative hierarchical models, each of which is unconditional at Level 2. A natural temptation is to estimate a "saturated" Level-1 model—that is, where all potential predictors are included with random slopes—and then to work backward deleting nonsignificant effects from the model. Unfortunately, such a strategy is generally not useful unless the Level-1 sample sizes are very large (e.g., sufficient to sustain stable OLS estimation of the specified Level-1 model in each separate unit). Even here, such a saturated model might require hundreds of iterations to converge and often will produce a large array of nonsignificant findings that offer little direction as to next steps. Intuitively, there is only a fixed amount of variation to be explained. If one overfits the model by specifying too many random Level-1 coefficients, the variation is partitioned into many little pieces, none of which is of much significance. The problem here is analogous to focusing a projector. If one moves beyond the proper range, the image loses focus.

In general, we have found it more productive to use a "step-up" strategy. Assuming some external theoretical guidance that has defined a relatively small set of Level-1 predictors, we build up from univariate to bivariate to trivariate (and so on) models based on promising submodels. Often the best subset of Level-1 predictors can be identified through preliminary modeling using OLS Level-1 analyses.

Empirical Methods to Guide Model Building at Level 1

In terms of a hierarchical analysis, two questions need to be addressed: (a) Is the fixed effect of X_{qij} significant? and (b) Is there any evidence of slope heterogeneity [i.e., Var(β_q) > 0]? Statistical evidence of slope heterogeneity includes the point estimates, $\hat{\tau}_{qq}$, and the corresponding homogeneity test statistics (χ^2 and likelihood-ratio tests introduced in Chapter 3). Also useful in this regard are the estimated reliabilities for the OLS intercepts and slopes.

When the reliabilities become small (e.g., < 0.05), the variances we wish to estimate are likely to be close to zero (or what is technically referred to as near the boundary of the parameter space.) Such cases cause a variety of numerical difficulties depending upon the particular iterative computing routines employed in the variance-covariance component estimation. Although some algorithms abnormally terminate (or require a fix-up to override such a termination), the EM algorithm simply slows down. In extreme cases it becomes tediously slow to converge. Inspection of the reliabilities may suggest that a random Level-1 coefficient be respecified as either fixed or nonrandomly varying. This respecified model may now converge very quickly.

Interestingly, the rate of convergence for the EM, as indicated by the number of iterations, is itself diagnostic. If the data are highly informative, the EM algorithm will converge rapidly (e.g., in less than 10 iterations). In contrast, if the model has an extensive number of random effects and the data are relatively sparse, hundreds of iterations may be needed. As a benchmark, the random-coefficient regression model estimated by Lee and Bryk (1989) and illustrated in chapter 5 took approximately 40 iterations to converge.

Inspection of the correlations among the Level-1 coefficients is also diagnostic (see vocabulary growth analysis in Chapter 6). If a high degree of collinearity or multicollinearity is found, too many random coefficients have been specified at Level 1 and a reduction in the dimensionality of **T** should be considered. At a minimum, one or more of the Level-1 coefficients should not be random.

In general, analysts must use some caution in specifying Level-1 coefficients as random. The number of variance-covariance components to be estimated in a two-level model (with homogeneous variance and independent errors at Level 1) is $r(r + 1)/2 + 1$, where r is the number of random Level-1 predictors in the model. Clearly, this number rapidly increases with r. As the number of random effects grows, significantly more information is required to obtain reasonable estimates of the variance-covariance components. For example, using the High School and Beyond data with about 60 students per school and 160 schools, we have found that three random coefficients plus a random intercept is about as rich a model as the data can sustain. (This number would increase if more observations per school were available.) One cannot be definitive about how many random effects can be specified because the maximum will depend on several factors: the magnitude of the variance components, the degree of intercorrelation among the random effects, and other characteristics of the data.

One additional caution is in order, however. Although the inferential and descriptive statistics may indicate that some τ_{qq} is zero or close to zero, this does not preclude the possibility of a nonrandomly varying specification for the corresponding β_{qj} . If theoretical arguments suggest that such effects might be present, the analyst should proceed with posing Level-2 models for β_{qj} . This occurred, for example, in the Lee and Bryk (1989) study on minority-gap effects discussed in Chapter 5. Prior research had indicated sector differences, and an effort to explain such differences as a function of school factors was certainly warranted. Again, evidence consistent with a null hypothesis does not mean it is true.

Finally, there is the question of whether a particular Level-1 predictor belongs in the model at all. To delete a variable, two conditions must apply: first, no evidence of slope heterogeneity, as discussed above; and second, no evidence of an "average" or fixed effect. In the latter case, the corresponding γ_{q0} would be small in magnitude and the t ratio would be nonsignificant.

Specification Issues at Level 1

The specification assumption implies that no Level-1 variable can be omitted from the model if that variable is both related to Y_{ij} and related to one of the Xs in the model. If such a variable is omitted, estimation of one or more of the βs will be biased. As a consequence, the Level-2 model for this β may also be biased. However, as we discuss below, there are conditions under which such bias will not occur.

We note that this assumption may be violated even if an omitted Level-1 predictor has, on average, no effect within units. That is, its fixed effect may be null, but failure to include it will still misspecify the Level-1 model if the predictor's effect varies from group to group and is related to other random Level-1 coefficients. For example, in Raudenbush, Kidchanapanish, and Kang's (1991) study of primary schools in Thailand, the fixed effect of student gender on mathematics achievement across Thai primary schools was null. However, the magnitude and direction of the effect varied from school to school. In some schools boys significantly outscored girls, whereas in other schools, girls scored higher.

Consequences of Level-1 Misspecification for Level-2 Estimates

Intercept Model. It is well known that failure to specify a Level-1 covariate can lead to a serious bias in the estimation of Level-2 predictors of the intercept. For example, there is available in the High School and Beyond data a measure of student's prior academic background (ACADEMIC BACKGROUND) that we have ignored so far in our analyses. If ACADEMIC BACKGROUND is related to math achievement, and if Catholic and public school students differ significantly on ACADEMIC BACKGROUND, then our previous estimates of the effect of SECTOR on β_{0j} will be biased.

This bias can be removed in one of two ways, depending upon the centering option selected for ACADEMIC BACKGROUND. If ACADEMIC BACKGROUND is entered at Level 1 and centered around its grand mean, each unit's intercept, β_{0j}, is adjusted for mean differences among schools on this variable, and this source of bias is thereby eliminated. Alternatively, ACADEMIC BACKGROUND could be added at Level 1 with group-mean centering. In this case, the bias is eliminated by including the school mean of ACADEMIC BACKGROUND as a Level-2 predictor of the intercept. The latter option is preferable if a compositional effect of ACADEMIC BACKGROUND exists (see Chapter 5) or if the ACADEMIC BACKGROUND slopes were treated as random.

Slope Model. Consequences of misspecification at Level 1 on the modeling of slopes at Level 2 are a bit more complex than for the intercept. These consequences are most easily understood in the context of a specific example. (For a formal derivation see the appendix to this chapter). Suppose that in the Level-1 model of Equation 9.1 a confounding variable, ACADEMIC BACKGROUND, should have been included. To illustrate the effects on the estimated γ coefficients in the slope model, we reanalyzed the data, adding ACADEMIC BACKGROUND as a predictor at Level 1. Table 9.1 provides the results. Formally, ACADEMIC BACKGROUND is a confounding variable at Level 1: it both predicts the outcome and is related to SES.

In order to restrict our attention at this point to consequences for the SES slope model, we centered ACADEMIC BACKGROUND about its school mean. As Table 9.1 indicates, the addition of ACADEMIC BACK-

TABLE 9.1 Confounding Effects of Academic Background[a]

Fixed Effect	*Original Model Estimates* *Coefficient*	*se*	*With Fixed Effect of ACADEMIC BACKGROUND Added* *Coefficient*	*se*
Model for school means, β_{0j}				
INTERCEPT, γ_{00}	13.73	0.20	13.74	0.20
MEAN SES, γ_{01}	4.54	0.48	4.55	0.48
SECTOR, γ_{02}	0.83	0.20	0.83	0.20
Model for SES slopes, β_{1j}				
INTERCEPT, γ_{10}	1.78	0.16	1.13	0.16
MEAN SES, γ_{11}	0.68	0.38	0.29	0.36
SECTOR, γ_{12}	−0.58	0.16	−0.39	0.15
Model for ACADEMIC BACKGROUND Slopes, β_{2j}				
INTERCEPT, γ_{20}			2.14	0.09

a. The data employed in this chapter are similar but not identical to that analyzed in Chapters 4 and 5. Because of missing information on the new Level-1 predictor, ACADEMIC BACKGROUND, the analytic sample is somewhat different here. Also MEAN SES is a school measure of social class, and not the simple average of the individual student's information used at Level 1. This has no effect on the illustrations of this chapter, but it does mean that results are not strictly comparable to those of earlier chapters.

GROUND under these conditions has no effect on the model for the intercept. (Note that $\hat{\gamma}_{01}$ and $\hat{\gamma}_{02}$ are virtually identical with and without ACADEMIC BACKGROUND.)

On the other hand, the estimated effects in the slope model have changed quite substantially. It is logical that the estimate of γ_{10} should be affected by the omission of ACADEMIC BACKGROUND. Because ACADEMIC BACKGROUND and SES are both positively related to achievement and positively related to each other, γ_{10}, which is the average SES slope within schools, ought to be smaller when ACADEMIC BACKGROUND is controlled. The results in Table 9.1 confirm this reasoning: The γ_{10} estimate diminishes from 1.78 to 1.13 when ACADEMIC BACKGROUND is added.

The sources of bias in estimating γ_{11} and γ_{12} are more complicated. These two coefficients are termed *cross-level interaction effects* because they involve the interaction between Level-2 variables (MEAN SES and SECTOR) and a Level-1 variable (SES). For an omitted Level-1 predictor to confound inferences about cross-level interactions, three conditions must hold (these are proved in the appendix to this chapter):

1. The omitted variable must be related to *Y*, controlling for other predictors in the model.
2. The omitted variable must be related to an *X* already included in the model.

TABLE 9.2 Random Coefficient Regression of ACADEMIC BACKGROUND on SES

Model

$$Y_{ij} = \beta_{0j} + \beta_{1j}(\text{SES})_j + r_{ij}$$

where Y_{ij} = academic background of student i in school j,

$$\beta_{0j} = \gamma_{00} + u_{0j}$$
$$\beta_{1j} = \gamma_{01} + u_{1j}$$

Fixed Effect	*Coefficient*	*se*	*t ratio*	
Mean intercept, γ_{00}	0.052	0.027	1.939	
Mean SES slope, γ_{01}	0.262	0.023	11.560	

Random Effect	*Variance Component*	*df*	χ^2	*p value*
INTERCEPT, u_{0j}	0.081	159	597.5	0.000
SES slope, u_{1j}	0.016	159	198.9	0.017

Exploratory regressions of β^*_{1j} on MEAN SES and SECTOR[a]

	Coefficient	*se*	*Approximate t-to-enter*
MEAN SES	−0.038	0.014	−2.750
SECTOR	−0.030	0.005	−5.591

a. Based on use of empirical Bayes residuals as described in this chapter.

3. The association between the omitted variable and X must itself vary from unit to unit; and the strength of this association between the omitted variable and X must be related to a Level-2 predictor.

It is clear from Table 9.1 that the failure to include ACADEMIC BACKGROUND biases estimates of γ_{11} and γ_{12}. In both cases, the magnitudes of their effects are substantially diminished after ACADEMIC BACKGROUND is added: The effect of MEAN SES on the SES slope drops from .68 to .29; the magnitude of the SECTOR effect goes from −.58 to −.39.

Each of the three conditions stated above apply in this case. Condition 1 can be examined through a simple regression analysis of math achievement on SES and ACADEMIC BACKGROUND. Not suprisingly, ACADEMIC BACKGROUND is related to math achievement even after controlling for SES. Conditions 2 and 3 can be investigated using a random-coefficient model that regresses ACADEMIC BACKGROUND on SES (see Table 9.2). Clearly, the mean ACADEMIC BACKGROUND– SES slope,

γ_{01}, is highly significant, $t = 11.56$ (condition 2). Further, there is evidence that these relationships vary across schools [Var(β_{1j}) = .016, p = .017], and that these slopes are significantly related to other school variables considered in the analysis, MEAN SES and SECTOR (condition 3; see t-to-enter statistics in the last panel of Table 9.2).

Errors of Measurement in Level-1 Predictors

Such errors can also bias estimates in the Level-2 model. If SES were measured with error, the β_{1j} estimates would be biased, and the mean slope, γ_{10}, would also be biased. In terms of the cross-level interactions, γ_{11} and γ_{12}, it is shown in the appendix to this chapter that bias results only if (a) the reliability of the SES measure varies from school to school; and (b) this variation in reliability is related to one or more Level-2 predictors included in the model.

Examining Assumptions About Level-1 Random Effects

Homogeneity of Variance

In most multilevel applications, the errors in the Level-1 model are assumed to have equal variance, σ^2. Because of limits on the amount of data available within each unit, investigators generally will wish to begin with this homogeneity assumption. (Some alternative specifications for the Level-1 variance were discussed in Chapters 5 and 6.) If the Level-1 variances are truly unequal but are assumed equal, no bias will be introduced into point estimation of the Level-2 coefficients. However, these estimates will be inefficient and the standard errors biased.

Once a tentative model has been specified, the investigator may test the homogeneity of Level-1 variances. Heterogeneity may have several causes:

1. One or more important Level-1 predictor variables may have been omitted from the model. If such a variable were distributed with unequal variance across groups, failure to include it would cause heterogeneity of variance at Level-1.
2. The effects of a Level-1 predictor that is random or nonrandomly varying may have been erroneously treated as fixed or omitted entirely from the model.
3. One or more units may have bad data. For example, a simple coding error could cause inflated variance in one or a few groups, yielding significant heterogeneity of variance overall.

4. Nonnormal data with heavy tails (i.e., more extreme observations than normally expected) can cause a significant test statistic for heterogeneity of variance. Parametric tests are sensitive to such nonnormality, and kurtosis (heavy tails) can masquerade as variance heterogeneity.

Because these causes are quite different in their implications, we advise investigation of the possible sources of heterogeneity before concluding that a more complex variance assumption is needed. For this purpose, it is useful to compute the standardized measure of dispersion for each group j introduced in Chapter 7:

$$d_j = \frac{\ln(S_j^2) - \left[\sum f_j \ln(S_j^2) / \sum f_j\right]}{(2/f_j)^{1/2}}. \qquad [9.5]$$

A simple and commonly used test statistic for homogeneity is

$$H = \sum d_j^2 , \qquad [9.6]$$

which has a large sample χ^2 distribution with $J - 1$ degrees of freedom under the homogeneity hypothesis. This test is appropriate when the data are normal and sample sizes per unit are 10 or more (Bartlett & Kendall, 1946; see also Raudenbush & Bryk, 1987).

A likelihood-ratio test can also be used to assess heterogeneity at Level 1. The model with homogeneous variance becomes the restricted model to be compared with a more general alternative (e.g., a different Level-1 variance, σ_j^2, for each of the J Level-2 units). The deviance statistics from these alternative models are compared using the standard procedure introduced in Chapter 3.

To illustrate, we tested the homogeneity of variance assumption after computing the model specified by Equations 9.1 and 9.2. The H statistic was 312.13 with 159 df, which is significant beyond the .001 level. This result indicates that heterogeneity of Level-1 variance exists among the 160 schools, and encourages closer scrutiny of the Level-1 model before proceeding further.

One possibility is that a few unusual schools account for most of the observed heterogeneity. In fact, a probability plot of the standardized dispersion measures suggests an unusually large number of schools with smaller than expected residual dispersion (see Figure 9.1). These cases are readily apparent in a stem and leaf of the d_j (see Figure 9.2). Next, we visually inspected data from the five most extreme cases identified in Figure 9.2.

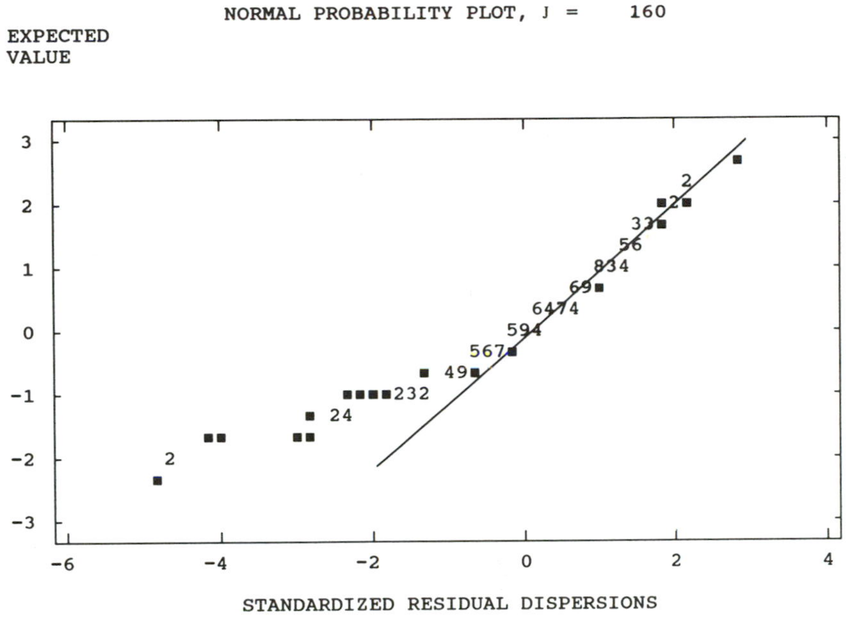

Figure 9.1. Probability Plot of Residual Dispersions for 160 High Schools[a]

a. The standardized residual dispersion is given by Equation 9.5.

The recorded information seemed accurate, and the problem appears to be an unusually homogeneous intake of students. This suggests that we consider including additional variables in Equation 9.1 in an attempt to remove at least some of the residual heterogeneity.

In general, a violation of the homogeneity assumption is not per se a serious problem for estimating either the Level-2 coefficients or their standard errors. We are principally concerned about it because such heterogeneity may indicate a possible misspecification of the Level-1 model. In particular, unidentified slope heterogeneity at Level 1 would appear as heterogeneity of Level-1 error variance. As noted earlier, such slope heterogeneity can bias estimates of the Level-2 coefficients.

A word of caution is in order about the standarized residuals and heterogeneity statistics illustrated above. Although these statistics can be informative, they are quite sensitive to violation of normality in the observed data. We also note that extreme individual values of d_j contribute most to the magnitude of the heterogeneity statistic, H. Hence, examining these, as we did above, can inform investigators about which types of units may

```
MINIMUM IS:         -4.878
LOWER HINGE IS:     -0.706
MEDIAN IS:           0.159
UPPER HINGE IS:      0.962
MAXIMUM IS:          2.789


           -4    86510
      ***OUTSIDE VALUES***
           -3    0
           -2    995
           -2    43333210
           -1    866555
           -1    33300
           -0 H  9998887777776666555
           -0    44444333322111110000000
            0 M  000000111111222233344
            0 H  555555666666777777788888889999
            1    000000111222223333444444
            1    555567889
            2    0111
            2    7
```

Figure 9.2. Stem-and-Leaf Plot of Residual Dispersions for 160 High Schools

have unusual variances. Some further investigation of the quality of data within certain units may be needed. In other cases, a transformation of Y may reduce the effect of heavy-tailed data. In other instances, we may identify a regular pattern where d_j is related to a particular unit characteristic such as sector. Such variables are candidates for inclusion in the Level-2 models as predictors for random Level-1 slope coefficients. (For a further discussion see Raudenbush and Bryk, 1987).

Normality Assumption

Nonnormality of the errors at Level 1 will not bias estimation of the Level-2 effects, but it will introduce bias into standard errors at both levels and therefore into the computation of confidence intervals and hypothesis tests. Little is currently known about the direction and severity of such effects.

Data normality can be checked by computing separate probability plots for each unit or, if the number of units J is large, by looking at a normal probability plot for the residuals pooled across units. (These pooled plots will be misleading in the presence of heterogeneity of variance, however.) A transformation of the outcome or one or more of the predictors may improve the normality of the error distribution.

Building the Level-2 Model

Much of what we have said about model building at Level 1 also applies at Level 2. Ideally the task should be theory-driven, where specific hypotheses are posed about expected relationships in each of the $Q + 1$ Level-2 equations. Again, a backward solution of entering all possible Level-2 predictors and removing the nonsignificant ones is generally not workable because of limits imposed by the number of Level-2 units and likely multicollinearity problems.

A common rule of thumb for a regression analysis is that one needs at least 10 observations for each predictor. The analogous rules for hierarchical models are a bit more complex. For predicting a single Level-2 outcome, for example, β_{0j}, the number of observations is the number of Level-2 units, J, and the conventional 10-observations rule can be applied against this count.

With multiple βs as Level-2 outcomes the total number of predictors that may be included in all Level-2 equations is not clear. If the βs were mutually independent, then the 10-observations rule would apply separately to each of the $Q + 1$ equations. We suspect that this rule is too liberal, however, with correlated outcomes and the possibility of multicollinearity both within and between equations. Therefore we urge a cautious approach examining possible collinearity among the Level-2 predictors and monitoring the standard errors of the estimates as new predictors are entered.

When adding fixed Level-1 predictors to the model, the intraclass correlation for each predictor is crucial. If this is null (for example when predictors are group-mean centered), the total number of observations for applying the 10-observations rule is the total number of Level-1 units. In contrast, as the intraclass correlation approaches 1.0, the number of Level-1 predictors that can be added is constrained by the number of Level-2 units, J.

If hierarchical analyses are to be used in an exploratory mode, we suggest dividing the Level-2 predictors into conceptually distinct subsets and fitting a submodel for each. The strongest predictors from these submodels might then be combined in an overall model. This exploratory approach was used by Bryk and Thum (1989) in an examination of school correlates of student absenteeism and dropping out.

TABLE 9.3 Correlations of Empirical Bayes and OLS residuals[a] (Level 2) with Other Potential School-Level Variables

School-Level	*Empirical Bayes*		*Ordinary Least Squares*	
Variables to Enter	*INTERCEPT*	*SES Slope*	*INTERCEPT*	*SES Slope*
Average # math courses	0.644	−0.348	0.643	−0.099
School size	−0.109	0.187	−0.095	0.109
High minority	−0.343	0.057	−0.340	−0.005
sd math courses	−0.289	0.336	−0.277	0.199
% academic program	0.634	−0.334	0.630	−0.093
Academic climate	0.595	−0.289	0.597	−0.060
Disciplinary climate	−0.469	0.327	−0.472	0.123

a. The OLS and empirical Bayes residuals are computed using the procedure illustrated by Equations 3.43 and 3.44.

Whenever hierarchical models involve both random intercepts and random or nonrandomly varying slopes, the analyst will usually want to develop a tentative model for the intercept, β_{0j}, before proceeding to fit models for the random slopes. This is akin in a general linear model analysis to fitting the main effects first before considering interaction effects. In a hierarchical analysis, the interactions of primary interest are cross-level. (Of course, interactions at just Level 1 or Level 2 are also possible.)

Empirical Methods to Guide Model Building at Level 2

The most direct evidence of whether a Level-2 predictor should be included is the magnitude of its estimated effect and related *t* ratio. Predictors with *t* ratios near or less than 1 are obvious candidates for exclusion from the model.

Analysis of Empirical Bayes Residuals

On the more exploratory side, an examination of the empirical Bayes residuals at Level 2 is often helpful. These empirical Bayes residuals exist for each group (even those with deficient rank data) and tend to be less infuenced by estimation error than do the OLS residuals (although these too can be used).

Table 9.3 presents simple Pearson correlations between both empirical Bayes and OLS residuals and school-level variables considered as potential candidates for entry into the Level-2 model. (The residuals are based on the Level-1 model of Equation 9.1 and an unconditional Level-2 model).

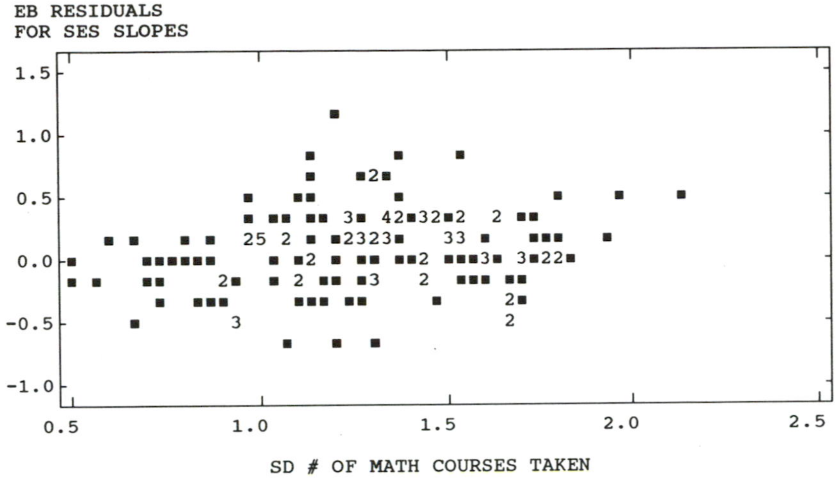

Figure 9.3. Plots of SES Slope Residuals Versus Excluded Variable (SD # OF MATH COURSES)

Note that the correlations with the intercept, β_{0j}, are quite similar for both empirical Bayes and OLS. Given the high reliability of β_{0j} (reported as .91 in Chapter 4), this is not surprising. The correlations involving the empirical Bayes residuals for the SES slope, however, are much stronger than those based on the OLS residuals. The larger sampling variability associated with $\hat{\beta}_{1j}$ (the estimated reliability of $\hat{\beta}_{1j}$ was .23 in Chapter 4), accounts for the much smaller correlations when using OLS residuals.

Plots of residuals against potential Level-2 predictor variables can also help to identify the functional form of these additional relations. Figure 9.3 plots the empirical Bayes residuals for the SES slopes against the standard deviation of the number of math courses taken in each school. SES slopes have a positive linear relationship with this school variable (r = .366 from Table 9.3). This suggests that the SES differentiation effects (i.e., SES slopes) are somewhat greater in schools where there is more diversity in math course taking.

Similarly, plotting the residuals against the predictors in the tentative model provides a graphical check on the adequacy of the structural portion for each Level-2 equation. In Figure 9.4, the empirical Bayes residuals for the SES slope from the fitted model of column 1 in Table 9.1 are plotted against MEAN SES. Because MEAN SES was included as a predictor of the SES slope, we expect homoscedastic residuals randomly dispersed

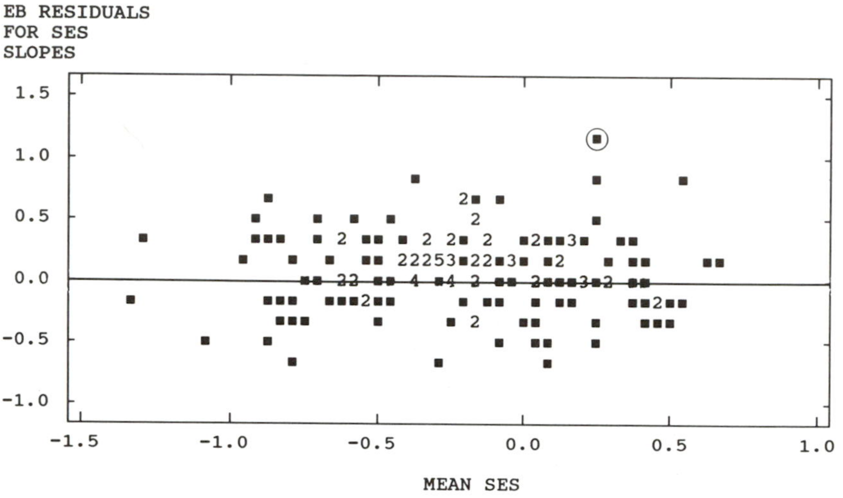

Figure 9.4. Plot of Empirical Bayes Residual for SES Slopes Versus Included Variable (MEAN SES)

around zero. With the exception perhaps of one case, circled in the plot, the assumption of a linear relationship between MEAN SES and the SES slope seems quite reasonable.

Approximate t-to-Enter Statistics

Another approach to investigating potential variables to be included in the Level-2 model involves a simple univariate regression of the empirical Bayes residuals from each of the $Q + 1$ equations on W variables that might be added to the model. One can compute an approximate "t-to-enter" statistic in this way. An example of these statistics was reported in the last panel of Table 9.2. These t statistics are often the best indicators for selecting W variables.

Although regression coefficients based on empirical Bayes residuals are preferable to those based on the OLS residuals, they still underestimate the effects of the W variables when actually included in the model. Fortunately, the standard errors for the regression coefficients are also underestimated by approximately the same proportion, and thus the t-to-enter statistics will often provide a good indication of the likely consequences. These statistics are, however, only approximate because the model is doubly multivariate with errors correlated across equations and multiple predictors for each equation. They will usually provide a good indication of the next *single* variable to enter *one* of the Level-2 equations. If several variables are entered simultaneously (e.g., one on each of several equations), the actual results may not follow the pattern suggested by these statistics.

Specification Issues at Level 2

A proper specification is assumed for each of the $Q + 1$ Level-2 equations. That is, the error term, u_{qj}, for each equation is assumed uncorrelated with predictors in that equation. This means that any omitted predictors are unrelated to those already included in the model. A corollary of this assumption is that all predictors (i.e., the W_js) are measured without error.

If a confounding variable (i.e., a significant predictor correlated with one or more of the Level-2 predictors already included in the equation) is ignored in one of these equations, estimation of one or more Level-2 coefficients in that equation will be biased. The degree of bias depends on the predictive power of the omitted variable and its strength of association with other variables in the model.

Further, misspecification of one equation can cause biased estimates in another equation. That is, an individual Level-2 equation could be properly specified and yet its estimated coefficient be biased. This bias is induced through the correlation among the errors in the properly and improperly specified equations. A specification test and ameliorative procedures for such cross-equation bias are described below.

Consequences of Level-2 Misspecification

Again, we revert to a specific example to illuminate the problem. For this purpose we assume Equations 9.1 and 9.2 are properly specified. Thus, the "correct" estimates appear in the first column of Table 9.4.

Assume that MEAN SES were incorrectly dropped from the intercept model. Results for this incorrect specification are reported in the second set of columns in Table 9.4. Because MEAN SES and SECTOR are positively correlated, deleting MEAN SES results in an overestimation of the SECTOR effect in the intercept equation by a factor of almost two from 0.83 to 1.56. Further, as noted above, the estimates in the SES slope model are also affected. The coefficient for MEAN SES, γ_{11}, is now inflated by a factor of 40% from 0.68 to 0.93. The misspecification of the intercept

TABLE 9.4 Illustration of Misspecification Effects

	Original Model		*MEAN SES Missing*		*Specification Test (Fixed SES Slopes)*	
	Coefficient	*se*	*Coefficient*	*se*	*Coefficient*	*se*
Model for school means, β_{0j}						
INTERCEPT, γ_{00}	13.73	0.20	12.90	0.23	12.90	0.23
MEAN SES, γ_{01}	4.53	0.48	—	—	—	—
SECTOR, γ_{02}	0.83	0.20	1.56	0.23	1.56	0.23
Model for SES slopes, β_{1j}						
INTERCEPT, γ_{10}	1.78	0.16	1.82	0.16	1.80	0.15
MEAN SES, γ_{11}	0.68	0.38	0.93	0.38	0.73	0.34
SECTOR, γ_{12}	–0.58	0.16	–0.62	0.16	–0.61	0.14

model has led to a distortion in the slope model as well. This has ocurred because the errors of the two models are correlated.

A Specification Test

The coefficient estimates for the intercept and slope equations are independent (and thus not influenced by a specification error in the other) if the sum of the sampling covariance between $\hat{\beta}_{0j}$ and $\hat{\beta}_{1j}$ and the covariance of the true β_{0j} and β_{1j} are zero. Although this condition will rarely arise in practice, the analyst can use this as the basis for a specification test. Specifically, centering the Level-1 predictors around their unit means guarantees that the sampling covariances with the intercept will be null; and constraining that slope to have a zero error term sets the parameter covariance of the slope and intercept to zero. This leads to a specification check to examine whether the estimates in each Level-2 equation have been distorted by misspecification in another equation.

The last set of columns in Table 9.4 demonstrates the specification check where the residual variance for the SES slope model has been set to zero. Even though the BASE model is seriously misspecified due to the omission of MEAN SES, notice that the γ estimates in the SES slope model are not nearly as distorted as in column 3. The fact that the results in columns 3 and 5 differ indicate a likely misspecification for the model in column 3. We caution, however, that a model with a Level-2 variance constrained to zero should be used only as a specification test (assuming that the corresponding variance component is really not zero). By setting the residual variance to zero we have overestimated the precision of the γ coefficients.

Note that the standard errors for the γs in the slope model in column 6 are artificially smaller than the corresponding estimates in column 2.

An Ameliorative Strategy

The biased estimates in a properly specified Level-2 equation that result from a misspecification in another Level-2 equation and correlated errors between these two equations can be avoided if the same predictor set is used for all $Q + 1$ equations. Formally, if the same predictor set is used in each equation *and* if the data are perfectly balanced (i.e., each school had the same sample size and the same set of SES values), the estimates of the Level-2 coefficients in the slope model would be independent of the estimated coefficients in the intercept model. Even when the data are unbalanced, the estimates in the slope model will be *asymptotically* independent of the estimates in the intercept model and they will be asymptotically unbiased.

In many applications, the analyst will not want to force every W in any of the $Q + 1$ equations into all of the $Q + 1$ equations. (Parsimony objects and so may your computer.) At a minimum, the investigator should check that any predictor included in one of the Level-2 equations but excluded from others is in fact nonsignificant. The exploratory analyses using empirical Bayes residuals described above can provide a useful check in this regard.

Errors of Measurement in Level-2 Predictors

Errors of measurement can be viewed as a specific form of a misspecification problem (see the chapter appendix). Thus, all of the concerns described above also apply to fallible Level-2 predictors. In general, if a Level-2 predictor is measured with error, its coefficient and possibly other Level-2 coefficients will be biased. The degree of bias depends on the explanatory power of the true predictor, the degree of unreliability of its measurement, and the intercorrelations among the predictors.

Examining Assumptions About Level-2 Random Effects

Homogeneity

We typically assume that the dispersion of the Level-2 random effects is homogeneous across the J units. A failure of this assumption could occur in the High School and Beyond data, for example, if schools in the Catholic sector had less variable random effects than did schools in the public sector. (Parenthetically, such sector differences might be of substantive interest.)

In terms of the fixed effects, the consequences of inappropriately assuming homogeneity would be a somewhat less than optimal weighting in estimating these effects, resulting in some loss of efficiency. The Level-2 coefficients estimates would, however, remain unbiased. In terms of the random effects, the shrinkage in β_j^* would be incorrect and result in an increased mean squared error for estimation of β_j.

Equality of dispersion in **T** can formally be tested against alternative hypotheses. For example, one might estimate separate **T** matrices for the Catholic and public sectors. This would add $r(r + 1)/2$ variance-covariance components to be estimated and a likelihood-ratio test could be employed to test the equality of the **T** matrices. Discovering the sources of such inequalities would be very much like the process described above for studying heterogeneity of σ^2.

Normality

Estimation of the fixed effects will not be biased by a failure of the normality assumption at Level 2. However, if the the Level-2 random effects have heavy tails, inferences based on normality may be sensitive to outliers. A failure of the normality assumption will affect the validity of the confidence intervals and hypothesis tests for the fixed effects. The nature of these effects depends upon the true shape of the distribution of the random effects. Seltzer (1990) discusses the types of distortion that can occur.

Checking for normality at Level 2 is complicated by the fact that the Level-2 outcomes, β_{qj}, are not directly observed. The empirical Bayes residuals can be plotted and the plots inspected for outlier values. Moreover, their marginal variances can be estimated so that they can be standardized and compared to the expected values of normal order statistics from the unit normal distribution. However, when the sample size per group, n_j, is small, these variance estimates will be quite uncertain, so that the true variance of the standardized residuals may be somewhat greater than unity.

Complicating the checking of the normality assumption is that the $Q + 1$ correlated random effects may be estimated per unit. A *Mahalanobis Distance measure* for each unit summarizes the degree of departure of the random effects from normality and allows detection of outliers. This statistic measures the distance between the residual estimates for each group relative to the expected distance based on the model.[1] Given sufficiently

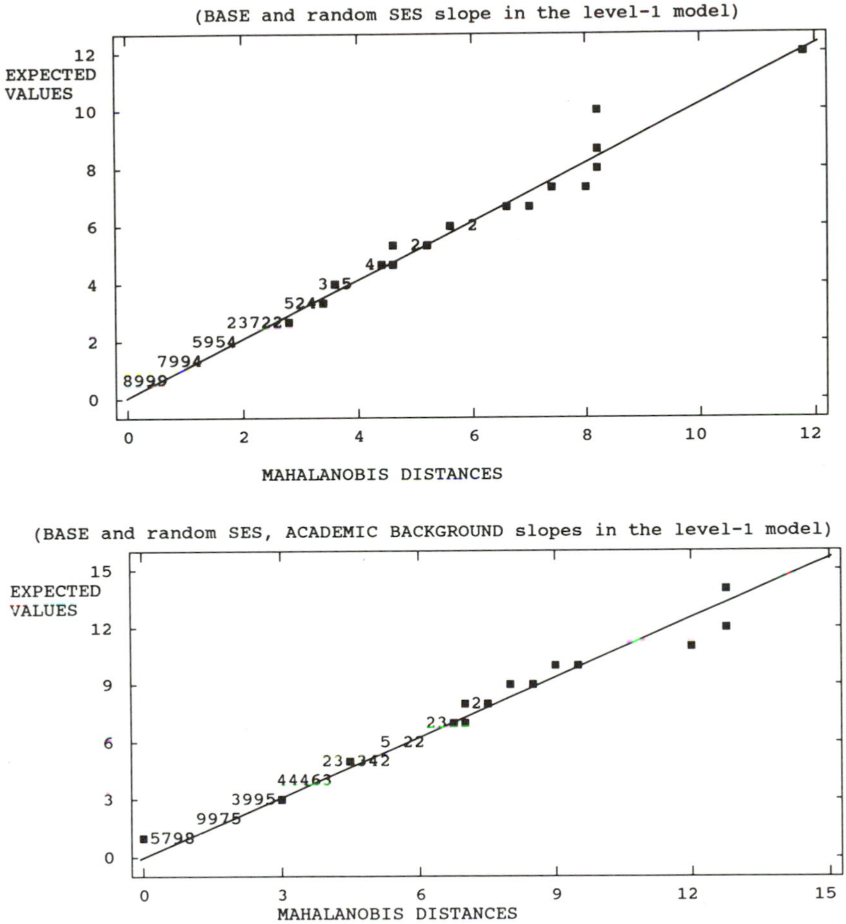

Figure 9.5. Mahalanobis Plots for Examining Normality Assumption

large samples at Level 1, this statistic will have a χ^2 distribution with Q + 1 degrees of freedom when the data are normal. Plotting the observed distance statistics against the expected order statistics allows graphical inspection of possible departures from normality. In addition, one can identify outlier units for further examination.

Figure 9.5 displays Mahalanobis Distance plots for two different models. The first plot is from a Level-1 model with a random intercept and SES slope. The second plot is based on a model where a random ACADEMIC

BACKGROUND slope has been added. Neither model appears grossly nonnormal.

If serious nonnormality is encountered at Level 2, procedures recently developed by Seltzer (1990) can be helpful. In particular, if the random effects at Level 2 have heavy tails, Seltzer has demonstrated that the *data augmentation* method of Tanner and Wong (1987) can be used to estimate the hierarchical linear model. In addition, his results show that a "*t* prior" for the Level-2 random effects provides robust estimates of the fixed effects. These estimates are less sensitive to outlier values at Level 2.

Validity of Inferences when Samples Are Small

In the special case of completely balanced data,[2] small sample theory for inferences about the fixed effects holds. For example, the estimated value of a fixed effect divided by its standard error will be distributed exactly as a *t* variate. Exact inference about fixed effects is possible in the balanced case because the point estimates of the fixed effects do not depend upon the variance components.[3]

In unbalanced cases we rely on large sample theory. Estimates of the fixed effects and their standard errors depend upon point estimates of each of the variance and covariance components in the model. Because of the mutual dependence of the point estimates of the fixed effects and the point estimates of the variance-covariance components, the exact sampling distributions of the resulting estimators are unknown. However, when maximum likelihood estimation is used, the large-sample properties of the maximum likelihood estimators are known. The question in this section is: How well does the large sample distribution theory work?

For any particular application, the answer depends upon the inferences sought. We consider below estimation of fixed effects γ, the variance-covariance components (σ^2 and $\mathbf{T}$), and the random effects, $\mathbf{u}$. To explicate basic principles and clarify the logic we illustrate with a one-way random-effects ANOVA model.

Inferences About the Fixed Effects

For any sample size, fixed-effects estimates are unbiased. However, in the unbalanced case, the standard error estimates for the fixed effects are generally too small, and hypothesis tests based on the unit normal reference distribution will be too liberal.

The point estimate of γ_{00} in the one-way random-effects ANOVA model is from Equation 3.9:

$$\hat{\gamma}_{00} = \sum (\hat{V}_j + \hat{\tau}_{00})^{-1} \bar{Y}_{.j} / \sum (\hat{V}_j + \hat{\tau}_{00})^{-1} , \qquad [9.7]$$

where

$$\hat{V}_j = \hat{\sigma}^2 / n_j ,$$

and

$$\bar{Y}_{.j} = \sum Y_{ij} / n_j .$$

The estimated standard error of $\hat{\gamma}_{00}$ is

$$[\hat{V}(\hat{\gamma}_{00})]^{1/2} = \left[\sum (\hat{V}_j + \hat{\tau}_{00})^{-1} \right]^{-1/2} . \qquad [9.8]$$

Note that, in general, the point estimate of γ_{00} and its estimated standard error are a function of estimates of σ^2 and τ_{00}. However, in the balanced case, this is not true:

$$\hat{\gamma}_{00} = \sum \bar{Y}_{..} / J . \qquad [9.9]$$

Clearly, in the balanced case, $\hat{\gamma}_{00}$ does not depend on σ^2 or τ_{00}. Further, $V(\hat{\gamma}_{00})$ requires only an estimate of $V + \tau_{00}$ and not the separate components. (The usual estimate of $V + \tau_{00}$ is just the mean square between groups divided by n.)

Thus in the balanced case,

$$(\hat{\gamma} - \gamma_o) / (\text{MS between} / nJ)^{1/2} \qquad [9.10]$$

will have a t distribution with $J - 1$ degrees of freedom under the null hypothesis H_0: $\gamma = \gamma_o$.

However, in the unbalanced case, no such exact test exists. We can say, however, that if σ^2 and τ_{00} are estimated by maximum likelihood, the large-sample distribution of

$$Z = (\hat{\gamma} - \gamma_o) / [V(\hat{\gamma})]^{1/2} \qquad [9.11]$$

is unit normal. In practice, however, use of a t reference distribution may be more appropriate. Fotiu (1989) simulated unbalanced data from hypothetical small-sample studies of classrooms in which both the intercept and slope from each classroom depended on the assignment of that class to an experimental or control condition. His results showed that using the t distribution rather than the unit normal as the reference distribution produced substantially more accurate hypothesis tests for the fixed effects.

Second, the estimate $V(\hat{\gamma}_{00})$ is negatively biased. The true variance of $\hat{\gamma}_{00}$ will be

$$\text{Var}(\hat{\gamma}_{00}) = \text{E}_\text{m}[\text{Var}_\text{c}(\hat{\gamma}_{00} \mid \hat{\tau}_{00}, \hat{\sigma}^2)] + \text{Var}_\text{m}[\text{E}_\text{c}(\hat{\gamma}_{00} \mid \hat{\tau}_{00}, \hat{\sigma}^2)], \quad [9.12]$$

where the expectation and variance E_m and Var_m are taken over the joint distribution of $\hat{\tau}_{00}$ and $\hat{\sigma}^2$ and E_c and Var_c are taken over the conditional distribution of $\hat{\gamma}_{00}$ given $\hat{\tau}_{00}$ and $\hat{\sigma}^2$. The second term, which is the bias under maximum likelihood estimation, is zero in the balanced case and will converge to zero as J increases in the unbalanced case. Even in many small-sample cases (which are not too badly unbalanced) this term will be very small.

Given small to moderate sample size J at Level 2, the key determinant of the size of the bias for $\hat{V}(\hat{\gamma}_{00})$ will be the sensitivity of the $\hat{\gamma}_{00}$ estimates to differential weighting. Recall from Equation 9.7 that the estimate for $\hat{\gamma}_{00}$ is a weighted average based on $(V_j + \tau_{00})^{-1}$. As τ_{00} approaches zero, these weights approach n_j/σ^2 and $\hat{\gamma}_{00}$ approaches the weighted mean $\Sigma n_j \bar{Y}_{.j} / \Sigma n_j$. In contrast, for nonzero τ_{00}, $\hat{\gamma}_{00} = \Sigma \lambda_j \bar{Y}_{.j} / \Sigma \lambda_j$ with $\lambda_j = \tau_{00} / [\tau_{00} + (\sigma^2/n_j)]$. Hence, as τ_{00} increases, λ_j approaches 1 and $\hat{\gamma}_{00}$ approximates the arithmetic mean $\Sigma \bar{Y}_{.j}/J$. If the weighted mean $\Sigma n_j \bar{Y}_{.j} / \Sigma n_j$ is highly discrepant from the arithmetic mean, the bias term in Equation 9.12 will be large and the hierarchical estimate of $V(\hat{\gamma}_{00})$ will be too small. If these weighted and unweighted averages are similar, the hierarchical estimate of $V(\hat{\gamma}_{00})$ will be nearly unbiased.

This analysis leads to the following general recommendations:

1. Use the t rather than the normal distribution to test hypotheses about γ.
2. Examine the sensitivity of the $\hat{\gamma}$ estimates to the choice of the weighting scheme. If the estimates are insensitive to the weighting scheme, use $V(\hat{\gamma})$ as the standard error estimate.
3. If the results are sensitive to the weighting scheme, t tests based on $V(\hat{\gamma})$ should be viewed as liberal. An exact solution is available through a Bayes approach. The Bayes estimates, which require substantial computation, take full account of the uncertainty about σ^2 and $\mathbf{T}$ in estimating the γs and their standard errors (Seltzer, 1990).

Inferences About the Variance Components

Inferences about the variance components, σ^2 and **T**, depend on the large-sample properties of maximum likelihood estimates. Technically, standard errors and hypothesis tests are based on the "information matrix" (see Chapter 10). Point estimates of σ^2 will generally be quite accurate in most applications. If σ^2 is assumed equal in every unit, then the precision of its estimation will depend on the total sample size ($N = \Sigma n_j$), which will typically be large. Similarly, likelihood-ratio tests and standard errors for σ^2 will tend to be accurate.

Problems may arise, however, if σ^2 is assumed to vary across Level-2 units. The key issue is the number of observations n_j upon which each σ_j^2 is estimated. In these applications, the sample size in each unit, n_j, should be large. On the other hand, if σ_1^2 and σ_2^2 are estimated for each of two school sectors (e.g., Catholic versus public) the accuracy of estimation of these σ^2s and the credibility of inferences about them will depend upon the total sample size in each sector.

In terms of **T** the accuracy of estimation depends upon the number of Level-2 units, J. Standard errors for **T** based on the information matrix require large J for credibility.

MLR Versus MLF. In Chapter 2 we introduced the distinction between the full and restricted likelihood. We noted that when J is small, MLF estimates for the **T** matrix can be too small and this problem will be exacerbated as the number of fixed effects in the model increases. However, the standard-error estimates for these elements will also tend to be proportionally too small. So hypotheses based on these standard errors will not be seriously biased by the use of the full as opposed to the restricted likelihood.

Type of Test. Chapter 2 introduced three types of tests for elements of **T**: a univariate χ^2 test, a univariate test based on the ratio of an estimate to its standard error, and a likelihood-ratio test that is generally multivariate (because it simultaneously tests two or more elements of **T**). Each of these tests is based on large sample theory. However, our experience suggests that the test using the estimated standard errors of the **T** elements are especially untrustworthy when sample sizes are small. These tests are based on the notion of constructing a confidence interval with the estimate at its center. Such a test is informative only if the likelihood is symmetric about the mode. In many cases, however, the likelihood will be highly skewed. This will be especially true when the true variance is small, which is when the test is most needed. In general, the smaller the variance component, the more data are needed to justify the large-sample normality approximation on which the test is based.

All of the tests for **T** elements depend asymptotically on J. That is, even if the sample size within units, n_j, were infinite, the tests would be accurate only if the number of units, J, were large. More investigation is needed, however, to discern the effects of small-sample sizes on the accuracy of these tests. We suspect that the likelihood for **T** can be quite skewed if each n_j is small, even if J is large, thus rendering test results inaccurate. One possibility is to graph the likelihood as suggested by Raudenbush and Bryk (1985). This procedure, however, becomes impractical when **T** is of high dimension.

Inferences About Random Level-1 Coefficients

Chapter 3 discussed procedures for constructing confidence intervals and tests for the random coefficients, β_j. We mentioned that exact tests are possible using separate OLS estimation for each unit. However, these intervals will be very large and the tests very conservative unless sample sizes per unit are quite large.

The alternative is to base intervals and tests on the empirical Bayes estimates, β_j^*. However, these tests do not reflect uncertainty about the variance components. Thus the intervals will be too short and the tests too liberal unless **T** and σ^2 are precisely determined.

MLR Versus MLF. The accuracy of inferences about the random coefficients using the empirical Bayes approach also depends upon choice of likelihood: MLF versus MLR. Inferences based on MLF require the assumption that the fixed effects in the model are given. Thus the MLF-based intervals will be shorter than those based on MLR.

In both cases, the intervals will be based on the posterior variance of the β_j element. A comparison of these posterior variances in the simple case of a balanced one-way random-effects ANOVA reveals the difference between the two:

$$\text{Var}(\beta_j \mid \text{MLR}) = \text{Var}(\beta_j \mid \text{MLF})\{1 + [n\,\tau_{00}/(J\sigma^2)]\}\,. \qquad [9.13]$$

The formula shows that as J (the number of Level-2 units) increases, the two converge. When J is small, the MLF variance estimate is especially unrealistic. The difference also depends on the ratio of τ_{00} to σ^2. As this ratio increases, the MLF variance becomes less realistic.

Appendix

Misspecification of the Level-1 Structural Model

Earlier we discussed the consequences of misspecification of the Level-1 model for estimation of the Level-2 coefficients. Restricting our attention to predictors of Level-1 slopes, we asserted that if three conditions were met, estimated effects would be biased. These conditions are (a) an omitted Level-1 variable must be related to *Y*; (b) it must be related to a Level-1 predictor already in the model; and (c) the statistical association between the omitted variable and this predictor must vary from unit to unit, and the degree of this statistical association must be related to one of the Level-2 predictors in the model. We prove these assertions below. We emphasize that the conditions do not apply to Level-2 predictors of the intercept.

Suppose that the true Level-1 model were

$$\mathbf{Y} = \mathbf{X}_1\beta_1 + \mathbf{X}_2\beta_2 + \mathbf{r}, \quad \mathbf{r} \sim N(\mathbf{0}, \sigma^2\mathbf{I}), \qquad [9.14]$$

where $\mathbf{Y}$ is a vector of outcomes, $\mathbf{X}_1$ and $\mathbf{X}_2$ are matrices of known predictors (with full column rank), β_1 and β_2 are vectors of unknown effects, and $\mathbf{r}$ is the vector of errors, where vectors and matrices are conformable. The variable $\mathbf{Y}$ is assumed to have a mean of zero with each group (i.e., the Level-1 model has no intercept).

Suppose, however, that the model actually estimated is

$$\mathbf{Y} = \mathbf{X}_1\beta_1 + \mathbf{e}, \qquad [9.15]$$

where $\mathbf{e} = \mathbf{X}_2\beta_2 + \mathbf{r}$. Then, using OLS regression within units,

$$\hat{\beta}_1 = (\mathbf{X}_1'\mathbf{X}_1)^{-1}\mathbf{X}_1'\mathbf{Y}$$

which has expectation

$$E(\hat{\beta}_1) = \beta_1 + (\mathbf{X}_1'\mathbf{X}_1)^{-1}\mathbf{X}_1'\mathbf{X}_2\beta_2. \qquad [9.16]$$

This reveals that $\hat{\beta}_1$ is a biased estimator of β_1 if two conditions hold: β_2 is nonnull; and the matrix of regression coefficients

$$\beta_{2\cdot 1} = (\mathbf{X}_1'\mathbf{X}_1)^{-1}\mathbf{X}_1'\mathbf{X}_2$$

is nonnull.

At Level 2, the true model is

$$\beta_1 = \mathbf{W}_1\gamma_1 + \mathbf{u}_1 , \qquad [9.17]$$

$$\beta_2 = \mathbf{W}_2\gamma_2 + \mathbf{u}_2 , \qquad [9.18]$$

where $\mathbf{W}_1$ and $\mathbf{W}_2$ are matrices of predictors, γ_1 and γ_2 are fixed-effect vectors, and $\mathbf{u}_1$ and $\mathbf{u}_2$ are random-error vectors. Hence the true combined model may be written

$$\mathbf{Y} = \mathbf{X}_1\mathbf{W}_1\gamma_1 + \mathbf{X}_2\mathbf{W}_2\gamma_2 + \varepsilon , \qquad [9.19]$$

where $\varepsilon = \mathbf{X}_1\mathbf{u}_1 + \mathbf{X}_2\mathbf{u}_2 + \mathbf{r}$. The model estimated, however, is

$$\mathbf{Y} = \mathbf{X}_1\mathbf{W}_1\gamma_1 + \varepsilon^* ,$$

where $\varepsilon^* = \mathbf{X}_1\mathbf{u}_1 + \mathbf{X}_2\beta_2 + \mathbf{r}$. Then the generalized least squares estimator of γ_1 will be

$$\hat{\gamma}_1 = (\mathbf{W}_1' \, \mathbf{V}^{*\,-1}\mathbf{W}_1)^{-1}\mathbf{W}_1' \, \mathbf{V}^{*\,-1}\hat{\beta}_1 , \qquad [9.20]$$

where $\mathbf{V}^*$ is the dispersion matrix of ε^*. The expectation of $\hat{\gamma}_1$ will be

$$\mathrm{E}(\hat{\gamma}_1) = \gamma_1 + (\mathbf{W}_1' \, \mathbf{V}^{*\,-1}\mathbf{W}_1)^{-1}\mathbf{W}_1' \, \mathbf{V}^{*\,-1}\beta_{2\cdot 1}\mathbf{W}_2\gamma_2 . \qquad [9.21]$$

The bias term will be null if any of the following conditions hold:

1. $\mathrm{E}(\beta_2) = \mathbf{W}_2\gamma_2 = 0$ (no association between $\mathbf{W}_2$ and β_2).
2. $\beta_{2\cdot 1} = 0$ (no association between $\mathbf{X}_1$ and $\mathbf{X}_2$).
3. $\beta_{2\cdot 1}$ is unrelated to $\mathbf{W}_1$. (Note that $(\mathbf{W}_1'\mathbf{V}^{*\,-1}\mathbf{W}_1)^{-1}\mathbf{W}_1'\mathbf{V}^{*\,-1}\beta_{2\cdot 1}$ is the matrix of regression coefficients in which $\beta_{2\cdot 1}$ is the outcome and $\mathbf{W}_1$ is the predictor.)

Hence the three conditions listed earlier must be satisfied for bias to occur.

Level-1 Predictors Measured with Error

Suppose that the true Level-1 model is

$$\mathbf{Y} = \mathbf{X}\beta + \mathbf{r} , \qquad [9.22]$$

but the estimated model is

$$\mathbf{Y} = \mathbf{X}_o\beta + \mathbf{r}^*,$$

where $\mathbf{X}_o = \mathbf{X} + \mathbf{E}$ is a fallible measure of $\mathbf{X}$ with error $\mathbf{E}$ having a null expectation. Then the true model may be written as

$$\mathbf{Y} = \mathbf{X}_o\beta - \mathbf{E}\beta + \mathbf{r}, \qquad [9.23]$$

and we have a special case of misspecification (Equations 9.14 and 9.15) with $\mathbf{X}_1 = \mathbf{X}_o$, $\mathbf{X}_2 = -\mathbf{E}$, and $\beta_1 = \beta_2 = \beta$. Hence the results of part one apply. Condition 1, that $E(\beta_2) = \mathbf{0}$, clearly does not apply. Now, however,

$$\beta_{2 \cdot 1} = -(\mathbf{X}_o' \mathbf{X}_o)^{-1}\mathbf{X}_o'\mathbf{E}$$

measures the degree of unreliability of $\mathbf{X}_o$ as a measure of $\mathbf{X}$. Our previous results imply that errors of measurement $\mathbf{E}$ will bias estimation of γ_1 if and only if (a) the measurement reliability varies from unit to unit; and (b) that reliability is related to elements of the Level-2 predictor matrix, $\mathbf{W}$.

Distortions in One Equation Arising from Misspecification of Another

Earlier we discussed the possibility that estimates of effects in one Level-2 equation could be biased by misspecification in another Level-2 equation. Yet we argued that such bias was detectable and possibly avoidable. To illustrate the properties of this bias, suppose that we have a simple Level-1 model:

$$Y_{ij} = \beta_{0j} + \beta_{1j}X_{ij} + r_{ij}, \quad r_{ij} \sim N(0, \sigma^2). \qquad [9.24]$$

The true Level-2 model is

$$\beta_{0j} = \alpha W_j + \delta Z_j + u_{0j} \qquad [9.25]$$

$$\beta_{1j} = \gamma W_j + u_{1j} \qquad [9.26]$$

where $\mathbf{u}_j \sim N(0, \mathbf{T})$.

Suppose, however, that the variable Z_j is omitted from Equation 9.25 so that this equation is misspecified. How will this misspecification affect estimation of Equation 9.26? Standard but tedious algebra reveals that the bias in $\hat{\gamma}$ will be

$$\text{Bias}(\hat{\gamma}) = \qquad [9.27]$$

$$\frac{\left(\sum W_j^2 c_j \Delta_{01j}\right)\left(\sum W_j Z_j c_j \Delta_{11j}\right) - \left(\sum W_j Z_j c_j \Delta_{01j}\right)\left(\sum W_j^2 c_j \Delta_{11j}\right)}{\left(\sum W_j^2 c_j \Delta_{11j}\right)\left(\sum W_j^2 c_j \Delta_{00j}\right) - \left(\sum W_j^2 c_j \Delta_{01j}\right)^2}$$

where

$$\Delta_{st} = \text{Cov}(\hat{\beta}_{sj}, \hat{\beta}_{tj}) = \tau_{st} + V_{st}, \quad s, t = 0, 1$$

$$c_j = (\Delta_{00j}\Delta_{11j} - \Delta_{01j}^2)^{-1},$$

and $\hat{\beta}_{sj}$ and $\hat{\beta}_{tj}$ are OLS estimators. Inspection of Equation 9.27 reveals the following:

1. If Δ_{st} are the same for every unit, such as when data are perfectly balanced, the bias $(\hat{\gamma}) = 0$.
2. If $\Delta_{01j} = 0$ in every unit (i.e., no intercept-slope covariance exists), the bias $(\hat{\gamma}) = 0$.
3. As the sample size per unit, n_j, increases for all j, the Δ_{stj} values converge to constants and bias $(\hat{\gamma}) \to 0$.

From these principles it is clear that group-mean centering of the predictors and constraining the slope β_{1j} to have zero variance as explained will constrain every Δ_{01j} to be zero and will therefore eliminate the bias in $\hat{\gamma}$. This provides the bias specification check.

Notes

1. Specifically, the Mahalanobis Distance is

$$u_j^{*\prime} V_j^{-1} u_j^*,$$

where u_j^* is the empirical Bayes estimate of the vector $\mathbf{u}_j$ of random effects for unit j, and V_j is the error dispersion of that vector. Specifically,

$$V_j = \sigma^2(X_j' X_j)^{-1} + \mathbf{T} - \text{Var}(W_j\hat{\gamma})$$

where Var $(W_j\hat{\gamma})$ is the dispersion matrix of the $P + 1$ elements of $W_j\hat{\gamma}$.

2. Completely balanced cases are an extremely restricted set. In a two-level hierarchy, the following conditions must hold for the data to be completely balanced:

a. Sample sizes within units must be equal.

b. The same set of Level-1 predictor values must be present within each unit.

c. For each of the $Q + 1$ Level-2 equations, the same set of predictor variables must be used.

d. Level-1 and Level-2 variance components must be constant for every unit.

3. In the balanced case, the Level-2 model is a classical multivariate linear model in which the OLS regression coefficients from each unit may be viewed as the outcome vectors distributed independently and identically as multivariate normal:

$$\hat{\beta}_j = \mathbf{W}_j\gamma + \mathbf{u}_j + \mathbf{e}_j\,, \quad \mathbf{u}_j + \mathbf{e}_j \sim \mathrm{N}(\mathbf{0}\,,\ \Sigma)$$

where $\Sigma = \sigma^2(\mathbf{X}'\mathbf{X})^{-1} + \mathbf{T}$. Only Σ need be estimated—that is, point estimates of σ^2 and $\mathbf{T}$ are not needed to estimate γ.

10 Technical Appendix

- The General Bayes Linear Model
- "No-Subscript" Notation for the Hierarchical Linear Model
- Estimation Theory and Computations
- Inferences About the Fixed Parameters

The General Bayes Linear Model

All of the models presented in this book may be viewed as particular cases of the general Bayes linear model

$$\mathbf{Y} = \mathbf{A}\theta + \mathbf{r}, \qquad \mathbf{r} \sim N(\mathbf{0}, \Psi), \qquad [10.1]$$

where the outcome vector $\mathbf{Y}$, the predictor matrix, $\mathbf{A}$, the parameter vector, θ, and the error vector, $\mathbf{r}$, are dimensioned conformably. The errors, $\mathbf{r}$, are presumed normally distributed with a mean vector of $\mathbf{0}$ and an arbitrary positive definite dispersion matrix, Ψ.

What distinguishes the model from the standard linear model of classical statistics is that we also specify a prior distribution for the parameter vector, θ:

$$\theta \sim N(\bar{\theta}, \Omega). \qquad [10.2]$$

Estimation theory for this and related models is presented in Lindley and Smith (1972) and Dempster et al. (1981). The key result is that θ, given $\mathbf{Y}$, Ψ, Ω, and $\bar{\theta}$, is normally distributed with mean vector θ^* and dispersion, $\mathbf{D}^*$, where

$$\theta^* = \mathbf{D}^*(\Omega^{-1}\bar{\theta} + \mathbf{A}'\Psi^{-1}\mathbf{Y}), \qquad [10.3]$$

and

$$\mathbf{D}^* = (\mathbf{A}'\Psi^{-1}\mathbf{A} + \Omega^{-1})^{-1}. \qquad [10.4]$$

To prove this result, we first note that Equations 10.1 and 10.2 imply that the joint distribution of **Y** and θ, given Ψ, Ω, and $\bar{\theta}$, is multivariate normal such that

$$\begin{bmatrix} \mathbf{Y} \\ \theta \end{bmatrix} \sim \mathrm{N}\left\{ \begin{bmatrix} \mathbf{A}\bar{\theta} \\ \bar{\theta} \end{bmatrix}, \begin{bmatrix} \mathbf{A}\Omega\mathbf{A}' + \Psi & \mathbf{A}\Omega \\ \Omega\mathbf{A}' & \Omega \end{bmatrix} \right\}. \qquad [10.5]$$

It follows from standard multivariate normal distribution theory (cf. Morrison, 1967, p. 88) that the conditional distribution of $\theta \mid \mathbf{Y}, \Psi, \Omega, \bar{\theta}$ is $\mathrm{N}(\theta^*, \mathbf{D}^*)$ with

$$\theta^* = \bar{\theta} + \Omega\mathbf{A}'(\mathbf{A}\Omega\mathbf{A}' + \Psi)^{-1}(\mathbf{Y} - \mathbf{A}\bar{\theta}) \qquad [10.6]$$

and

$$\mathbf{D}^* = \Omega - \Omega\mathbf{A}'(\mathbf{A}\Omega\mathbf{A}' + \Psi)^{-1}\mathbf{A}\Omega. \qquad [10.7]$$

However, by theorem 3 in Smith (1973),

$$(\mathbf{A}\Omega\mathbf{A}' + \Psi)^{-1} = \Psi^{-1} - \Psi^{-1}\mathbf{A}(\mathbf{A}'\Psi^{-1}\mathbf{A} + \Omega^{-1})^{-1}\mathbf{A}'\Psi^{-1}. \qquad [10.8]$$

Substituting Equation 10.8 into Equation 10.7 and setting $Q = \mathbf{A}'\Psi^{-1}\mathbf{A}$ yields

$$\begin{aligned} \mathbf{D}^* &= \Omega - \Omega\mathbf{Q}[\mathbf{I} - (\mathbf{Q} + \Omega^{-1})^{-1}\mathbf{Q}]\Omega \\ &= \Omega - \Omega\mathbf{Q}(\mathbf{Q} + \Omega^{-1})^{-1} \\ &= \Omega[\mathbf{I} - \mathbf{Q}(\mathbf{Q} + \Omega^{-1})^{-1}]. \end{aligned}$$

Expressing **I** as $(\mathbf{Q} + \Omega^{-1})(\mathbf{Q} + \Omega^{-1})^{-1}$ and simplifying yields

$$\mathbf{D}^* = (\mathbf{Q} + \Omega^{-1})^{-1}. \qquad [10.9]$$

Substituting Equation 10.8 into Equation 10.6 yields

$$\theta^* = \bar{\theta} + [\Omega\mathbf{A}'\Psi^{-1} - \Omega\mathbf{Q}(\mathbf{Q} + \Omega^{-1})^{-1}\mathbf{A}'\Psi^{-1}](\mathbf{Y} - \mathbf{A}\bar{\theta}) \qquad [10.10]$$

$$= \bar{\theta} + \Omega[\mathbf{I} - \mathbf{Q}(\mathbf{Q} + \Omega^{-1})^{-1}]\mathbf{A}'\Psi^{-1}(\mathbf{Y} - \mathbf{A}\bar{\theta})$$

$$= \bar{\theta} + \mathbf{D}^*\mathbf{A}'\Psi^{-1}(\mathbf{Y} - \mathbf{A}\bar{\theta})$$

$$= \mathbf{D}^*\mathbf{A}'\Psi^{-1}\mathbf{Y} + (\mathbf{I} - \mathbf{D}^*\mathbf{A}'\Psi^{-1}\mathbf{A})\bar{\theta}$$

$$\theta^* = \mathbf{D}^*(\Omega^{-1}\bar{\theta} + \mathbf{A}'\Psi^{-1}\mathbf{Y})\,.$$

The Likelihood Function. Viewing $\mathbf{Y}$ and θ as random and Ψ and Ω as parameters to be estimated, the likelihood is the marginal density of $\mathbf{Y}$ viewed as a function of the parameters Ψ and Ω. We denote this density as $f(\mathbf{Y} \mid \Psi, \Omega, \bar{\theta})$. However, in all of the applications in this book it is sensible and convenient to assume that $\bar{\theta} = \mathbf{0}$. Following Dempster et al. (1981), this density may therefore be written as

$$f(\mathbf{Y} \mid \Psi, \Omega) = g(\mathbf{Y} \mid \theta, \Psi, \Omega)\, h(\theta \mid \Psi, \Omega)/p(\theta \mid \mathbf{Y}, \Psi, \Omega)\,, \quad [10.11]$$

where f, g, h, and p are probability density functions. Thus,

$$f(\mathbf{Y} \mid \Psi, \Omega) \propto |\Psi|^{-1/2} \exp[-\tfrac{1}{2}(\mathbf{Y} - \mathbf{A}\theta)'\Psi^{-1}(\mathbf{Y} - \mathbf{A}\theta)] \quad [10.12]$$

$$\times |\Omega|^{-1/2} \exp(-\tfrac{1}{2}\theta'\Omega^{-1}\theta)$$

$$\div |\mathbf{D}^*|^{-1/2} \exp[-\tfrac{1}{2}(\theta - \theta^*)'\mathbf{D}^{*\,-1}(\theta - \theta^*)]$$

leading to the result

$$f(\mathbf{Y} \mid \Psi, \Omega) \propto |\Psi|^{-1/2} |\Omega|^{-1/2} |\mathbf{D}^*|^{1/2} \exp(-\tfrac{1}{2}\mathbf{Q}^*) \quad [10.13]$$

where

$$\mathbf{Q}^* = \mathbf{Y}'\Psi^{-1}(\mathbf{Y} - \mathbf{A}\theta^*)\,.$$

The key steps in the proof involve collecting terms in the exponent and simplifying. Terms in θ disappear, leaving $\mathbf{Q}^*$ defined as above. See Dempster et al. (1981) for detailed steps.

Inference. An approximate Bayes solution to the problem of finding inferences about θ requires first maximizing the likelihood given by Equation 10.11 with respect to Ψ and Ω. The maximum likelihood point estimates of Ψ and Ω are then substituted into the formulas for the posterior mean and dispersion of θ given $\mathbf{Y}$, Ψ, and Ω (Equations 10.3 and 10.4), and inferences are then based upon the posterior distribution of $\theta \mid \mathbf{Y},\Psi,\Omega$. This posterior distribution is a first-order aproximation of the distribution of $\theta \mid \mathbf{Y}$ (Deeley & Lindley, 1981) upon which exact Bayes inference would be based. This approximation to a Bayes solution has been termed the empirical Bayes approach (see the review by Morris, 1983). It is the estimation strategy introduced in Chapter 3 and used in the HLM computer program of Bryk et al. (1988).

The exact Bayes solution to the problem of inference for θ requires the specification of a prior distribution for the dispersion parameters Ψ and Ω. One then computes the joint posterior distribution of θ, Ψ, and Ω given $\mathbf{Y}$. To make inferences about θ requires integration of the joint posterior with respect to Ψ and Ω. The resulting inferences take fully into account the uncertainty about the dispersion parameters, which the empirical Bayes estimates do not. However, the exact Bayes solution poses serious computational problems. Because the empirical Bayes approach is computationally efficient and the results are asymptotically equivalent to the exact Bayes results, it often provides a sensible analytic approach.

Several strategies are actually available for maximizing the likelihood. In the applications in this book, we have employed the HLM program, which uses the EM algorithm of Dempster et al. (1977). With this method, the computations needed on each iteration are quite simple, the estimates are well conditioned to lie within the parameter space, and the solution is highly robust to poor starting values. Other examples of EM applications of the type presented here include Dempster et al. (1981), Laird and Ware (1982), Strenio et al. (1983), and Mason et al. (1983).

Other methods for maximizing the likelihood include Fisher scoring (Longford [1987]; see Aitkin & Longford [1986] and de Leeuw and Kreft [1986] for applications) and iterative generalized least squares (Goldstein, 1986, 1987). Kreft et al. (1990) have extensively compared computer packages using the various methods. Although the various approaches differ in terms of user interface, data requirements, and treatment of certain boundary value problems, the results produced by these approaches are highly similar in the vast majority of applications.

"No-Subscript" Notation for the Hierarchical Linear Model

Below we show how specific two- and three-level models may be written without subscripts and then translated into the terms of the general model. Once this translation has been accomplished, computational formulae for the models of interest can be derived from the results for the general model given by Equations 10.9, 10.10, and 10.13.

Two-Level Model

Level-1 Model. Within each unit, j, we formulate the model

$$\mathbf{Y}_j = \mathbf{X}_j \beta_j + \mathbf{r}_j , \quad \mathbf{r}_j \sim \mathrm{N}(\mathbf{0}, \Psi_j), \qquad [10.14]$$

where $\mathbf{Y}_j$ is vector of outcomes, $\mathbf{X}_j$ is a matrix of known Level-1 predictors, β_j is a vector of unknown Level-1 coefficients, and $\mathbf{r}_j$ is an error vector at Level-1 assumed normally distributed with dispersion Ψ_j. By stacking the models from each unit $j = 1, \ldots, J$, we may write the model for all of the data without subscripts:

$$\mathbf{Y} = \mathbf{X}\beta + \mathbf{r} , \quad \mathbf{r} \sim \mathrm{N}(\mathbf{0}, \Psi), \qquad [10.15]$$

where

$$\mathbf{Y} = (\mathbf{Y}_1', \mathbf{Y}_2', \ldots, \mathbf{Y}_J')',$$

$$\beta = (\beta_1', \beta_2', \ldots, \beta_J')',$$

$$\mathbf{r} = (\mathbf{r}_1', \mathbf{r}_2', \ldots, \mathbf{r}_J')',$$

$$\mathbf{X} = \begin{pmatrix} \mathbf{X}_1 & 0 & \ldots & 0 \\ 0 & \mathbf{X}_2 & \ldots & 0 \\ \cdot & \cdot & \ldots & \cdot \\ \cdot & \cdot & \ldots & \cdot \\ \cdot & \cdot & \ldots & \cdot \\ 0 & 0 & \ldots & \mathbf{X}_J \end{pmatrix} \quad \text{and} \quad \Psi = \begin{pmatrix} \Psi_1 & 0 & \ldots & 0 \\ 0 & \Psi_2 & \ldots & 0 \\ \cdot & \cdot & \ldots & \cdot \\ \cdot & \cdot & \ldots & \cdot \\ \cdot & \cdot & \ldots & \cdot \\ 0 & 0 & \ldots & \Psi_J \end{pmatrix}.$$

Level-2 Model. The vector of coefficients β_j is conceived as varying over the population of J units

$$\beta_j = \mathbf{W}_j \gamma + \mathbf{u}_j , \qquad [10.16]$$

where γ is a vector of fixed effects, $\mathbf{u}_j$ is a vector of Level-2 random effects, and $\mathbf{W}_j$ is a matrix of known Level-2 predictors. Each $\mathbf{u}_j$ is assumed independently normally distributed with **0** mean and common dispersion matrix, τ [i.e., $\mathbf{u}_j \sim N(\mathbf{0}, \tau)$].[1]

Again, by stacking the models across units, the Level-2 model may also be written without subscripts as

$$\beta = \mathbf{W}\gamma + \mathbf{u}\,, \qquad \mathbf{u} \sim N(\mathbf{0}\,,\ \mathbf{T})\,, \tag{10.17}$$

where

$$\mathbf{W} = (\,\mathbf{W}_1'\,, \mathbf{W}_2'\,, \ldots, \mathbf{W}_J')'\,,$$

$$\mathbf{u} = (\mathbf{u}_1'\,, \mathbf{u}_2'\,, \ldots, \mathbf{u}_J')'\,,$$

$$\mathbf{T} = \begin{pmatrix} \tau & 0 & \ldots & 0 \\ 0 & \tau & \ldots & 0 \\ \cdot & \cdot & \ldots & \cdot \\ \cdot & \cdot & \ldots & \cdot \\ \cdot & \cdot & \ldots & \cdot \\ 0 & 0 & \ldots & \tau \end{pmatrix}.$$

Combined Model. If we substitute Equation 10.17 into Equation 10.15, we obtain the single model

$$\mathbf{Y} = \mathbf{XW}\gamma + \mathbf{Xu} + \mathbf{r}\,, \tag{10.18}$$

which is a special case of a mixed model

$$\mathbf{Y} = \mathbf{A}_1\theta_1 + \mathbf{A}_2\theta_2 + \mathbf{r} \tag{10.19}$$

with

$$\mathbf{A}_1 = \mathbf{XW}\,, \quad \mathbf{A}_2 = \mathbf{X}\,, \quad \theta_1 = \gamma\,, \quad \text{and } \theta_2 = \mathbf{u}\,,$$

where **Y** is the outcome vector, the θ_1 vector contains unknown fixed effects, the θ_2 vector includes the unknown Level-2 random effects, $\mathbf{A}_1$ and $\mathbf{A}_2$ are known predictor matrices, and **r** is vector of random effects.

The mixed-model formulation is especially useful if some elements of **u** are constrained to be zero (as when fixed or nonrandomly varying Level-1 coefficients are specified), θ_2 becomes the nonzero subset of **u**, and $\mathbf{A}_2$ is the corresponding subset of **X**. Thus the mixed model of Equation 10.19

is more general than Equation 10.18, which we refer to as the fully hierarchical model.

Three-Level Model

The three-level model may be similarly reformulated without subscripts. Suppose, for example, that a person-level model (Level 1) is written as

$$\mathbf{Y}_{jk} = \mathbf{A}_{jk}\pi_{jk} + \mathbf{e}_{jk} \qquad [10.20]$$

for the vector of outcomes in classroom j of school k. The classroom-level model (Level 2) for π_{jk} may therefore be written

$$\pi_{jk} = \mathbf{X}_{jk}\beta_k + \mathbf{r}_{jk}\,. \qquad [10.21]$$

The stacking procedure employed for the two-level case may now be used to eliminate the j subscript within school k. The classroom equations would be concatenated within each school as if each school had a two-level model. A second stacking procedure concatentating models across schools will rid the model of the k subscript. The result is a mixed model:

$$\mathbf{Y} = \mathbf{A}_1\theta_1 + \mathbf{A}_2\theta_2 + \mathbf{A}_3\theta_3 + \mathbf{r}\,, \qquad [10.22]$$

where θ_1 is again the vector of fixed effects, θ_2 contains the random effects that vary across schools but not across classsrooms, θ_3 contains the random effects that vary across classrooms, and $\mathbf{r}$ contains the Level-1 random effects varying across persons within classrooms.

Estimation Theory and Computations

Two-Level MLR

In Chapter 3 we introduced the distinction between MLR and MLF. Dempster et al. (1981) describe this distinction in detail. Under MLR a prior distribution is formulated for θ_1, whereas under MLF, θ_1 is conceived as a fixed, unknown parameter. The consequence is that under MLR, estimates of covariance components take into account uncertainty about θ_1, whereas under MLF they do not. In the MLR case we assume a noninformative prior distribution for the fixed effects of Equation 10.19:

$$\boldsymbol{\theta}_1 \sim N(\mathbf{0}, \Gamma). \qquad [10.23]$$

It is convenient and sensible to assume that $\boldsymbol{\theta}_1$ has a prior mean of $\mathbf{0}$ because the prior dispersion Γ will be assumed arbitrarily large. That is, if $\Gamma^{-1} \rightarrow \mathbf{0}$ the prior location is arbitrary. Thus the mixed model of Equation 10.19 becomes

$$\mathbf{Y} = \mathbf{A}_1\boldsymbol{\theta}_1 + \mathbf{A}_2\boldsymbol{\theta}_2 + \mathbf{r} \qquad [10.24]$$

with

$$\boldsymbol{\theta}_1 \sim N(\mathbf{0}, \Gamma), \quad \boldsymbol{\theta}_2 \sim N(\mathbf{0}, \mathbf{T}), \quad \text{and } \mathbf{r} \sim N(\mathbf{0}, \sigma^2\mathbf{I}).$$

Hence, this mixed model is a special case of the general Bayes linear model (Equation 10.1) with the following substitutions:

$$\mathbf{A} = [\mathbf{A}_1 \mid \mathbf{A}_2],$$

$$\boldsymbol{\theta} = \begin{bmatrix} \boldsymbol{\theta}_1 \\ \boldsymbol{\theta}_2 \end{bmatrix} \qquad \bar{\boldsymbol{\theta}} = \begin{bmatrix} \mathbf{0} \\ \mathbf{0} \end{bmatrix} \qquad \Omega = \begin{bmatrix} \Gamma & \mathbf{0} \\ \mathbf{0} & \mathbf{T} \end{bmatrix},$$

and

$$\Psi = \sigma^2\mathbf{I}.$$

Because the two models are equivalent, the posterior distribution of $\boldsymbol{\theta}_1, \boldsymbol{\theta}_2 \mid \mathbf{Y}, \sigma^2, \Gamma, \mathbf{T}$ follows from Equations 10.3 and 10.4 after appropriate substitutions. The posterior dispersion based on the general model is

$$\mathbf{D}^*_\theta = (\mathbf{A}'\Psi^{-1}\mathbf{A} + \Omega^{-1})^{-1},$$

which, after substitution, in our case becomes

$$\mathbf{D}^*_\theta = \begin{bmatrix} \mathrm{Var}(\boldsymbol{\theta}_1 \mid \mathbf{Y}, \sigma^2, \mathbf{T}) & \mathrm{Cov}(\boldsymbol{\theta}_1, \boldsymbol{\theta}_2 \mid \mathbf{Y}, \sigma^2, \mathbf{T}) \\ \mathrm{Cov}(\boldsymbol{\theta}_2, \boldsymbol{\theta}_1 \mid \mathbf{Y}, \sigma^2, \mathbf{T}) & \mathrm{Var}(\boldsymbol{\theta}_2 \mid \mathbf{Y}, \sigma^2, \mathbf{T}) \end{bmatrix} \qquad [10.25]$$

$$= \sigma^2 \begin{bmatrix} \mathbf{A}_1'\mathbf{A}_1 + \sigma^2\Gamma^{-1} & \mathbf{A}_1'\mathbf{A}_2 \\ \mathbf{A}_2'\mathbf{A}_1 & \mathbf{A}_2'\mathbf{A}_2 + \sigma^2\mathbf{T}^{-1} \end{bmatrix}^{-1}.$$

Standard methods for inverting a symmetric partitioned matrix (Morrison, 1967, p. 88), yield

$$\begin{bmatrix} \mathbf{A} & \mathbf{B} \\ \mathbf{B}' & \mathbf{C} \end{bmatrix}^{-1} = \begin{bmatrix} \mathbf{D}^*_{11} & \mathbf{D}^*_{12} \\ \mathbf{D}^*_{21} & \mathbf{D}^*_{22} \end{bmatrix}$$

with

$$\mathbf{D}^*_{11} = (\mathbf{A} - \mathbf{B}\mathbf{C}^{-1}\mathbf{B}')^{-1} ,$$

$$\mathbf{D}^*_{12} = -\mathbf{D}^*_{11}\mathbf{B}\mathbf{C}^{-1} ,$$

$$\mathbf{D}^*_{21} = \mathbf{D}^{*\prime}_{12} ,$$

and

$$\mathbf{D}^*_{22} = \mathbf{C}^{-1} + \mathbf{C}^{-1}\mathbf{B}'\mathbf{D}^*_{11}\mathbf{B}\mathbf{C}^{-1} .$$

Making the appropriate substitutions and letting $\boldsymbol{\Gamma}^{-1} \rightarrow \mathbf{0}$, we have

$$\mathbf{D}^*_{11} = \mathrm{Var}(\theta_1 \mid \mathbf{Y},\ \sigma^2,\ \mathbf{T}) = \sigma^2\mathbf{V}_{11} \qquad [10.26]$$

with

$$\mathbf{V}_{11} = [\mathbf{A}_1'\mathbf{A}_1 - \mathbf{A}_1'\mathbf{A}_2\mathbf{C}^{-1}\mathbf{A}_2'\mathbf{A}_1]^{-1} \qquad [10.27]$$

where

$$\mathbf{C} = \mathbf{A}_2'\mathbf{A}_2 + \sigma^2\mathbf{T}^{-1} .$$

The covariance terms follow:

$$\mathbf{D}^*_{12} = -\mathbf{D}^*_{11}\mathbf{A}_1'\mathbf{A}_2\mathbf{C}^{-1} . \qquad [10.28]$$

The posterior variance of $\theta_2 \mid \mathbf{Y},\sigma^2,\mathbf{T}$ is

$$\mathbf{D}^*_{22} = \sigma^2\mathbf{V}_{22} \qquad [10.29]$$

where

$$\mathbf{V}_{22} = \mathbf{C}^{-1} + \mathbf{C}^{-1}\mathbf{A}_2'\mathbf{A}_1\mathbf{V}_{11}\mathbf{A}_1'\mathbf{A}_2\mathbf{C}^{-1} .$$

To find the posterior expectations, we can make appropriate substitutions into Equation 10.3, that is,

$$E(\theta \mid \mathbf{Y},\ \sigma^2,\ \mathbf{T}) = \mathbf{D}^*(\Omega^{-1}\bar{\theta} + \mathbf{A}'\Psi^{-1}\mathbf{Y}) = \mathbf{D}^*\mathbf{A}'\Psi^{-1}\mathbf{Y}$$

because $\bar{\theta} = \mathbf{0}$. Translating into the terms of the mixed model, we have

$$\mathbf{D}^*\mathbf{A}'\Psi^{-1}\mathbf{Y} = \begin{bmatrix} E(\theta_1 \mid \mathbf{Y},\ \sigma^2,\ \mathbf{T}) \\ E(\theta_2 \mid \mathbf{Y},\ \sigma^2,\ \mathbf{T}) \end{bmatrix} = \sigma^{-2}\begin{bmatrix} \mathbf{D}^*_{11} & \mathbf{D}^*_{12} \\ \mathbf{D}^*_{21} & \mathbf{D}^*_{22} \end{bmatrix} \begin{bmatrix} \mathbf{A}'_1\mathbf{Y} \\ \mathbf{A}'_2\mathbf{Y} \end{bmatrix}$$

which upon substitution and simplification yields the posterior expectations, θ^*:

$$\begin{bmatrix} \theta^*_1 \\ \theta^*_2 \end{bmatrix} = \begin{bmatrix} \mathbf{V}_{11}\mathbf{A}'_1(\mathbf{I} - \mathbf{A}_2\mathbf{C}^{-1}\mathbf{A}'_2)\mathbf{Y} \\ \mathbf{C}^{-1}\mathbf{A}'_2(\mathbf{Y} - \mathbf{A}_1\theta^*_1) \end{bmatrix}. \qquad [10.30]$$

To summarize, by making appropriate substitutions, we have utilized our results from the general Bayesian linear model to find the joint posterior distribution of θ_1 and θ_2 given the data, $\mathbf{Y}$, and the dispersion parameters, σ^2 and $\mathbf{T}$.

Computational Formulae

To perform computation requires that we translate the no-subscript results back to the subscripted results. Further, we rearrange the formulae so that all computations are based on the sufficient statistics

$$\mathbf{A}'_{1j}\mathbf{A}_{1j}, \quad \mathbf{A}'_{1j}\mathbf{A}_{2j}, \quad \mathbf{A}'_{2j}\mathbf{A}_{2j}, \quad \mathbf{A}'_{1j}\mathbf{Y}_j, \quad \mathbf{A}'_{2j}\mathbf{Y}_j,$$

which we denote as $\mathbf{S}_{11j}$, $\mathbf{S}_{12j}$ $\mathbf{S}_{22j}$, $\mathbf{S}_{1yj}$, and $\mathbf{S}_{2yj}$, respectively. Given that the Level-1 variance matrix is $\sigma^2\mathbf{I}$, these statistics need to be computed only once and saved for use during each iteration. This means that if *N* is the total number of Level-1 observations and *J* is the number of Level-2 units, the effective sample size for the computation is *J*. This enormously increases computational efficiency when *J/N* is small, as is common, for example, in school effects research.

Convenient formulae for the posterior means and dispersions are

$$\theta^*_1 = \mathbf{V}_{11}\left[\sum \mathbf{S}_{1yj} - \sum \mathbf{S}_{12j}\mathbf{C}_j^{-1}\mathbf{S}_{2yj}\right], \qquad [10.31]$$

$$\mathbf{D}^*_{11} = \sigma^2 \mathbf{V}_{11}, \qquad [10.32]$$

$$\theta^*_{2j} = \mathbf{C}_j^{-1}(\mathbf{S}_{2yj} - \mathbf{S}_{21j}\theta^*_1), \qquad [10.33]$$

$$\mathbf{D}^*_{22j} = \sigma^2 \mathbf{V}_{22j}, \qquad [10.34]$$

and

$$\mathbf{D}^*_{12j} = -\mathbf{D}^*_{11}\mathbf{S}_{12j}\mathbf{C}_j^{-1}, \qquad [10.35]$$

where

$$\mathbf{C}_j = \mathbf{S}_{22j} + \sigma^2 \tau^{-1},$$

$$\mathbf{V}_{11} = \left[\sum \mathbf{S}_{11j} - \sum \mathbf{S}_{12j}\mathbf{C}_j^{-1}\mathbf{S}_{21j}\right]^{-1},$$

and

$$\mathbf{V}_{22j} = \mathbf{C}_j^{-1} + \mathbf{C}_j^{-1}\mathbf{S}_{21j}\mathbf{V}_{11}\mathbf{S}_{12j}\mathbf{C}_j^{-1}.$$

The Likelihood

Translating the log-likelihood for the general model into the two-level MLR case yields the following equivalences:

$$\log|\Psi| = N\log(\sigma^2)$$

$$\log|\Omega| \propto \log|\Gamma| + \log|\mathbf{T}|.$$

However, we assume that $|\Gamma|$, though arbitrarily large, is a known constant. Therefore,

$$\log|\Omega| \propto \log|\mathbf{T}| = J\log|\tau|.$$

Finally,

$$\log|\mathbf{D}^*| = \log\begin{vmatrix}\mathbf{D}^*_{11} & \mathbf{D}^*_{12}\\ \mathbf{D}^*_{21} & \mathbf{D}^*_{22}\end{vmatrix}. \qquad [10.36]$$

Using standard formulae for the determinant of a partitioned matrix facilitates substantial simplification of Equation 10.36:

$$|\mathbf{D}^*| = |\mathbf{D}^*_{11}||\mathbf{D}^*_{22} - \mathbf{D}^*_{21}\mathbf{D}^{*-1}_{11}\mathbf{D}^*_{12}|$$
$$= \sigma^{2F}|\mathbf{V}_{11}|\sigma^{2JR}|\mathbf{V}_{22} - \mathbf{V}_{21}\mathbf{V}^{-1}_{11}\mathbf{V}_{12}|,$$

where F is the number of fixed effects in the model, R is the number of random effects (per Level-2 unit) and

$$\mathbf{V}_{22} - \mathbf{V}_{21}\mathbf{V}^{-1}_{11}\mathbf{V}_{12} = \mathbf{C}^{-1}$$

so that

$$\log|\mathbf{D}^*| = (F + JR)\log(\sigma^2) + \log|\mathbf{V}_{11}| + \sum \log|\mathbf{C}^{-1}_j|. \qquad [10.37]$$

The result is that

$$\log[f(\mathbf{Y}|\sigma^2, \tau)] \propto -(N - JR - F)\log(\sigma^2) - J\log|\tau| + \log|\mathbf{V}_{11}| \qquad [10.38]$$
$$+ \sum \log|\mathbf{C}^{-1}_j| - \sum \mathbf{Q}^*_j,$$

where

$$\mathbf{Q}^*_j = \mathbf{Y}'_j(\mathbf{Y}_j - \mathbf{A}_{1j}\theta^*_1 - \mathbf{A}_{2j}\theta^*_{2j})/\sigma^2.$$

EM Algorithm

An EM algorithm can readily be constructed to maximize the log likelihood given by Equation 10.38 (Dempster et al., 1981). Suppose that the unknown effects θ_1 and θ_2, in addition to the actual data $\mathbf{Y}$, had been observed. We shall refer to $\mathbf{Y}$, θ_1, and θ_2 as the "complete data." Then the log of the complete-data likelihood

$$\log[f(\mathbf{Y}, \theta_1, \theta_2|\sigma^2, \tau)] \propto -N\log(\sigma^2) - J\log|\tau| \qquad [10.39]$$
$$- \sum \mathbf{r}'_j\mathbf{r}_j/\sigma^2 - \sum \theta'_{2j}\tau^{-1}\theta_{2j}$$

would easily be maximized with respect to the parameters σ^2, τ by computing

$$\hat{\sigma}^2 = \sum \mathbf{r}'_j\mathbf{r}_j/N \qquad [10.40]$$

and

$$\hat{\tau} = J^{-1} \sum \theta_{2j} \theta'_{2j} . \qquad [10.41]$$

Of course, θ_1 and θ_2 have not been observed so that $\Sigma \mathbf{r}'_j \mathbf{r}_j$ and $\Sigma \theta_{2j} \theta'_{2j}$ cannot be computed. However, these complete data-sufficient statistics can be estimated by means of their conditional expectations given the data $\mathbf{Y}$ and current estimates of σ^2 and τ. These expectations are

$$E\left(\sum \mathbf{r}'_j \mathbf{r}_j \mid \mathbf{Y},\ \sigma^2,\ \tau\right) = E[(\mathbf{Y} - \mathbf{A}\theta)'(\mathbf{Y} - \mathbf{A}\theta) \mid \mathbf{Y},\ \sigma^2,\ \tau] \qquad [10.42]$$

$$= E[(\mathbf{Y} - \mathbf{A}\theta^* + \mathbf{A}\theta^* - \mathbf{A}\theta)'(\mathbf{Y} - \mathbf{A}\theta^* + \mathbf{A}\theta^* - \mathbf{A}\theta) \mid \mathbf{Y},\ \sigma^2,\ \tau]$$

$$= (\mathbf{Y} - \mathbf{A}\theta^*)'(\mathbf{Y} - \mathbf{A}\theta^*) + E[(\theta - \theta^*)'\mathbf{A}'\mathbf{A}(\theta - \theta^*) \mid \mathbf{Y},\ \sigma^2,\ \tau]$$

where

$$\mathbf{Y} - \mathbf{A}\theta^* = \mathbf{Y} - \mathbf{A}_1\theta_1^* - \mathbf{A}_2\theta_2^*$$

and

$$E[(\theta - \theta^*)'\mathbf{A}'\mathbf{A}(\theta - \theta^*) \mid \mathbf{Y},\ \sigma^2,\ \tau] = \mathrm{tr}(\mathbf{A}'\mathbf{A}\mathbf{D}^*) \qquad [10.43]$$

$$= \mathrm{tr}\begin{bmatrix} \mathbf{A}'_1\mathbf{A}_1 & \mathbf{A}'_1\mathbf{A}_2 \\ \mathbf{A}'_2\mathbf{A}_1 & \mathbf{A}'_2\mathbf{A}_2 \end{bmatrix} \begin{bmatrix} \mathbf{D}^*_{11} & \mathbf{D}^*_{12} \\ \mathbf{D}^*_{21} & \mathbf{D}^*_{22} \end{bmatrix} .$$

A computationally convenient formula for Equation 10.43 is

$$\sigma^2\left[F - \mathrm{tr}\left(\mathbf{V}_{11} \sum \mathbf{S}_{12j}\mathbf{C}_j^{-1}\mathbf{S}_{21j}\right) + \mathrm{tr}\left(\sum \mathbf{V}_{22j}\mathbf{S}_{22j}\right)\right] .$$

The expected complete data-sufficient statistic for τ is simply

$$E\left(\sum \theta_{2j}\theta'_{2j} \mid \mathbf{Y},\ \sigma^2,\ \tau\right) = \sum \theta^*_{2j}\theta^{*\prime}_{2j} + \sigma^2 \sum \mathbf{V}_{22j} . \qquad [10.44]$$

The EM algorithm begins with some convenient starting estimates of σ^2 and τ. Conditional on these, the complete data sufficient statistics are then computed by means of Equations 10.43 and 10.44. This is the so-called E or expectation step. These estimated complete data-sufficient statistics are then used for $\hat{\sigma}^2$ and $\hat{\tau}$ (Equations 10.40 and 10.41) to generate values for

θ_1^* and θ_2^* in the M (or maximization) step. These new values of $\hat{\theta}_1^*$ and $\hat{\theta}_2^*$ provide input for the next cycle's E-step.

Two-Level MLF

In the MLR formulation, the random quantities are θ_1, θ_2, and **Y**, and σ^2 and **T** are treated as fixed quantities.[2] In MLF, only θ_2 and **Y** are random; the likelihood will depend upon the fixed quantities θ_1, σ^2, and **T**. Hence the model is

$$\mathbf{Y} = \mathbf{A}_1\theta_1 + \mathbf{A}_2\theta_2 + \mathbf{r},$$

with

$$\theta_2 \sim N(\mathbf{0}, \mathbf{T})$$

and

$$\mathbf{r} \sim N(\mathbf{0}, \sigma^2\mathbf{I}).$$

Following Dempster et al. (1981), we rewrite the model as

$$\mathbf{d} = \mathbf{Y} - \mathbf{A}_1\theta_1 = \mathbf{A}_2\theta_2 + \mathbf{r}, \qquad [10.45]$$

from which it becomes clear that the two-level MLF is a special case of the general Bayes linear model (Equation 10.1), with

$$\mathbf{Y} = \mathbf{d}, \quad \mathbf{A} = \mathbf{A}_2, \quad \theta = \theta_2, \quad \Psi = \sigma^2\mathbf{I}, \quad \text{and} \quad \Omega = \mathbf{T}.$$

Hence, the posterior mean and variance of $\theta_2 \mid \mathbf{Y}, \sigma^2, \mathbf{T}, \theta_1$ are provided directly by Equations 10.3 and 10.4 after making the above substitutions. This yields

$$\theta_2^* = \mathbf{C}^{-1}\mathbf{A}_2'(\mathbf{Y} - \mathbf{A}_1\theta_1) \qquad [10.46]$$

and

$$\mathbf{D}_{22}^* = \sigma^2\mathbf{C}^{-1} \qquad [10.47]$$

where as before

$$\mathbf{C}^{-1} = (\mathbf{A}_2'\mathbf{A}_2 + \sigma^2\mathbf{T}^{-1})^{-1}.$$

MLF Likelihood

The log-likelihood for the general model provided in Equation 10.11, after substitution, is now proportional to

$$\log[f(\mathbf{Y} \mid \sigma^2, \tau, \theta_1)] \propto -(N - JR)\log(\sigma^2) - J\log|\tau| + \sum \log|\mathbf{C}_j^{-1}| - \sum \mathbf{d}_j'(\mathbf{d}_j - \mathbf{A}_{2j}\theta_{2j}^*)/\sigma^2. \quad [10.48]$$

EM Algorithm

Again, the likelihood given by Equation 10.48 can be maximized by means of an EM algorithm, and, in fact, the computations are substantially simpler for MLF than for MLR. Given knowledge of θ_2 and $\mathbf{Y}$, the log-likelihood function of these complete data is

$$\log[f(\mathbf{Y}, \theta_2 \mid \theta_1, \sigma^2, \tau)] \propto -N\log(\sigma^2) - J\log|\tau| - \sum (\mathbf{d}_j - \mathbf{A}_{2j}\theta_{2j})'(\mathbf{d}_j - \mathbf{A}_{2j}\theta_{2j})/\sigma^2 - \sum \theta_{2j}'\tau^{-1}\theta_{2j}. \quad [10.49]$$

This complete-data log-likelihood is easily maximized with respect to θ_1, σ^2, τ:

$$\hat{\theta}_1 = \left(\sum \mathbf{A}_{1j}'\mathbf{A}_{1j}\right)^{-1} \sum \mathbf{A}_{1j}'(\mathbf{Y}_j - \mathbf{A}_{2j}\theta_{2j}) \quad [10.50]$$

$$\hat{\sigma}^2 = \sum (\mathbf{d}_j - \mathbf{A}_{2j}\theta_{2j})'(\mathbf{d}_j - \mathbf{A}_{2j}\theta_{2j})/N \quad [10.51]$$

$$\hat{\tau} = J^{-1} \sum \theta_{2j}\theta_{2j}'. \quad [10.52]$$

During the EM algorithm's E-step, the conditional expectations of the complete data-sufficient statistics are computed:

$$E\left[\left(\sum \mathbf{A}_{1j}'\mathbf{A}_{1j}\right)^{-1} \sum (\mathbf{Y}_j - \mathbf{A}_{2j}\theta_{2j}) \mid \mathbf{Y}, \theta_1, \sigma^2, \tau\right] \quad [10.53]$$

$$= \left(\sum \mathbf{A}_{1j}'\mathbf{A}_{1j}\right)^{-1} \sum (\mathbf{Y}_j - \mathbf{A}_{2j}\theta_{2j}^*),$$

$$E\left[\sum (\mathbf{d}_j - \mathbf{A}_{2j}\theta_{2j})'(\mathbf{d}_j - \mathbf{A}_{2j}\theta_{2j}) \mid \mathbf{Y}, \theta_1, \sigma^2, \tau\right] \quad [10.54]$$

$$= \sum (\mathbf{d}_j - \mathbf{A}_{2j}\theta^*_{2j})'(\mathbf{d}_j - \mathbf{A}_{2j}\theta^*_{2j}) + \sigma^2 \mathrm{tr}\left[\sum \mathbf{A}'_{2j}\mathbf{A}_{2j}\mathbf{C}_j^{-1}\right],$$

and

$$E\left(\sum \theta_{2j}\theta'_{2j} \mid \mathbf{Y}, \theta_1, \sigma^2, \tau\right) = \sum \theta^*_{2j}\theta^{*\prime}_{2j} + \sigma^2 \sum \mathbf{C}_j^{-1}. \quad [10.55]$$

These computations depend on the same sufficient statistics used by MLR. Alternately computing the E and M steps maximizes the likelihood given by Equation 10.48. However, the resulting estimates of τ do not take into account the uncertainty about θ_1.

Three-Level MLF

In Chapter 6, we illustrated application of three-level models. The three-level mixed model may be written without subscripts as

$$\mathbf{Y} = \mathbf{A}_1\theta_1 + \mathbf{A}_2\theta_2 + \mathbf{A}_3\theta_3 + \mathbf{r}, \quad [10.56]$$

where the θ_1 vector contains the fixed effects, θ_2 contains the random effects at Level 3, θ_3 contains the Level-2 random effects, and $\mathbf{r}$ contains the errors at Level 1. If one views the random quantities as

$$\mathbf{r} \sim N(\mathbf{0}, \sigma^2\mathbf{I})$$

$$\theta_2 \sim N(\mathbf{0}, \mathbf{T}_\beta),$$

$$\theta_3 \sim N(\mathbf{0}, \mathbf{T}_\pi),$$

and the fixed parameters as θ_1, σ^2, $\mathbf{T}_\pi$, and $\mathbf{T}_\beta$, then this three-level model becomes a special case of the two-level MLF model. We rewrite Equation 10.45 as

$$\mathbf{d} = \mathbf{A}_2\theta_2 + \mathbf{A}_3\theta_3 + \mathbf{r}. \quad [10.57]$$

The following substitutions translate the two-level MLF formulae into the three-level MLF formulae:

Two-level MLF	*Three-level MLF*	
$\mathbf{A}_2$	$[\mathbf{A}_2 \mid \mathbf{A}_3]$,	[10.58]
θ_2	$\begin{bmatrix} \theta_2 \\ \theta_3 \end{bmatrix}$,	[10.59]
$\mathbf{T}$	$\begin{bmatrix} \mathbf{T}_\beta & 0 \\ 0 & \mathbf{T}_\pi \end{bmatrix}$,	[10.60]
$\mathbf{D}^*_{2\,2}$	$\begin{bmatrix} \mathbf{D}^*_{2\,2} & \mathbf{D}^*_{2\,3} \\ \mathbf{D}^*_{3\,2} & \mathbf{D}^*_{3\,3} \end{bmatrix}$,	[10.61]
θ^*_2	$\begin{bmatrix} \theta^*_2 \\ \theta^*_3 \end{bmatrix}$,	[10.62]

where

$$\mathbf{D}^*_{2\,2} = \sigma^2 \mathbf{V}_{2\,2} \text{ with } \mathbf{V}_{2\,2} = [\sigma^2 \mathbf{T}_\beta^{-1} + \mathbf{A}_2'\mathbf{M}\mathbf{A}_2]^{-1}$$

$$\mathbf{D}^*_{2\,3} = \sigma^2 \mathbf{V}_{2\,3} \text{ with } \mathbf{V}_{2\,3} = -\mathbf{V}_{2\,2}\mathbf{A}_2'\mathbf{A}_3\mathbf{C}^{-1}$$

$$\mathbf{D}^*_{3\,2} = \mathbf{D}^{*\prime}_{2\,3}$$

$$\mathbf{D}^*_{3\,3} = \sigma^2 \mathbf{V}_{3\,3} \text{ with } \mathbf{V}_{3\,3} = \mathbf{C}^{-1} + \mathbf{C}^{-1}\mathbf{A}_3'\mathbf{A}_2\mathbf{V}_{2\,2}\mathbf{A}_2'\mathbf{A}_3\mathbf{C}^{-1}$$

$$\theta^*_2 = \mathbf{V}_{2\,2}\mathbf{A}_2'\mathbf{M}\mathbf{d}$$

$$\theta^*_3 = \mathbf{C}^{-1}\mathbf{A}_3'(\mathbf{d} - \mathbf{A}_2\theta^*_2),$$

with

$$\mathbf{C} = \mathbf{A}_3'\mathbf{A}_3 + \sigma^2\mathbf{T}_\pi^{-1}$$

and

$$\mathbf{M} = \mathbf{I} - \mathbf{A}_3\mathbf{C}^{-1}\mathbf{A}_3'.$$

Three-Level MLF Likelihood

The log-likelihood for the three-level MLF follows directly from the log-likelihood for the two-level MLF after appropriate substitution:

$$\log[f(\mathbf{Y} \mid \theta_1, \sigma^2, \tau_\pi, \tau_\beta)] \quad [10.63]$$

$$\propto -(T - KR_2 - JR_3)\log(\sigma^2) - K\log|\tau_\beta|$$

$$- J\log|\tau_\pi| + \sum \log|\mathbf{V}_{2\,2\,k}| + \sum\sum \log|\mathbf{C}_{j\,k}^{-1}| - \sum\sum \mathbf{Q}_{j\,k}^*/\sigma^2,$$

where T is the total number of Level-1 units, J is the total number of Level-2 units, K is the number of Level-3 units, R_2 is the dimension of θ_{2k}, R_3 is the dimension of θ_{3jk}, and

$$\mathbf{Q}_{j\,k}^* = \mathbf{d}_{j\,k}'(\mathbf{d}_{j\,k} - \mathbf{A}_{2\,j\,k}\theta_{2\,k}^* - \mathbf{A}_{3\,j\,k}\theta_{j\,k}^*),$$

where

$$\mathbf{d}_{j\,k} = \mathbf{Y}_{j\,k} - \mathbf{A}_{1\,j\,k}\theta_1 .$$

EM Algorithm

The complete-data likelihood for the three-level MLF follows Equation 10.49:

$$\log[f(\mathbf{Y}, \theta_2, \theta_3 \mid \theta_1, \sigma^2, \tau_\pi, \tau_\beta)] \quad [10.64]$$

$$= -N\log(\sigma^2) - K\log|\tau_\beta| - J\log|\tau_\pi|$$

$$- \sum\sum (\mathbf{d}_{j\,k} - \mathbf{A}_{2\,j\,k}\theta_{2\,k} - \mathbf{A}_{3\,j\,k}\theta_{3\,j\,k})'(\mathbf{d}_{j\,k} - \mathbf{A}_{2\,j\,k}\theta_{2\,k} - \mathbf{A}_{3\,j\,k}\theta_{3\,j\,k})/\sigma^2$$

$$- \sum \theta_{2\,k}'\tau_\beta^{-1}\theta_{2\,k} - \sum\sum \theta_{3\,j\,k}'\tau_\pi^{-1}\theta_{3\,j\,k}.$$

Therefore, the complete-data maximum likelihood estimates are

$$\hat{\theta}_1 = \left(\sum\sum \mathbf{A}_{1\,j\,k}'\mathbf{A}_{1\,j\,k}\right)^{-1}\sum\sum \mathbf{A}_{1\,j\,k}'(\mathbf{Y}_{j\,k} - \mathbf{A}_{2\,j\,k}\theta_{2\,k} - \mathbf{A}_{3\,j\,k}\theta_{3\,j\,k}) \quad [10.65]$$

$$\hat{\sigma}^2 = \sum\sum \mathbf{r}_{j\,k}'\mathbf{r}_{j\,k}/\mathrm{T} \quad [10.66]$$

$$\hat{\tau}_\pi = J^{-1}\sum\sum \theta_{3\,j\,k}\theta_{3\,j\,k}' \quad [10.67]$$

and

$$\hat{\tau}_\beta = K^{-1} \sum \theta_{2k} \theta'_{2k} \qquad [10.68]$$

where

$$\mathbf{r}_{jk} = \mathbf{Y}_{jk} - \mathbf{A}_{1jk}\theta_1 - \mathbf{A}_{2jk}\theta_{2k} - \mathbf{A}_{3jk}\theta_{3jk}.$$

The complete data-sufficient statistic for θ_1 is found by substituting θ^*_{2k} and θ^*_{3jk} into Equation 10.65. For σ^2, we have

$$E\left(\sum \sum \mathbf{r}'_{jk}\mathbf{r}_{jk} \mid \theta_1, \sigma^2, \tau_\pi, \tau_\beta\right) = \sum \mathbf{r}^{*\prime}_{jk}\mathbf{r}^*_{jk} \qquad [10.69]$$

$$+ \sigma^2 \operatorname{tr}\left[\sum\left(\sum \mathbf{A}'_{2jk}\mathbf{M}^2_{jk}\mathbf{A}_{2jk}\right)\mathbf{V}_{22k}\right]$$

$$+ \sigma^2 \operatorname{tr}\left(\sum \sum \mathbf{A}'_{3jk}\mathbf{A}_{3jk}\mathbf{C}^{-1}_{jk}\right),$$

where $\mathbf{r}^*_{jk} = \mathbf{r}_{jk}$ with θ^*_{2k} and θ^*_{3jk} substituted for θ_{2k} and θ_{3jk}.

The complete data-sufficient statistics for τ_π and τ_β are

$$E\left(\sum \sum \theta_{3jk}\theta'_{3jk} \mid \mathbf{Y}, \theta_1, \sigma^2, \tau_\pi, \tau_\beta\right) = \sum \sum \theta^*_{3jk}\theta^{*\prime}_{3jk} \qquad [10.70]$$

$$+ \sigma^2 \sum \sum \mathbf{V}_{33jk}$$

and

$$E\left(\sum \theta_{2k}\theta'_{2k} \mid \mathbf{Y}, \theta_1, \sigma^2, \tau_\pi, \tau_\beta\right) = \sum \theta^*_{2k}\theta^{*\prime}_{2k} + \sigma^2 \sum \mathbf{V}_{22k}. \qquad [10.71]$$

The reader may have noticed the similarity between the formulae for the two-level MLR computations and those for the three-level MLF computations. Indeed, going from MLF to MLR effectively adds a level to the computational complexity.

Two-Level *V*-Known Model

Chapter 7 illustrated applications of what we called the *V*-known model. This involves a two-level MLR estimation. The Level-1 model is

$$\mathbf{d}_j = \delta_j + \mathbf{e}_j, \quad \mathbf{e}_j \sim \mathrm{N}(\mathbf{0}, \mathbf{V}_j) \qquad [10.72]$$

where δ_j is a vector of effects estimated by the statistic $\mathbf{d}_j$. It must be assumed that $\mathbf{d}_j$ is an unbiased estimator of δ_j with a multivariate normal sampling distribution having dispersion $\mathbf{V}_j$, where $\mathbf{V}_j$ is a known, positive definite variance-covariance matrix.

At Level 2, the model is

$$\delta_j = \mathbf{W}_j \gamma + \mathbf{u}_j, \quad \mathbf{u}_j \sim \mathrm{N}(\mathbf{0}, \tau). \qquad [10.73]$$

Combining these two models and deleting subscripts yields

$$\mathbf{d} = \mathbf{W}\gamma + \mathbf{u} + \mathbf{e}, \quad \mathbf{u} + \mathbf{e} \sim \mathrm{N}(\mathbf{0}, \Delta), \qquad [10.74]$$

with $\Delta = \mathbf{V} + \mathbf{T}$. If we assign γ a noninformative prior distribution such that $\gamma \sim \mathrm{N}(\mathbf{0}, \Gamma)$, with $\Gamma^{-1} \to \mathbf{0}$, we have a special case of the general Bayes model (Equation 10.1) with the following substitutions:

$$\mathbf{Y} = \mathbf{d}, \quad \mathbf{A} = [\mathbf{W} \mid \mathbf{I}], \quad \theta = \begin{bmatrix} \gamma \\ \mathbf{u} \end{bmatrix}, \quad \Psi = \mathbf{V},$$

and

$$\Omega = \begin{bmatrix} \Gamma & \mathbf{0} \\ \mathbf{0} & \mathbf{T} \end{bmatrix}.$$

Hence, it is straightforward to compute the posterior distribution of $\gamma, \mathbf{u} \mid \mathbf{d}, \mathbf{T}, \Gamma$ (with $\mathbf{V}$ known). These are normal with expectations $(\gamma^*, \mathbf{u}^*)$, dispersions $(\mathbf{D}^*_{11}, \mathbf{D}^*_{22})$, and covariance $\mathbf{D}^*_{12}$, where

$$\gamma^* = (\mathbf{W}'\Delta^{-1}\mathbf{W})^{-1}\mathbf{W}'\Delta^{-1}\mathbf{d} \qquad [10.75]$$

$$\mathbf{u}^* = \Lambda(\mathbf{d} - \mathbf{W}\gamma^*) \qquad [10.76]$$

$$\mathbf{D}^*_{11} = (\mathbf{W}'\Delta^{-1}\mathbf{W})^{-1} \qquad [10.77]$$

$$\mathbf{D}^*_{12} = -\mathbf{D}^*_{11}\mathbf{W}'\Lambda' \qquad [10.78]$$

$$\mathbf{D}^*_{21} = \mathbf{D}^{*\prime}_{12} \qquad [10.79]$$

$$\mathbf{D}^*_{22} = (\mathbf{V}^{-1} + \mathbf{T}^{-1})^{-1} + \Lambda\mathbf{W}\mathbf{D}_{11}\mathbf{W}'\Lambda' \qquad [10.80]$$

where

$$\Lambda = (\mathbf{V}^{-1} + \mathbf{T}^{-1})^{-1}\mathbf{V}^{-1},$$

or, equivalently,

$$\Lambda = \mathbf{T}(\mathbf{T} + \mathbf{V})^{-1}.$$

To prove this result, we note first that the posterior dispersion for the general model (Equation 10.4)—that is,

$$\mathbf{D}^* = (\mathbf{A}'\Psi^{-1}\mathbf{A} + \Omega^{-1})^{-1}$$

becomes

$$\mathbf{D}^* = \begin{bmatrix} \mathbf{D}^*_{11} & \mathbf{D}^*_{12} \\ \mathbf{D}^*_{21} & \mathbf{D}^*_{22} \end{bmatrix} = \begin{bmatrix} \mathbf{W}'\mathbf{V}^{-1}\mathbf{W} + \Gamma^{-1} & \mathbf{W}'\mathbf{V}^{-1} \\ \mathbf{V}^{-1}\mathbf{W} & \mathbf{V}^{-1} + \mathbf{T}^{-1} \end{bmatrix}^{-1}$$

in the V-known model. Using standard methods for inverting a partitioned matrix and letting $\Gamma^{-1} \to 0$ yields

$$\begin{aligned} \mathbf{D}^*_{11} &= [\mathbf{W}'\mathbf{V}^{-1}\mathbf{W} - \mathbf{W}'\mathbf{V}^{-1}(\mathbf{V}^{-1} + \mathbf{T}^{-1})^{-1}\mathbf{V}^{-1}\mathbf{W}]^{-1} \\ &= [\mathbf{W}'\mathbf{V}^{-1}(\mathbf{I} - \Lambda)\mathbf{W}]^{-1} \\ &= (\mathbf{W}'\Delta^{-1}\mathbf{W})^{-1} \end{aligned}$$

$$\mathbf{D}^*_{12} = -\mathbf{D}^*_{11}\mathbf{W}'\mathbf{V}^{-1}(\mathbf{V}^{-1} + \mathbf{T}^{-1})^{-1} = -\mathbf{D}^*_{11}\mathbf{W}'\Lambda'$$

$$\mathbf{D}^*_{21} = \mathbf{D}^{*\prime}_{12}$$

and

$$\mathbf{D}^*_{22} = \mathbf{L}^{-1} + \Lambda\mathbf{W}\mathbf{D}^*_{11}\mathbf{W}'\Lambda'$$

where

$$\mathbf{L} = \mathbf{V}^{-1} + \mathbf{T}^{-1}.$$

To find the posterior expectations, we postmultiply the joint posterior dispersion $\mathbf{D}^*$ by

$$\mathbf{A}'\Psi^{-1}\mathbf{Y} = \begin{bmatrix} \mathbf{W}'\mathbf{V}^{-1}\mathbf{d} \\ \mathbf{V}^{-1}\mathbf{d} \end{bmatrix}$$

which yields

$$\begin{aligned}
\gamma^* &= \mathbf{D}_{1\,1}^*\mathbf{W}'\mathbf{V}^{-1}\mathbf{d} + \mathbf{D}_{1\,2}^*\mathbf{V}^{-1}\mathbf{d} \\
&= \mathbf{D}_{1\,1}^*\mathbf{W}'\mathbf{V}^{-1}\mathbf{d} - \mathbf{D}_{1\,1}^*\mathbf{W}'\Lambda'\mathbf{V}^{-1}\mathbf{d} \\
&= \mathbf{D}_{1\,1}^*\mathbf{W}'\mathbf{V}^{-1}(\mathbf{I} - \Lambda)\mathbf{d} \\
&= \mathbf{D}_{1\,1}^*\mathbf{W}'\Delta^{-1}\mathbf{d}\,;
\end{aligned}$$

$$\begin{aligned}
\mathbf{u}^* &= \mathbf{D}_{2\,1}^*\mathbf{W}'\mathbf{V}^{-1}\mathbf{d} + \mathbf{D}_{2\,2}^*\mathbf{V}^{-1}\mathbf{d} \\
&= -\Lambda\mathbf{W}\mathbf{D}_{1\,1}^*\mathbf{W}'\mathbf{V}^{-1}\mathbf{d} + (\mathbf{L}^{-1} + \Lambda\mathbf{W}\mathbf{D}_{1\,1}^*\mathbf{W}'\Lambda')\mathbf{V}^{-1}\mathbf{d} \\
&= \Lambda\mathbf{d} - \Lambda\mathbf{W}\mathbf{D}_{1\,1}^*\mathbf{W}'(\mathbf{I} - \Lambda)'\mathbf{V}^{-1}\mathbf{d} \\
&= \Lambda(\mathbf{d} - \mathbf{W}\gamma^*)\,.
\end{aligned}$$

Likelihood Function

A computationally convenient form of the log-likelihood follows directly from the MLR likelihood (Equation 10.38):

$$\log[f(\mathbf{d} \mid \tau)] \propto -\sum \log|\mathbf{V}_j| - J\log|\tau| - \log\left|\sum \mathbf{W}_j'\Delta_j^{-1}\mathbf{W}_j\right| \quad [10.81]$$
$$-\sum |\mathbf{L}_j| - \sum \mathbf{d}_j'\Delta_j^{-1}(\mathbf{d}_j - \mathbf{W}_j\gamma^*)\,,$$

where

$$\Delta_j = \mathbf{V}_j + \tau \quad \text{and} \quad \mathbf{L}_j = \mathbf{V}_j + \tau\,.$$

EM Algorithm

The EM computations are particularly simple in this case because only τ need be estimated. The log of the complete data likelihood is just

$$\log[f(\mathbf{u} \mid \tau)] \propto -J \log|\tau| - \frac{1}{2}\sum \mathbf{u}_j'\tau^{-1}\mathbf{u}_j , \qquad [10.82]$$

which is maximized by

$$\hat{\tau} = J^{-1}\sum \mathbf{u}_j\mathbf{u}_j' . \qquad [10.83]$$

The conditional expectation of the complete data-sufficient statistic is

$$E\left(\sum \mathbf{u}_j\mathbf{u}_j' \mid \mathbf{Y}, \tau\right) = \sum \mathbf{u}_j^*\mathbf{u}_j^{*\prime} + \sum \mathbf{D}_{22j}^* , \qquad [10.84]$$

where

$$\mathbf{D}_{22j}^* = \mathbf{L}_j^{-1} + \Lambda_j\mathbf{W}_j\mathbf{D}_{11}^*\mathbf{W}_j'\Lambda_j' .$$

Inferences About the Fixed Parameters

Chapter 3 discusses statistical inference for hierarchical models. Using MLR, inferences about the fixed effects, θ_1, and the random effects, θ_2, are based on their posterior distribution given restricted maximum likelihood estimates of σ^2 and $\mathbf{T}$. Inferences about the parameters σ^2 and $\mathbf{T}$, however, are based on likelihood-ratio tests or on the information matrix, the negative inverse of which yields large-sample standard errors.

Using MLF (two-level case), inferences about θ_2 are based on its posterior distribution given maximum likelihood estimates of θ_1, σ^2, and $\mathbf{T}$. Inferences about the latter parameters are based on likelihood-ratio tests or the information matrix.

In this section, we provide the needed formulae for the information matrices in the two-level cases. We begin with MLF, which is substantially simpler than the MLR formulation. To simplify the notation in this section we shall drop the "2" subscript from $\mathbf{A}_2$, though $\mathbf{A}_1$ will remain subscripted. Also, we shall now use $\mathbf{V}$ to represent $\text{Var}(\mathbf{Y}) = \mathbf{ATA}' + \sigma^2\mathbf{I}$.

Information Matrix, MLF

Using no-subscript notation, the two-level MLF log-likelihood may be written as

$$\lambda = \log[f(\mathbf{Y} \mid \sigma^2, \mathbf{T}, \theta_1)] = -\frac{N}{2}\log(2\pi) - \frac{1}{2}\log|\mathbf{V}| - \frac{1}{2}\mathbf{d}'\mathbf{V}^{-1}\mathbf{d} \qquad [10.85]$$

where

$$\mathbf{V} = \mathbf{ATA}' + \sigma^2\mathbf{I}$$

and

$$\mathbf{d} = \mathbf{Y} - \mathbf{A}_1\theta_1 .$$

Longford (1987) provides the vector of first derivatives and the matrix of expected second derivatives. To see how these can be found, suppose that φ and φ' are arbitrary elements of (σ^2, **T**). Then

$$\partial(\log|\mathbf{V}|)/\partial\varphi = \mathrm{tr}(\mathbf{V}^{-1}\partial\mathbf{V}/\partial\varphi) \qquad [10.86]$$

$$\partial(\mathbf{V}^{-1})/\partial\varphi = -\mathbf{V}^{-1}(\partial\mathbf{V}/\partial\varphi)\mathbf{V}^{-1} . \qquad [10.87]$$

The form of $\partial\mathbf{V}/\partial\varphi$ depends upon which parameter φ represents:

$$\partial\mathbf{V}/\partial(\sigma^2) = \mathbf{I}$$

$$\partial\mathbf{V}/\partial\tau_{ij} = \mathbf{ADA}'$$

$$\partial\mathbf{V}/\partial\tau_{kl} = \mathbf{AEA}' ,$$

where **D** contains all zeros except for element (i, j) and (j, i) which take on the value of unity. Thus only a single nonzero value will exist if $i = j$. Similarly, **E** contains zeros except for elements (k, l) and (l, k), which take on the value of unity.

First Derivatives. These definitions lead to expressions for the first derivative with respect to the variance-covariance parameters:

$$\partial\lambda/\partial\varphi = -\frac{1}{2}\,\mathrm{tr}(\mathbf{V}^{-1}\partial\mathbf{V}/\partial\varphi) + \frac{1}{2}\,\mathbf{d}'[\mathbf{V}^{-1}\partial\mathbf{V}/\partial\varphi\mathbf{V}^{-1}]\mathbf{d} \qquad [10.88]$$

so that

$$\partial\lambda/\partial\sigma^2 = -\frac{1}{2}\,\mathrm{tr}(\mathbf{V}^{-1}) + \frac{1}{2}\,\mathbf{d}'\mathbf{V}^{-2}\mathbf{d} \qquad [10.89]$$

$$\partial\lambda/\partial\tau_{ij} = -\frac{1}{2}\,\mathrm{tr}(\mathbf{V}^{-1}\mathbf{ADA}') + \frac{1}{2}\,\mathbf{d}'\mathbf{V}^{-1}\mathbf{ADA}'\mathbf{V}^{-1}\mathbf{d} \qquad [10.90]$$

$$= -\frac{1}{2}\,\mathrm{tr}(\mathbf{A}'\mathbf{V}^{-1}\mathbf{AD}) + \frac{1}{2}\,\mathbf{d}'\mathbf{V}^{-1}\mathbf{ADA}'\mathbf{V}^{-1}\mathbf{d}\,.$$

For θ_1, we have a standard case of a generalized least squares model where

$$\partial\lambda/\partial\theta_1 = -\mathbf{A}_1'\mathbf{V}^{-1}\mathbf{d}\,. \qquad [10.91]$$

Second Derivatives. Taking the expected values of the second derivative of Equation 10.88 with respect to φ' yields a generic expression

$$E(\partial^2\lambda/\partial\varphi\partial\varphi') = -\frac{1}{2}\,\mathrm{tr}[(\partial\mathbf{V}^{-1}/\partial\varphi')(\partial\mathbf{V}/\partial\varphi)] \qquad [10.92]$$

$$+\frac{1}{2}\,E\{\mathbf{d}'[(\partial\mathbf{V}^{-1}/\partial\varphi')(\partial\mathbf{V}/\partial\varphi)\mathbf{V}^{-1} + \mathbf{V}^{-1}(\partial\mathbf{V}/\partial\varphi)(\partial\mathbf{V}^{-1}/\partial\varphi')]\mathbf{d}\}$$

$$= -\frac{1}{2}\,\mathrm{tr}[\mathbf{V}^{-1}(\partial\mathbf{V}/\partial\varphi')\mathbf{V}^{-1}(\partial\mathbf{V}/\partial\varphi)]\,.$$

[Note that $E(\partial^2\lambda/\partial\varphi\partial\theta_1)$ is null for every φ.] We employ the fact that the expected value of the quadratic form $\mathbf{d}'\mathbf{Q}\mathbf{d}$ is $\mathrm{tr}(\mathbf{QV})$ and then simplify. The results are

$$E[\partial^2\lambda/(\partial\sigma^2)^2] = -\frac{1}{2}\,\mathrm{tr}(\mathbf{V}^{-2})\,, \qquad [10.93]$$

$$E[\partial^2\lambda/(\partial\tau_{ij}\partial\tau_{kl})] = -\frac{1}{2}\,\mathrm{tr}[(\mathbf{A}'\mathbf{V}^{-1}\mathbf{AD})(\mathbf{A}'\mathbf{V}^{-1}\mathbf{AE})]\,, \qquad [10.94]$$

$$E[\partial^2\lambda/(\partial\sigma^2\partial d\tau_{ij})] = -\frac{1}{2}\,\mathrm{tr}(\mathbf{A}'\mathbf{V}^{-2}\mathbf{AD})\,. \qquad [10.95]$$

Translation into computational formulas is facilitated by the fact that

$$\mathbf{V}^{-1} = (\mathbf{ATA}' + \sigma^2\mathbf{I})^{-1} = \sigma^{-2}\mathbf{I} - \sigma^{-4}\mathbf{A}(\mathbf{A}'\mathbf{A}\sigma^{-2} + \mathbf{T}^{-1})^{-1}\mathbf{A}' = \sigma^{-2}\mathbf{M}$$

where $\mathbf{M} = \mathbf{I} - \mathbf{AC}^{-1}\mathbf{A}'$, with $\mathbf{C} = \mathbf{A}'\mathbf{A} + \sigma^2\mathbf{T}^{-1}$. The largest matrix to be inverted is $\mathbf{C}$, which is block diagonal with elements $\mathbf{C}_j = \mathbf{A}_j'\mathbf{A}_j + \sigma^2\tau^{-1}$. Each $\mathbf{C}_j$ is of order R, where R is the number of random effects per unit. Longford (1987) provides further computational details.

For θ_1, the result is standard

$$E[\partial^2\lambda/(\mathbf{d}\theta_1)^2] = -\mathbf{AV}^{-1}\mathbf{A} = -\sigma^2\mathbf{A}'\mathbf{MA}\,. \qquad [10.96]$$

Information Matrix, MLR

The computational formulae for the information matrix for MLR are substantially more complex than are those for MLF. To derive these formulae, we note first that a convenient expression for the MLR likelihood can be obtained by integrating the MLF likelihood with respect to θ_1 :

$$f(\mathbf{Y} \mid \sigma^2, \mathbf{T}) = \int f(\mathbf{Y} \mid \theta_1, \sigma^2, \mathbf{T})\partial\theta_1\,. \qquad [10.97]$$

This integration is justifiable if we view the likelihood as proportional to the joint posterior distribution of θ_1, σ^2, and $\mathbf{T}$ given $\mathbf{Y}$. The integration is facilitated by partitioning

$$\mathbf{d}'\mathbf{V}^{-1}\mathbf{d} = \hat{\mathbf{d}}'\mathbf{V}^{-1}\hat{\mathbf{d}} + (\hat{\theta}_1 - \theta_1)'\mathbf{A}_1'\mathbf{V}^{-1}\mathbf{A}_1(\hat{\theta}_1 - \theta_1)\,,$$

where

$$\hat{\mathbf{d}} = \mathbf{Y} - \mathbf{A}_1\hat{\theta}_1 \quad \text{and} \quad \hat{\theta}_1 = (\mathbf{A}_1'\mathbf{V}^{-1}\mathbf{A}_1)^{-1}\mathbf{A}_1'\mathbf{V}^{-1}\mathbf{Y}\,.$$

A second useful result is the integral

$$\int \exp\left[-\frac{1}{2}(\hat{\theta}_1 - \theta_1)'\mathbf{A}_1'\mathbf{V}^{-1}\mathbf{A}_1(\hat{\theta}_1 - \theta_1)\right]\partial\theta_1 = (2\pi)^{F/2} \mid \mathbf{A}_1'\mathbf{V}^{-1}\mathbf{A}_1 \mid^{-1/2}. \qquad [10.98]$$

From these two results one can deduce that, apart from a constant,

$$\log\left[\int f(\mathbf{Y} \mid \theta_1, \sigma^2, \mathbf{T})\partial\theta_1\right] \qquad [10.99]$$

$$= \lambda_{MLR} = \lambda_{MLF} - \frac{1}{2}\log\mid \mathbf{M} \mid + \frac{1}{2}(\hat{\theta}_1 - \theta_1)'\mathbf{M}(\hat{\theta}_1 - \theta_1)\,,$$

with $\mathbf{M} = \mathbf{A}_1'\mathbf{V}^{-1}\mathbf{A}_1$.

This expression makes it clear that the information matrix for MLR will be equal to the information matrix for MLF with the addition of the expected second derivatives of the second and third terms of Equation 10.99.

The following derivatives are useful in finding the MLR information matrix:

$$\partial\mathbf{M}/\partial\varphi = \mathbf{A}_1'\mathbf{G}\mathbf{A}_1$$

and

$$\partial\hat{\theta}_1/\partial\varphi = \mathbf{M}^{-1}\mathbf{A}_1'\mathbf{G}\hat{\mathbf{d}} ,$$

where

$$\mathbf{G} = \partial\mathbf{V}^{-1}/\partial\varphi .$$

From these definitions, it follows that

$$\partial(\log|\,\mathbf{M}\,|)/\partial\varphi = \mathrm{tr}[\mathbf{M}^{-1}(\partial\mathbf{M}/\partial\varphi)] = \mathrm{tr}(\mathbf{M}^{-1}\mathbf{A}_1'\mathbf{G}\mathbf{A}_1)$$

and

$$\partial[(\hat{\theta}_1 - \theta_1)'\mathbf{M}(\hat{\theta}_1 - \theta_1)]/\partial\varphi$$
$$= \hat{\mathbf{d}}'\mathbf{G}\mathbf{A}_1(\hat{\theta}_1 - \theta_1) + (\hat{\theta}_1 - \theta_1)'\mathbf{A}_1'\mathbf{G}\mathbf{A}_1(\hat{\theta}_1 - \theta_1) + (\hat{\theta}_1 - \theta_1)'\mathbf{A}_1'\mathbf{G}\hat{\mathbf{d}} .$$

The second derivative of log|**M**| is

$$\partial^2\log|\,\mathbf{M}\,|/\partial\varphi\partial\varphi' = \mathrm{tr}(\mathbf{A}_1'\mathbf{H}\mathbf{V}\mathbf{G}\mathbf{A}_1\mathbf{M}^{-1}) + \mathrm{tr}(\mathbf{A}_1'\mathbf{G}\mathbf{V}\mathbf{H}\mathbf{A}_1\mathbf{M}^{-1}) - \mathrm{tr}(\mathbf{A}_1'\mathbf{G}\mathbf{A}_1\mathbf{M}^{-1}\mathbf{A}_1'\mathbf{H}\mathbf{A}_1\mathbf{M}^{-1}) \quad [10.100]$$

where $\mathbf{H} = \partial\mathbf{V}^{-1}/\partial\varphi'$.

The expected second derivative of the quadratic form $(\hat{\theta}_1 - \theta_1)'\mathbf{M}(\hat{\theta}_1 - \theta_1)$ is twice the negative of Equation 10.100. Substituting τ_{ij}, and σ^2 for φ and σ^2 and τ_{kl} for φ' then leads the following formulae for the negative of the MLR information matrix:

$$E[\partial^2\lambda_{MLR}/(\partial\sigma^2)^2] = E[\partial^2\lambda_{MLF}/(\partial\sigma^2)^2] - \mathrm{tr}(\mathbf{M}^{-1}\mathbf{A}_1'\mathbf{V}^{-3}\mathbf{A}_1) + \tfrac{1}{2}\mathrm{tr}(\mathbf{M}^{-1}\mathbf{A}_1'\mathbf{V}^{-2}\mathbf{A}_1)^2 , \quad [10.101]$$

$$E[\partial^2\lambda_{MLR}/(\partial\tau_{ij}\partial\tau_{kl})] = E[\partial^2\lambda_{MLF}/(\partial\tau_{ij}\partial\tau_{kl})] \qquad [10.102]$$

$$+\frac{1}{2}\,\mathrm{tr}(\mathbf{M}^{-1}\mathbf{R}_{1\,2}\mathbf{E}\mathbf{R}_{2\,2}\mathbf{D}\mathbf{R}_{2\,1})$$

$$+\frac{1}{2}\,\mathrm{tr}(\mathbf{M}^{-1}\mathbf{R}_{1\,2}\mathbf{D}\mathbf{R}_{2\,2}\mathbf{E}\mathbf{R}_{2\,1})$$

$$-\frac{1}{2}\,\mathrm{tr}(\mathbf{M}^{-1}\mathbf{R}_{1\,2}\mathbf{D}\mathbf{R}_{2\,1}\mathbf{M}^{-1}\mathbf{R}_{1\,2}\mathbf{E}\mathbf{R}_{2\,1}),$$

where $\mathbf{R}_{st} = \mathbf{A}_s'\mathbf{V}^{-1}\mathbf{A}_t$, $s = 1, 2$; and

$$E[\partial^2\lambda_{MLR}/(\partial\sigma^2\partial\tau_{ij})] = E[\partial^2(\lambda_{MLF})/(\partial\sigma^2\partial\tau_{ij})] \qquad [10.103]$$

$$+\frac{1}{2}\,\mathrm{tr}(\mathbf{M}^{-1}\mathbf{A}_1'\mathbf{V}^{-2}\mathbf{A}_2\mathbf{D}\mathbf{R}_{2\,1})$$

$$+\frac{1}{2}\,\mathrm{tr}(\mathbf{M}^{-1}\mathbf{R}_{1\,2}\mathbf{D}\mathbf{A}_2'\mathbf{V}^{-2}\mathbf{A}_1)$$

$$-\frac{1}{2}\,\mathrm{tr}(\mathbf{M}^{-1}\mathbf{R}_{1\,2}\mathbf{D}\mathbf{R}_{2\,1}\mathbf{M}^{-1}\mathbf{A}_1'\mathbf{V}^{-2}\mathbf{A}_1).$$

These formulas can be converted into computational formulas as follows:

$$\mathbf{M} = \sigma^{-2}\left(\sum \mathbf{S}_{1\,1j} - \sum \mathbf{S}_{1\,2j}\mathbf{C}_j^{-1}\mathbf{S}_{2\,1j}\right)$$

$$\mathbf{R}_{2\,2j} = \mathbf{S}_{2\,2j}\mathbf{C}_j^{-1}\tau^{-1}$$

$$\mathbf{R}_{1\,2j} = \mathbf{S}_{1\,2j}\mathbf{C}_j^{-1}\tau^{-1}$$

$$\mathbf{A}_{1j}\mathbf{V}_j^{-2}\mathbf{A}_{1j} = \sigma^{-2}(\mathbf{M}_j - \mathbf{R}_{1\,2j}\mathbf{C}_j^{-1}\mathbf{S}_{2\,1j})$$

$$\mathbf{A}_{1j}'\mathbf{V}_j^{-2}\mathbf{A}_{1j} = \mathbf{S}_{1\,2j}(\mathbf{C}_j^{-1}\tau^{-1})^2;$$

and

$$\mathbf{A}_1'\mathbf{V}^{-3}\mathbf{A}_1 = \sigma^{-2}\left(\sum \mathbf{A}_{1j}'\mathbf{V}_j^{-2}\mathbf{A}_{1j} - \sum \mathbf{A}_{1j}'\mathbf{V}_j^{-2}\mathbf{A}_{2j}\mathbf{C}_j^{-1}\mathbf{S}_{2\,1j}\right).$$

Notes

1. We introduce a different notation for the Level-2 dispersion matrix in order to facilitate the analytic aims of this chapter. Specifically, τ is now defined as a matrix rather than an element of a matrix as in the preceding chapters.

2. θ_1 is considered random in the sense that it has a prior distribution. The parameters σ^2 and **T** are considered fixed. Thus, the use of terms *fixed* and *random* in this appendix deviate from the terminology generally employed elsewhere in this text, where θ_1 is described as a vector of fixed effects, θ_2 as random and σ^2 and **T** as variance-covariance components. This unfortunate complexity is needed in order to properly distinguish MLF and MLR estimation.

References

Aitkin, M., Anderson, D., & Hinde, J. (1981). Statistical modeling of data on teaching styles. *Journal of the Royal Statistical Society, Series A, 144*(4), 419-461.

Aitkin, M., & Longford, N. (1986). Statistical modeling issues in school effectiveness studies. *Journal of the Royal Statistical Society, Series A, 149*(1), 1-43.

Anderson, T. W. (1984). *An Introduction to Multivariate Statistical Analysis* (2nd ed.). New York: John Wiley.

Bartlett, M. S., & Kendall, D. G. (1946). The statistical analysis of variances-heterogeneity and the logarithmic transformation. *Journal of the Royal Statistical Society,* (Suppl. 8), 128-138.

Becker, B. J. (1988). Synthesizing standardized mean-change measures. *British Journal of Mathematical and Statistical Psychology, 41,* 257-278.

Bereiter, C. (1963). Some persisting dilemmas in the measurement of change. In C. W. Harris (Ed.), *Problems in the measurement of change* (pp. 3-20). Madison: University of Wisconsin Press.

Blomqvist, N. (1977). On the relation between change and initial value. *Journal of the American Statistical Association, 72,* 746-749.

Box, G. E. P., & Tiao, G. C. (1973). *Bayesian inference in statistical analysis.* Reading, MA: Addison-Wesley.

Braun, H. I., Jones, D. H., Rubin, D. B., & Thayer, D. T. (1983). Empirical Bayes estimation of coefficients in the general linear model from data of deficient rank. *Psychometrika, 489*(2), 171-181.

Bryk, A. S., & Driscoll, M. E. (1988). *An empirical investigation of school as a community.* Madison: University of Wisconsin Research Center on Effective Secondary Schools.

Bryk, A. S., & Frank, F. (1991). The specialization of teachers' work: An initial exploration. In S. W. Raudenbush & J. D. Willms (Eds.), *Schools, classrooms, and pupils: International studies of schooling from a multilevel perspective* (pp. 185-204). Orlando, FL: Academic Press.

Bryk, A. S., & Raudenbush, S. W. (1987). Application of hierarchical linear models to assessing change. *Psychological Bulletin, 101*(1), 147-158.

Bryk, A. S., & Raudenbush, S. W. (1988). On heterogeneity of variance in experimental studies: A challenge to conventional interpretations. *Psychological Bulletin, 104*(3), 396-404.

Bryk, A. S., Raudenbush, S. W., Seltzer, M., & Congdon, R. (1988). *An introduction to HLM: Computer program and user's guide* (2nd ed.). Chicago: University of Chicago Department of Education.

Bryk, A. S., & Thum, Y. M. (1989). The effects of high school on dropping out: An exploratory investigation. *American Educational Research Journal, 26,* 353-384.

Bryk, A. S., & Weisberg, H. I. (1977). Use of the nonequivalent control group design when subjects are growing. *Psychological Bulletin, 84,* 950-962.

Burstein, L. (1980). The analysis of multi-level data in educational research and evaluation. *Review of Research in Education, 8,* 158-233.

Carter, D. L. (1970). The effect of teacher expectations on the self-esteem and academic performance of seventh grade students. *Dissertation Abstracts International, 31,* 4539-A. (University Microfilms No. 7107612)

Carter, L. F. (1984). The sustaining effects study of compensatory and elementary education. *Educational Researcher, 13*(7), 4-13.

Claiborn, W. (1969). Expectancy effects in the classroom: A failure to replicate. *Journal of Educational Psychology, 60,* 377-383.

Coleman, J. S., Hoffer, T., Kilgore, S. B. (1982). *High school achievement: Public, Catholic and other schools compared.* New York: Basic Books.

Conn, L. K., Edwards, C. N., Rosenthal, R., & Crowne, D. (1968). Perception of emotion and response to teachers' expectancy by elementary school children. *Psychological Reports, 22,* 27-34.

Cook, T. D., & Campbell, D. T. (1979). *Quasi-experimentation.* New York: Rand McNally.

Cronbach, L. J. (1976). *Research on classrooms and schools: Formulations of questions design and analysis.* Occasional paper. Stanford, CA: Stanford Evaluation Consortium.

Deeley, J. J., &. Lindley, D. V. (1981). Bayes empirical Bayes. *Journal of the American Statistical Association, 76,* 833-841.

de Leeuw, J., & Kreft, I. (1986). Random coefficient models for multilevel analysis. *Journal of Educational Statistics, 11*(1), 57-85.

Dempster, A. P., Laird, N. M., & Rubin, D. B. (1977). Maximum likelihood from incomplete data via the EM algorithm. *Journal of the Royal Statistical Society, Series B, 39,* 1-8.

Dempster, A. P., Rubin, D. B., & Tsutakawa, R. K. (1981). Estimation in covariance components models. *Journal of the American Statistical Association, 76,* 341-353.

Efron, B., & Morris, C. (1975). Data analysis using Stein's estimator and its generalizations. *Journal of the American Statistical Association, 74,* 311-319.

Elston, R. C., & Grizzle, J. E. (1962). Estimation of time response curves and their confidence bands. *Biometrics, 18,* 148-159.

Englert, C. S., Raphael, T. E., Anderson, L. M., Anthony, H. M., Fear, K. L., & Gregg, S. L. (1988). *A case for writing intervention: Strategies for writing informational text.* East Lansing: Michigan State University, Institute for Research on Teaching.

Erbring, L., & Young, A. A. (1979). Individuals and social structure: Contextual effects as endogenous feedback. *Sociological Methods and Research, 7,* 396-430.

Evans, J., & Rosenthal, R. (1969). Interpersonal self-fulfilling prophecies: Further extrapolations from the laboratory to the classroom. *Proceedings of the 77th Annual Convention of the American Psychological Association, 4,* 371-372.

Fielder, W. R., Cohen, R. D., & Feeney, S. (1971). An attempt to replicate the teacher expectancy effect. *Psychological Association, 4,* 371-372.

Fine, L. (1972). The effects of positive teacher expectancy on the reading achievement of pupils in grade two. *Dissertation Abstracts International, 33,* 1510-A. (University Microfilms No. 7227180)

Firebaugh, G. (1978). A rule for inferring individual level relationships from aggregate data. *American Sociological Review, 43,* 557-572.

Fleming, E., & Anttonen, R. (1971). Teacher expectancy or my fair lady. *American Educational Research Journal, 8,* 241-252.

Flowers, C. E. (1966). Effects of an arbitrary accelerated group placement on the tested academic achievement of educationally disadvantaged students. *Dissertation Abstracts International, 27,* 991-A. (University Microfilms No. 6610288)

Fotiu, R. P. (1989). *A comparison of the EM and data augmentation algorithms on simulated small sample hierarchical data from research on education.* Unpublished doctoral dissertation, Michigan State University, East Lansing.

Frank, K., & Seltzer, M. (1990, April). *Using the hierarchical linear model to model growth in reading achievement.* Paper presented at the Annual Meeting of the American Educational Research Association, Boston, MA.

Ginsburg, R. E. (1970). An examination of the relationship between teacher expectations and student performance on a test of intellectual functioning. *Dissertation Abstracts International, 31,* 3337-A. (University Microfilms No. 710922)

Glass, G. V. (1976). Primary, secondary, and meta-analysis of research. *Educational Researcher, 5,* 3-8.

Goldstein, H. I. (1986). Multilevel mixed linear model analysis using iterative generalized least squares. *Biometrika, 73*(1), 43-56.

Goldstein, H. I. (1987). *Multilevel models in educational and social research.* London: Oxford University Press.

Greiger, R. M., II. (1970). The effects of teacher expectancies on the intelligence of students and the behaviors of teachers. *Dissertation Abstracts International, 31,* 3338-A. (University Microfilms No. 7114791)

Haney, W. (1980). Units and levels of analysis in large-scale evaluation. In *New directions for methodology of social and behavioral science* (Vol. 6, pp. 1-15). San Francisco: Jossey-Bass.

Harris, C. W. (1963). *Problems in the measurement of change.* Madison: University of Wisconsin Press.

Hauser, R. M. (1970). Context and consex: A cautionary tale. *American Journal of Sociology, 74,* 587-611.

Hedges, L. V. (1981). Distribution theory for Glass's estimator of effect size and related estimators. *Journal of the American Statistical Association, 74,* 311-319.

Hedges, L. V. (1982). Fitting continuous models to effect size data. *Journal of Educational Statistics, Winter, 7*(4), 245-270.

Hedges, L. V., & Olkin, I. O. (1983). Regression Models in research synthesis. *American Statistician, 37,* 137-140.

Hedges, L. V., & Olkin, I. O. (1985). *Statistical methods for meta-analysis.* Orlando, FL: Academic Press.

Henrickson, H. A. (1970). An investigation of the influence of teacher expectation upon the intellectual and academic performance of disadvantaged children. *Dissertation Abstracts International, 31,* 6278-A. (University Microfilms No. 7114791)

Hunter, J. E., & Schmidt, F. L. (1990). *Methods of meta-analysis: Correcting error and bias in research findings.* Newbury Park, CA: Sage.

Huttenlocher, J. E., Haight, W., Bryk, A. S., & Seltzer, M. (1991). Early vocabulary growth: Relation to language input and gender. *Developmental Psychology, 27*(2), 236-249.

James, W., & Stein, C. (1961). Estimation with quadratic loss. In J. Neyman (Ed.), *Proceedings of the Fourth Berkeley Symposium on Mathematical Statistics and Probability* (Vol. 1, pp. 361-379). Berkeley: University of California Press.

Jennrich, R. I., & Schlucter, M. D. (1986). Unbalanced repeated measures models with structured covariance matrices. *Biometrics, 42,* 805-820.

Jose, J., & Cody, J. (1971). Teacher-pupil interaction as it relates to attempted changes in teacher expectancy of academic ability achievement. *American Educational Research Journal, 8,* 39-49.

Kelley, T. L. (1927). *The interpretation of educational measurements.* New York: World Books.

Keshock, J. D. (1970). An investigation of the effects of the expectancy phenomenon upon the intelligence, achievement, and motivation of inner-city elementary school children. *Dissertation Abstracts International, 32,* 243-A. (University Microfilms No. 7119010)

Kester, S. W., & Letchworth, G. A. (1972). Communication of teacher expectations and their effects on achievement and attitudes of secondary school students. *Journal of Educational Research, 66,* 51-55.

Kirk, R. E. (1982). *Experimental design: Procedures of the behavioral sciences.* Belmont, CA: Wadsworth.

Kreft, I. G., de Leeuw, J., & Kim, K. (1990). *Comparing four different statistical packages for hierarchical linear regression: Genmod, HLM, ML2, and VARCL* (Statistics Series No. 50). Los Angeles: University of California at Los Angeles.

Laird, N. M., & Ware, H. (1982). Random-effects models for longitudinal data. *Biometrics, 38,* 963-974.

Lee, V., & Bryk, A. S. (1989). A multilevel model of the social distribution of high school achievement. *Sociology of Education, 62,* 172-192.

Lee, V. E., & Smith, J. B. (1991). Sex discrimination in teachers' salary. In S. W. Raudenbush & J. D. Willms (Eds.), *Schools, classrooms, and pupils: International studies of schooling from a multilevel perspective* (pp. 225-247). Orlando, FL: Academic Press.

Lindley, D. V., & Smith, A. F. M. (1972). Bayes estimates for the linear model. *Journal of the Royal Statistical Society, Series B, 34,* 1-41.

Longford, N. T. (1987). A fast scoring algorithm for maximum likelihood estimation in unbalanced mixed models with nested random effects. *Biometrika, 74*(4), 817-827.

Longford, N. T. (1988). Fisher scoring algorithm for variance component analysis of data with multilevel structure. In R. D. Bock (Ed.), *Multilevel analysis of educational data* (pp. 297-310). Orlando, FL: Academic Press.

Lord, F. M. (1980). *Applications of item response theory to practical testing problems.* Hillsdale, NJ: Laurence Erlbaum.

Louis, T. A., & Spiro, A., III. (1984). *Fitting first order auto-regressive models with covariates* (Tech. Rep.). Cambridge, MA: Harvard University School of Public Health, Department of Biostatistics.

Mason, W. M., Anderson, A. F., & Hayat, N. (1988). *Manual for GENMOD.* Ann Arbor: University of Michigan, Population Studies Center.

Mason, W. M., Wong, G. M., & Entwistle, B. (1983). Contextual analysis through the multilevel linear model. In S. Leinhardt (Ed.), *Sociological methodology* (pp. 72-103). San Francisco: Jossey-Bass.

Maxwell, M. L. (1970). A study of the effects of teachers' expectations on the IQ and academic performance of children. *Dissertation Abstracts International, 31,* 3345-A. (University Microfilms No. 710125)

Morris, C. N. (1983). Parametric empirical Bayes inference: Theory and applications. *Journal of the American Statistical Association, 78,* 47-65.

Morrison, D. F. (1967). *Multivariate statistical methods.* New York: McGraw-Hill.

Pallas, A. M. (1988). School climate in American high schools. *Teachers College Record, 89*(4), 541-554.

Paterson, L. (1990). *The use of multilevel models to estimate school effects: A report commissioned by the Scottish Education Department.* Edinburgh: University of Edinburgh, Centre for Educational Sociology.

Pellegrini, R., & Hicks, R. (1972). Prophecy effects and tutorial instruction for the disadvantaged child. *American Educational Research Journal, 9,* 413-419.

Rabash, J., Prosser, R., & Goldstein, H. (1989). *ML2: Software for two-level analysis. Users' guide.* London: University of London, Institute of Education.

Raffe, D. (1991). Assessing the impact of a decentralized initiative: The British technical and vocational initiative. In S. W. Raudenbush & J. D. Willms (Eds.), *Schools, classrooms, and pupils: International studies of schooling from a multilevel perspective* (pp. 149-166). Orlando, FL: Academic Press.

Raudenbush, S. W. (1984a). Applications of a hierarchical linear model in educational research. *Dissertation Abstracts International, 45,* 1713A.

Raudenbush, S. W. (1984b). Magnitude of teacher expectancy effects on pupil IQ as a function of the credibility of expectancy induction: A synthesis of findings from 18 experiments. *Journal of Educational Psychology, 76*(1), 85-97.

Raudenbush, S. W. (1988). Educational applications of hierarchical linear models: A review. *Journal of Educational Statistics, 13*(20), 85-116.

Raudenbush, S. W., & Bryk, A. S. (1985). Empirical Bayes meta-analysis. *Journal of Educational Statistics, 10,* 75-98.

Raudenbush, S. W., & Bryk, A. S. (1986). A hierarchical model for studying school effects. *Sociology of Education, 59,* 1-17.

Raudenbush, S. W., & Bryk, A. S. (1987). Examining correlates of diversity. *Journal of Educational Statistics, 12,* 241-269.

Raudenbush, S. W., Kidchanapanish, S., & Kang, S. J. (1991). The effects of pre-primary access and quality on educational achievement in Thailand. *Comparative Education Review, 35,* 255-273.

Raudenbush, S. W., Rowan, B., & Cheong, F. Y. (1991). *Teaching for higher-order thinking in secondary schools: Effects of curriculum, teacher preparation, and school organization.* East Lansing: Michigan State University, College of Education.

Raudenbush, S. W., Rowan, B., & Kang, S. J. (1991). A multilevel, multivariate model for school climate with estimation via the EM algorithm and application to US high school data. *Journal of Educational Statistics, 16,* 295-330.

Raudenbush, S. W., & Willms, J. D. (Eds.). (1991). *Schools, classrooms, and pupils: International studies of schooling from a multilevel perspective.* Orlando, FL: Academic Press.

Rogosa, D. R., Brand, D., & Zimowski, M. (1982). A growth curve approach to the measurement of change. *Psychological Bulletin, 90,* 726-748.

Rogosa, D. R., & Willett, B. (1985). Understanding correlates of change by modeling individual differences in growth. *Psychometrica, 50,* 203-228.

Rosenberg, B. (1973). Linear regression with randomly dispersed parameters. *Biometrika, 60,* 61-75.

Rosenthal, R. (1987). Pygmalion effects: Existence, magnitude, and social importance. *Educational Researcher, 16,* 37-41.

Rosenthal, R., Baratz, S., & Hall, C. M. (1974). Teacher behavior, teacher expectations, and gains in pupils' rated creativity. *Journal of Genetic Psychology, 124,* 115-121.

Rosenthal, R., & Jacobson, L. (1968). *Pygmalion in the classroom.* New York: Holt, Rinehart & Winston.

Rosenthal, R., & Rubin, D. B. (1982). Comparing effect sizes of independent studies. *Psychology Bulletin, 92,* 500-504.

Rubin, D. B. (1980). Using empirical Bayes techniques in the Law School Validity Studies. *Journal of the American Statistical Association, 75,* 801-827.

Seltzer, M. (1990). *The use of data augmentation in fitting hierarchical models to educational data.* Unpublished doctoral dissertation, University of Chicago.

Smith, A. F. M. (1973). A general Bayesian linear model. *Journal of the Royal Statistical Society, Series B, 35,* 61-75.

Strenio, J. L. F., Weisberg, H. I., & Bryk, A. S. (1983). Empirical Bayes estimation of individual growth curve parameters and their relationship to covariates. *Biometrics, 39,* 71-86.

Swamy, P. A. V. (1973). Criteria, constraints, and multi-collinearity in random coefficient regression models. *Annals of Economic and Social Measurement, 2*(4), 429-450.

Tanner, M. A., & Wong, W. H. (1987). The calculation of posterior distribution by data augmentation [with discusssion]. *Journal of the American Statistical Association, 82,* 528- 550.

Ware, J. H. (1985). Linear models for the analysis of longitudinal studies. *American Statistician, 39*(2), 95-101.

Willett, J. B. (1988). Questions and answers in the measurement of change. In E. Rothkopf (Ed.), *Review of research in education (1988-89)* (pp. 345-422). Washington, DC: American Educational Research Association.

Willms, J. D. (1986). Social class segregation and its relationship to pupils' examination results in Scotland. *American Sociological Review, 55,* 224-241.

Wineburg, S. (1987). The self-fulfillment of the self-fulfilling prophecy. *Educational Researcher, 16*(9), 28-37.

Zuzovsky, R., & Aitkin, M. (1991). Curricular change and science achievement in Israeli elementary schools. In S. W. Raudenbush & J. D. Willms (Eds.), *Schools, classrooms, and pupils: International studies of schooling from a multilevel perspective* (pp. 25-36). Orlando, FL: Academic Press.

About the Authors

Anthony S. Bryk is a Professor of Education at the University of Chicago and Director of its Center for School Improvement. His methodological work has focused on issues in the measurement of change and research on school effects. He has published this work in a variety of journals including *Psychological Bulletin*, *Sociology of Education*, and *Journal of Educational Statistics*. His substantive research focuses on school organization and its effects on teachers and students. He has co-authored with Valerie Lee a book on Catholic high schools to be published by Harvard University Press.

Stephen W. Raudenbush is an Associate Professor at the College of Education, Michigan State University. He has published articles on the statistical theory of hierarchical linear models and research synthesis in the *Journal of Educational Statistics* and *Psychological Bulletin* and has collaborated on numerous studies that use these techniques to illuminate the effects of schooling on student outcomes. He has co-edited with J. Douglas Willms a volume of applications of these methods entitled *Pupils, Classrooms, and Schools: International Studies of Schooling from a Multilevel Perspective*.